INSIGHT MEDITATION

Insight Meditation

WORKBOOK

Sharon Salzberg

AND

Joseph Goldstein

SOUNDS TRUE
BOULDER, COLORADO

Insight Meditation
© 2001 Sharon Salzberg and Joseph Goldstein
All rights reserved.
No part of this book may be used or reproduced in any manner without written permission from
the authors and publisher. Published 2001.

Portions of this book have been excerpted from *Insight Meditation Correspondence Course Workbook*
© 1996 Sharon Salzberg and Joseph Goldstein.

Sharon Salzberg and Joseph Goldstein.
   Insight Meditation
ISBN 1-56455-906-8

For information on meditation retreats with Sharon Salzberg and Joseph Goldstein, write:
Insight Meditation Society, 1230 Pleasant Street, Barre, MA 01005 / www.dharma.org/ims.htm

Compiled and edited by Jennifer Woodhull.
Design by Sarah Chesnutt.

For a complete catalog of audios, videos, and music, contact:
Sounds True, PO Box 8010, Boulder, CO 80306-8010 / Ph. 800-333-9185 / www.soundstrue.com

CONTENTS

We would like to thank Jennifer Woodhull for the immense amount of outstanding work she put into this project. It wouldn't have happened without her. And much appreciation also to Gyano Gibson and Susan O'Brien for their invaluable help and support. Thanks also to Sounds True, especially Sarah Chesnutt, Joe Ditta, and Peter McGoldrick.

INTRODUCTION

Welcome to *Insight Meditation.* Your compact discs and this workbook will take you step by step through a comprehensive training course in basic meditation. The cards included in the box list various helpful teachings that are explored throughout this workbook.

This course is rooted in the Buddhist style of *vipassana,* or insight meditation, but these fundamental techniques for sharpening your awareness and releasing painful mental habits are useful no matter what your religious or spiritual orientation.

It's not necessary to affiliate with any belief system in order to benefit from *Insight Meditation.* These mindfulness practices can support your existing spiritual path, whether it's a structured practice like Christianity or Judaism, or simply a personal sense of your relationship with the great questions of human existence.

What to Expect

Insight Meditation comprises two compact discs, this workbook, and a set of informational cards.
This workbook contains:

- information on meditation resources
- suggestions for setting up a meditation space and a daily practice
- Buddhist teachings about meditation and life
- Q&A sessions that clarify practical issues new meditators tend to encounter
- exercises to help you deepen your understanding and experience of meditation (and space to respond to them)

- tips for taking your meditative awareness into the world and for troubleshooting problem areas in your practice
- glossaries of Pali, Sanskrit, and other terms
- a list of books and tapes you can use to further your study of meditation

Each lesson elaborates a facet of developing awareness, using different objects and emphases. Taken together, they constitute a complete description of a path of meditation.

The workbook progresses from the basic theory of mindfulness (Lesson One) through suggestions on how to infuse all of your life activities with clarity and awareness (Last Words). Along the way, you'll learn how to work with mental and physical hindrances to meditation; the meaning and implications of *karma* (the law of cause and effect); how to find peace in the midst of life's challenges; and many other aspects of Buddhist psychology and awareness practice.

Each compact disc features three guided meditations, which will help you to explore the direct experience of meditation. They're set up to simulate as closely as possible the ambience of an actual practice session at a retreat center like the Insight Meditation Society.

Every lesson in the workbook includes a guided meditation that you can record yourself for playback during solitary sitting or read out loud at group sessions. Six of these meditations also appear on the CDs. The text versions are somewhat longer than the recorded ones, so you can also use them to gradually increase the length of your sessions.

I have discovered that all human evil comes from this, man's being unable to sit still in a room.

—BLAISE PASCAL

Before you listen to the guided meditations, have your meditation space set up (see page 6 for suggestions). Take your seat, ready to meditate for approximately twenty minutes. You'll notice that each meditation begins and ends with the traditional sound of a gong. If you have one, you may find it helpful to use a gong to begin and end any meditations you record yourself.

The cards feature helpful references to some of the Buddha's famous "lists." These lists − the five precepts, the eight vicissitudes, and so on − serve to summarize profound teachings, making them easier to memorize and apply in your everyday life. Some lessons encourage you to display a particular card that week in order to support your practice. You might also select cards, systematically or at random, to remind yourself of the respective teachings. Each card bears a page or lesson reference that will take you to an in-depth discussion of the list it features.

How to Use This Workbook

Each meditator has her or his own pace, logistical needs, and level of connection with the practice. However, there are general guidelines that will help you get the most out of this course. We recommend that you:

- establish your meditation space and schedule before beginning to read and work with Lesson One
- read each lesson in sequence
- explore the related guided meditation and exercises for at least a week before moving on to the next lesson

Insight Meditation has been carefully structured to take you progressively deeper into the practice of meditation. Although it's a good idea to go back and review previous lessons, you'll find yourself missing crucial information and experiences if you skip lessons to jump ahead. It's important to remember that the purpose of meditation is to deepen your awareness of your own reality. This course is designed to lead you, step by step, in that direction.

Each lesson includes a set of exercises. The spaces provided for your responses are intentionally short. The point is not to produce pages of description about your meditation practice, but to go to the heart of your experience. If you choose to respond to the exercise questions, you'll find that doing so helps clarify both your intellectual and heartfelt understandings of the meditative process.

Plunge Right In

Meditation is a lifelong practice that develops at a rate consistent with the amount of time and effort you devote to it. This course is designed to offer you a graduated path leading to the everyday experience of mindfulness. You'll find it most fruitful and meaningful when you take it a step at a time, contemplating each lesson and entering into the accompanying guided meditation fully before proceeding to the next lesson.

On the other hand, there's no reason to delay beginning your meditation practice. The profound gifts of awareness, compassion, and direct experience are always available to us. The sooner you discover them, the more deeply you can explore them during this lifetime. Should you let your practice lapse during this course, just return to the last lesson you remember reading (or, if you like, to the beginning) and start again.

Ideally, you should work your way up from the twenty-minute guided meditations supplied here to daily sessions of at least forty-five minutes. But meditation is not a coercive activity – it's something we do with interest, a sense of exploration, happiness, and joy. If forty-five minutes seems daunting or undesirable in any way, shorten your sessions. It may be that, on a given day, it's more appropriate for you to sit for fifteen minutes, or even just for five.

The Buddha taught the doctrine of the "Middle Way": a path that avoids extremes and remains centered in the reality of the present moment. In this spirit, we encourage you to find your own pace – neither rushing nor hesitating. As you progress in the course, you'll learn how to determine what pace is best for you, and your trust in that understanding will grow.

An Introduction to Vipassana Meditation

People have practiced some form of meditation, or quieting the mind, since the beginning of recorded history. Every major world religion (and many lesser-known spiritual traditions) includes a contemplative component.

Vipassana (pronounced vuh-*pah*-suhn-a), the style of meditation taught in this course, can be traced directly to the way the Buddha himself practiced, and is common to all Buddhist traditions. It is characterized by concentration and mindfulness. Vipassana meditation is designed to quiet the mind and refine our awareness, so that we can experience the truth of our lives directly with a minimum of distraction and obscuration.

The practice of Buddhist meditation can be said to be nontheistic – that is, not dependent on belief in an external deity. Buddhism simply reflects back to us that the degree of our own liberation is dependent on the extent of our own effort. So the Buddha's style of meditation is compatible with any spiritual path, whether theistic or nontheistic. The practice of mindful awareness is an invaluable tool to anyone seeking spiritual awakening, mental clarity, or peace of mind.

What You Need to Meditate

You don't need elaborate equipment or supplies to meditate. Many people simply sit on a chair, or use sofa or floor cushions they already have. Appendix A (page 209) describes the full range of commercially available meditation cushions and benches. It also gives you some contact information for vendors. Review this information and acquire an appropriate support before starting to work with the materials in this course. We recommend that you experiment with varying heights and degrees of firmness before investing in a meditation support of your own.

The Story of the Buddha

The meditation techniques presented in this course were originally taught by the Buddha, four to five hundred years before the birth of Christ. "Buddha" means "Awakened One," and refers to a prince who is believed to have lived in the Ganges Valley of northeastern India. He is sometimes called Gautama Buddha (Gautama was his family name) or Sakyamuni Buddha, the "Silent Sage of the Sakyas" (his tribe). His personal name was Siddhartha.

Legend has it that when the Buddha was born, astrologers told his father that the child would become either a mighty king, or – if he witnessed much suffering – a great religious leader. Wanting his son to rule in the worldly realm, Siddhartha's father went to enormous lengths to shield the young prince from encountering suffering. He was lavished with every conceivable pleasure and comfort, but forbidden to leave the palace grounds.

Finally, however, the prince persuaded his charioteer to take him into the city. There, he saw an old person, a sick person, a corpse, and a holy man. These traditional Four Signs led to a protracted inner search for the meaning of life. Siddhartha left his family at the age of twenty-nine to become a homeless spiritual seeker.

> *There is no savior in Buddhism. You have to do it for yourself. No one else will meditate for you.*
>
> —ROSHI JIYU KENNETT

After six years of severe ascetic practices, Siddhartha realized that the path of self-mortification was not leading to the enlightenment he sought. This understanding is the basis of the "Middle Way" of Buddhism: a spiritual path that avoids extremes of asceticism and indulgence.

Finally, the aspiring Buddha resolved to sit in meditation under a tree until he attained full realization. While meditating, it is said, he did battle with Mara – known as "the killer of life" and "the killer of virtue" – who tempted and mocked him. But the Buddha overcame these obstacles through the strength of his determination and achieved enlightenment, a state of clear understanding about the nature of reality, under the tree now known as the *Bodhi* tree in the town of Bodh Gaya (bodhi means "awake").

Buddhists respect the Buddha as a human being who found a way to break through delusion and find true happiness. Thus, rather than regarding him as a deity with extraordinary spiritual powers, practitioners take heart from the Buddha's example and commit themselves to emulating his accomplishment through their own practice of meditation.

How to Cultivate
a Daily Meditation Practice

The emphasis in meditation practice is on the word "practice." It's a lifelong journey, a process of learning to come back to your clear, unobstructed experience. Touching in daily with this profound practice will yield the greatest impact throughout your life.

Just as painful habits take time to unravel, helpful habits take time to instill. Here are some suggestions to help you establish a daily meditation habit. None of these ideas is a hard and fast rule. Try using them instead as tools to support your intention.

- Plan to meditate at about the same time every day. Some people find it best to sit right after they get up, while others find it easier to practice in the afternoon or at bedtime. Experiment to find what time works best for you.

- Establish a meditation corner you can use every day. It could be in your bedroom or living room; in a basement or attic; or on a porch. Wherever you sit, pick a place where you can be relatively undisturbed during your meditation sessions. If you can't dedicate this space exclusively to meditation, make sure you can easily carry your chair, cushion, or bench to and from it each day.

- Some meditators like to bring inspiring objects to their meditation space: an image, some incense, or possibly a book from which you can read a short passage before meditating. The resource list at the end of this workbook (page 224) will give you some ideas of good books to use for this purpose.

- Sit as long as you can every day. An ideal session will last forty-five minutes to an hour (the guided meditations on your *Insight Meditation* CDs last about twenty minutes each). But even five minutes of sitting or walking will help you cultivate and maintain your awareness as you continue through your day.

- Determine before you take your seat how long you'll meditate; likewise, decide beforehand how long you'll walk. This tactic eliminates the potential for discursive decision-making during your session.

- You can sit quietly, or use any of the guided meditations in this course. Until you complete the workbook, it's recommended that you use only the meditations you've worked with so far. This is because each lesson builds on those preceding it, making the meditations much richer when practiced in the context of the course structure.

❧ Keep it simple. The purpose of your practice is not to induce any particular state of mind, but to bring added clarity to whatever experience you're having in the moment. An attitude of openness and curiosity will help you to let go of judgments, expectations, and other obstacles that keep you from being present.

THE KALYANA MITTA

In this tradition of Buddhist meditation, teachers are referred to as *kalyana mitta*. This is a word in the Pali language meaning "spiritual friend." The Buddha himself was known as a kalyana mitta, in that out of compassion he pointed the way to liberation.

One of the Buddha's disciples once said to him: "It seems, venerable sir, that half the holy life is having good spiritual friends." The Buddha replied: "In fact, the whole of the holy life is having good spiritual friends." Each of us can benefit greatly from having friends who genuinely support our spiritual journey.

Some of our own teachers are mentioned in the talks contained in this course. One of them is Anagarika Munindra, an accomplished Bengali meditation teacher and scholar who studied and practiced for many years in Burma under the guidance of Mahasi Sayadaw (one of the great masters of this century). Another of our teachers is Nani Bala Barua (known as Dipa Ma), a Bengali woman who practiced under the guidance of Munindra in Burma. She embodied the qualities of love and wisdom to an extraordinary extent.

We have also practiced with U Pandita Sayadaw, one of the most renowned Burmese teachers of insight meditation. The great clarity of his teaching derives from his mastery of both study and practice. We highly recommend a book of his talks called *In This Very Life: The Liberation Teachings of the Buddha* (see resource list, page 226).

Some of the Tibetan teachers with whom we have studied include Kalu Rinpoche, Tulku Urgyen Rinpoche, and Nyoshul Khen Rinpoche. They have all been great inspirations in our own practice, and wonderful examples of liberating compassion.

The teachings in *Insight Meditation* have come to us from these teachers. May they be of benefit to all beings.

Sharon Salzberg
Joseph Goldstein

An Interview with Joseph Goldstein and Sharon Salzberg

Teachers Sharon Salzberg and Joseph Goldstein began meditating nearly thirty years ago. What first drew them to the path of awareness? How can their experience help us today, as we begin practicing ourselves? Sharon and Joseph answer some of these questions in this interview.

Sounds True: What motivated you to begin meditating?

Sharon Salzberg: I was a college student, had become acquainted with Buddhism, and had a deep intuition that meditation was the key to resolving my personal suffering.

Joseph Goldstein: I was in the Peace Corps in Thailand and started going to some discussion groups at Buddhist temples. After I had asked many, many questions, one monk finally suggested I try meditating. The possibility of a systematic inner journey was tremendously exciting.

ST: How did meditation fit with the religious training or understanding you inherited from your family?

SS: Meditation wasn't particularly connected to my early family belief systems.

JG: There was neither much conflict nor connection. I think my interest in meditation came more from my study of philosophy. I had a strong desire to understand my life.

ST: Did you find your family and friends thinking meditation was weird? How did you deal with judgments and other negative reactions to your practice?

JG: Mostly, there was support from family and friends. And I was so inspired by my practice, I wasn't much shaken by whatever negative comments did come.

SS: Society in general considered meditation weird in 1974, when we first came back from India. The reactions of others never took away the healing and obvious benefit of the practice.

ST: At what point did you make a lifelong commitment to meditation? What brought you to that decision?

JG: It's something that has unfolded quite organically, rather than coming from a decision. It quite simply feels to be the most important and rewarding thing in my life.

SS: I started practice in 1971, knew from the first moment it was important, and have never stopped. I don't recall "deciding" on a lifelong commitment — it just is.

ST: What is the most common misconception you've encountered about meditation?

JG: People often think meditation means thinking about something, reflecting on or mulling something over. In mindfulness practice the idea is to be aware of what's arising (thoughts included), but not to particularly think about what's happening.

SS: The most widespread misunderstanding I've seen is that the goal of meditation is to cease thinking, or to only have pleasant and wonderful experiences. It isn't that at all, but rather to be free, whatever experience is happening.

ST: How has meditation affected you? How would your life be different if you didn't meditate?

SS: Not meditating is an inconceivable thing to contemplate – meditation practice forms the basis of integrity, connection, and compassion in my life.

JG: It's hard to imagine my life without meditation practice. It provides a context of meaning for my life and an inner spaciousness, peace, and understanding.

ST: From your own experience, what is your best advice to beginning meditators?

JG: Whenever your mind wanders, simply begin again. All the rest will follow quite naturally.

SS: I will share what my teacher Munindra told me at the beginning: "Just put your body there." The experience of practice will always change, but it doesn't matter – our continued commitment to awareness is what's important.

THE NOBLE EIGHTFOLD PATH

*What is this Middle Way, the knowledge of which the Buddha has gained,
which leads to insight, which leads to wisdom, which conduces to calm, to knowledge,
to insight, to Nirvana? It is the Noble Eightfold Path.*

— WILLIAM JOHNSTON

In the lessons that follow, you'll see references to right effort, right action, and so on. These qualities are drawn from the Buddha's Noble Eightfold Path, which he realized at his enlightenment and included in his first teaching. The Eightfold Path delineates the course of conduct that leads to happiness. It consists of:

- right understanding
- right thought
- right speech
- right action
- right livelihood
- right effort
- right mindfulness
- right concentration

In each case, "right" means acting in a way that causes no harm, cuts through delusion, and expresses a balanced way of working with each of these factors. The steps are sometimes referred to as "wise understanding," "wise thought," and so on. Right understanding and right thought are said to lead to the accomplishment of wisdom.

Right speech, right action, and right livelihood are associated with ethical conduct, as expressed through the five precepts introduced in Lesson One. Right effort, right mindfulness, and right concentration describe the mental discipline required to follow the path of meditation.

INTRODUCTORY GLOSSARY

Each lesson in this workbook features a short glossary that defines some of the words and terms encountered in that lesson. This introductory glossary is designed to clarify some elementary meditation vocabulary.

Abhidhamma: "special doctrine" [Pali]; the body of Buddhist teachings devoted to human psychology

bodhi: "awake" [Pali, Sanskrit]

buddha: "awakened one"; specifically, Sakyamuni Buddha

enlightenment: a state of clear understanding about the nature of reality; a state of mind that is free of greed, hatred, and ignorance

gomden: "meditation cushion" [Tibetan]; a firm, rectangular meditation support

kalyana mitta: "spiritual friend" [Pali]

Middle Way: a spiritual path that avoids extremes of self-mortification and self-indulgence, as taught by the Buddha

sit: to sit in formal meditation

Theravada: "path of the elders" [Pali]; the form of Buddhism found through most of Southeast Asia (vipassana meditation is a central part of this tradition)

vipassana: "to see clearly" [Pali]; insight; the style of meditation taught in this course

walk: to practice formal walking meditation

zabuton: "sitting mat" [Japanese]

zafu: "sitting cushion" [Japanese]

LESSON ONE

THE POWER OF MINDFULNESS

"With an eye made quiet by the power of harmony and the deep power of joy, we see into the life of things." These words from the poet William Wordsworth quite beautifully reflect the process of meditation. For this, of course, is what we want: to see into the life of things, to be in touch, to be connected, to feel at home in our own lives. We don't want to live out our days mechanically, unaware, disconnected, and lost in the shadow of our conditioning.

One of the things that has always inspired me about the Theravada Buddhist tradition is that the Buddha is never described as a god or a deity. He was a human being. He was born as a prince, and lived in tremendous luxury. His call to awakening came when he saw a sick person, an old person, a corpse, and finally, a renunciate. These encounters prompted some very deep questions. The Buddha (who was then still Prince Siddhartha) essentially asked himself, "What does it mean to be born into a human body — a helpless, vulnerable, dependent child? What does it mean to grow old, whether we like it or not?"

The young prince saw that the very nature of the body is to break down, through age, injury, or illness. He asked himself, "What does it mean to exist within a body that is subject to sickness? What does it mean to die — to know that this is our future, whether we like it or not?"

No amount of protestation, grief, or longing for it to be otherwise makes any difference to the facts of our vulnerability and mortality. It's nonsensical to imagine that we might wake up one morning, look in the mirror, and say, "Okay, I've thought about it very carefully, and I've weighed all the pros and cons, and I've decided not to die" – or, "Okay, I've suffered enough. No more fear, no more grief, no more desire. I'm done." We can try that approach, but we find that thinking we can finally control the conditions of human existence doesn't lead to an abiding sense of peace.

These conditions are beyond our absolute control – just like the human mind, with its constantly changing cascade of impressions, thoughts, feelings, and images. We might wake up in the morning and feel very frightened; then, by the afternoon, we feel happy and full of faith. When evening falls, we're filled with doubt and sorrow. Even our inner world is constantly changing, beyond our control.

Having seen these truths in his own experience, the Buddha asked, "Given the nature of the body and the mind, where is happiness – true, abiding happiness – to be found? Where is happiness to be found that is not dependent on physical or mental conditions?" No one could answer his questions, and so the Buddha began a practice of awareness to discover the answers for himself.

It is taught that everything the Buddha did discover came from the power of his awareness. Nothing was just given to him. The clarity of his own mind enabled him to ask these questions – and find the answers. Because we are human beings, just as he was, we have the same capacity to understand our experience and release ourselves from the rollercoaster of capricious thoughts and emotions.

> *If you are new to practice it's important to realize that simply to sit on that cushion for fifteen minutes is a victory.*
>
> — CHARLOTTE JOKO BECK

The Buddha's questions reflect the kind of inquiry that might bring us to a spiritual search. We sense that irrespective of changing conditions, we have an ability to feel at home in our lives; to be kind to ourselves; to have a sense of fulfillment and happiness. Discovering that capacity in ourselves is the process of meditation. It's coming to find, abide in, and trust that unusual happiness.

The Buddha's quest to answer the most basic and meaningful of human questions led him to meditation. When we undertake this kind of practice, we find that it is embedded in the mythology – the language, imagery, and stories – of a particular tradition, which is Buddhism. But meditating is not at all about being a Buddhist. It has nothing to do with adopting a dogma or exchanging one set of beliefs for another. The essential point is not to consider oneself a Buddhist or anything else. Rather, we take heart from the Buddha's example and recognize that every one of us has the same capacity to ask our most personal and important questions – and to use the power of our own awareness to find the answers.

The entire purpose of meditation practice is to learn how to harness, refine, and sensitize this quite incredible power of awareness. No one is telling us to believe this or that answer to life's most profound questions. By simply becoming deeply aware of our own experience, we find the answers there. We discover that we can actually find happiness that doesn't depend on control or predictability. We have a choice other than to live out our entire lives without ever understanding why our moments of happiness seem so transient and unreliable.

THE TWO PILLARS OF MEDITATION

The first pillar of meditation is concentration. Concentration is the development of stability of mind, a gathering in and focusing of our normally scattered energy. The state of concentration that we develop in meditation practice is tranquil, at ease, relaxed, open, yielding, gentle, and soft. We let things be; we don't try to hold on to experiences. This state is also alert — it's not about getting so tranquil that we just fall asleep. It's awake, present, and deeply connected with what's going on. This is the balance that we work with in developing concentration.

The other main pillar of meditation is the quality of mindfulness. That means being aware of what is going on as it actually arises — not being lost in our conclusions or judgments about it; our fantasies of what it means; our hopes; our fears; our aversion. Rather, mindfulness helps us to see nakedly and directly: "This is what is happening right now." Through mindfulness, we pay attention to our pleasant experiences, our painful experiences, and our neutral experiences — the sum total of what life brings us.

The Persian poet Rumi said, "How long will we fill our pockets like children, with dirt and stones? Let the world go. Holding it, we never know ourselves, never are airborne."

By "let the world go," Rumi means we should let go of our addictions, obsessions, conclusions, and self-images, and see what is actually there. Then we will know ourselves; then we can be free of the burdens that keep us from taking flight. That's the quality of mindfulness: connecting deeply and directly with what is actually happening.

This means that mindfulness can go everywhere. It's not limited to a certain situation, or a degree of familiarity; nor to convention, past experiences, or expectations. The power of mindfulness opens and connects us to the entire range of our experience.

We say that mindfulness doesn't take the shape of what it's watching. In other words, it remains free in the face of what's going on at the same time as being completely aware of it. We can be aware of a beautiful state, like love or joy; we can be aware of very difficult states, like grief and sorrow; we can be aware of pleasure in the body; we can be aware of pain in the body. We can be aware of states of great silence and quiet, and we can be aware when we're trying to meditate and people are making a lot of noise around us. We can be aware of the sound, and we can be mindful of our reaction to the sound. None of these states of mind or external conditions is a problem. Everything becomes an object of meditation in the field of mindfulness.

Mindfulness is a capacity that we experience when we're not so distracted. Then we can be aware of what's going on without adding our hopes, fears, and decisions to that experience.

Once, Joseph and I were teaching a meditation program together. We were sitting in the kitchen of this little retreat center, having a cup of tea, when one of the participants burst into the room, clearly in a lot of distress. He said to Joseph, "I just had this really terrible experience."

Joseph said, "Well, what happened?"

And the participant said, "I was meditating and I felt all of this tension in my jaw, and I realized what an incredibly uptight person I am, and how I always have been and I always will be, and it's never going to change, and I'm just — I'm going to be this way for the entire rest of my life!"

And Joseph said, "You mean you felt a lot of tension in your jaw."

And he said, "Yes, and it's ruined my entire life, and I've never been able to get close to anybody because I'm so uptight, and I'll never be able to achieve real intimacy with anybody, and it's just terrible!"

Joseph said to him, "You mean, you felt a lot of tension in your jaw."

And he said, "Oh, yeah, I'm so incredibly uptight, it's horrible, I'm such an awful person, I'm so limited!"

It was really interesting to watch this exchange. It was like a ping-pong tournament, going back and forth — different ways of seeing reality, you might say; different aspects of reality.

Finally, Joseph said, "Why are you adding a miserable self-image to a painful experience?"

Yet this is what we do. We have an experience in the moment, like tension in the jaw, and we elaborate an entire story about it. "This is what I am, this is who I always will be, this is never going to change, this means this about myself" — and on and on it goes. We use mindfulness to bring us back as close as we can get to the direct experience. Only then can we see the simple truth of things, in an innocent way, with clarity. Now we're truly connected to what's going on, rather than bound and lost in these concepts about ourselves and who we are and what we're confined to, and so on.

THE WORLD OF CONCEPTS

I was eating lunch while on retreat in Burma once when I bit down on a whole chili pepper in the food. My mouth caught on fire. Shortly after lunch, I had an interview with my teacher, whose name is Sayadaw U Pandita – "Sayadaw" is a title meaning "teacher," and U Pandita is his name. I asked him, "Why do Burmese people like the taste of chilis so much?"

And he said, "We don't like the taste of chilis so much."

"Then why do you put so many in the food?" I asked.

"Well, we believe here in Burma that that stinging, burning sensation you get when you bite down on the chili will clear your palate; it's very good for your digestion; it's very good for your health. So we put a lot of them in the food."

We went on to talk about different ways of experiencing reality. There's a certain universal level to our experience: I bite down on a chili pepper, a Burmese person bites down on a chili pepper, and there's that same stinging, burning sensation. That's one level of our experience.

We are as much as we see. Faith is sight and knowledge.

— HENRY DAVID THOREAU

There's another level, on which a Burmese person biting down on the chili pepper might feel that stinging, burning sensation and think, "Oh, good, I'm clearing my palate, aiding my digestion, doing some very good things for my health." Whereas I bit down on the chili pepper, experienced the same sensation, and thought, "This is terrible, I've got to get out of this country, I've got to go to Thailand, I've got to get a salad. This is just horrible."

It's not that the ideas and concepts we hold about our experience are meaningless in our lives. We can't get rid of them, and we wouldn't want to. They're very helpful to us as we navigate our way through the world. The problem is that they come up so quickly that we're barely even aware of what the direct experience is: in this case, simply a stinging, burning sensation. Instead of simply feeling that, I immediately interpreted my experience as a profound realization about being in the wrong place, having to make intense changes, and so forth.

Concepts are formed by our hopes, fears, past conditioning, belief systems, ideas about things, and ideas about ourselves. This is a very valid world, but it's not the world of direct experience. Through mindfulness, we see the concept as simply a concept, and we come back in touch as closely as we can with the direct experience. Then we can see things anew, not so distorted or colored by our conditioning. When we see things clearly for what they are, we can begin to ask, "What's the nature of this?" In my case, the answer was simply, "The nature of this is to sting and burn," rather than, "The nature of this is an intolerable affront that makes it impossible for me to remain in Burma."

NON-DOING

Our habitual response, as human beings, is to try to prolong pleasure and avoid pain. When the experience we're aware of is pleasant, we typically try to keep it, to claim it for ourselves, to control it so that it continues to give us pleasure. When the experience is unpleasant, we're conditioned to push it away. We're afraid of it and consider it bad. We may even consider ourselves bad, just because this experience has arisen. We judge it – and we judge ourselves mercilessly. When the experience is neutral, our habit is to space out, to lose touch, to be deluded, to be confused. In meditation, by contrast, we have a direct experience in the moment, and we leave it as it is. We don't follow it up with conditioned reactions. This is why we sometimes call meditation "non-doing."

The unleashed power of the atom has changed everything save our modes of thinking.

—ALBERT EINSTEIN

Meditation is the act of not being swept away by all of these mind habits that we ordinarily have and do. Instead, we begin relaxing, being fully present with what is, being aware of it, touching it deeply, being touched by it, and seeing what is happening in the simplest and most direct fashion possible.

You might think of the metaphor of somebody walking a tightrope. As you're walking along, your most important practice is balance: to be at ease, not too tight, not too lax. The same is true of meditation. You simply stay as balanced as you can. As you're taking one step at a time on your tightrope, all kinds of things come whizzing by your head: sights and sounds and emotions and physical states and realizations and memories.

If these experiences are pleasant, we're trained to reach out and grab them – and obviously, if we're up on a tightrope and reach out like that, we lose our balance and fall. If the experiences are painful or difficult, we're conditioned to shove them away, or to recoil in fear. Once again, we lose our balance and fall off the tightrope. If the experiences are neutral, we're trained to just space out. We're not fully alive; we tend to be not entirely awake in times that aren't strikingly pleasant or unpleasant. If we're half asleep or distracted while on a tightrope, of course, we'll fall off.

So to stay on the tightrope, we have to pay attention. When we lose our balance and fall off, however, we don't land in a safety net or plunge to the ground. Instead, we land on another tightrope and begin again with the experience of this very moment: "Here it is again, something arising; another opportunity to connect; another opportunity to be mindful."

THE PATH TO DEATHLESSNESS

One of the Buddha's most provocative quotations is: "Those who are heedful or mindful are on the path to the deathless. Those who are heedless, those who are mindless, are as if dead already." To be heedless is to walk through life driven by our conditioning, lost in our concepts, and out of touch with the actual direct, living experience of this moment. And to live that way isn't really living at all.

To be heedful is to use concentration and mindfulness in order to make our minds clear, open, and expansive. Then we can begin to see the laws of nature for ourselves. We can see that everything changes; we can see the true nature of the body and the true nature of the mind. Only then can we discover happiness that is not based upon simply getting our needs met temporarily.

I was once staying with a young friend – he was about four years old at the time. I noticed that whenever he didn't get what he wanted, or something went wrong, or one of his toys broke, he would start screaming, "Nobody in this house loves me any more!" In his internal experience, an unmet desire made him feel as though all the love in the universe had been withdrawn from him.

You don't have to be a child to feel that way. Whatever our age, we can easily feel that happiness is only possible if things are a certain way, and if they stay that way. When we see the world through these eyes, what we call "happiness" is a very fragile entity. We want the body to never change, we want the mind to never change – yet the evidence is all around us that everything is in a state of constant change.

PRACTICE

One significant quality of meditation practice is that it's very pragmatic. It's not a scholarly pursuit, or tied to a belief system. We don't have to admire the accomplishments of somebody like the Buddha from afar. Meditation is a living reality that touches all aspects of our lives.

Early on in my own meditation practice, one of my teachers said to me, "The Buddha's enlightenment solved the Buddha's problem; now you solve yours." What is so extraordinarily empowering about the process of meditation is that we find out we can solve our problem: the problem of continually being disappointed as the things we pin our happiness on dissolve and reassemble in new forms. Meditation is not dependent on somebody else giving us something. The truth is not something anyone else can give us; and by the same token, nobody can take it away from us. It's been called "self-witnessed truth": the understanding that comes to us through the power of our own clear seeing. It's by way of this process that we come to sense the meaning of our own lives.

MEDITATION AND EVERYDAY LIFE

Meditation can't bring us to these insights, however, without a firm foundation. We build this foundation with our actions in the world: how we treat ourselves and others through our activity and speech. It really isn't possible to compartmentalize or fragment one's being. We may experience it that way, but actually, our lives are seamless. What we do when we sit formally in meditation is absolutely reflected in how we live, and how we live is absolutely reflected in what happens when we sit on the cushion.

The act of meditation, far from being a purely psychic exercise, actually draws moral practice and unfolding insight into a continuum.

— NEIL GORDON

Many years ago, when Joseph and I were first teaching meditation in this country, we brought over one of our teachers from Asia. We'd been here for a little while, and some interest was springing up in the practice. Various meditation communities had begun to form. We took our teacher around to all these places rather proudly. At one point, we said to him, "What do you think about this wonderful thing? Here is this Asian tradition taking root in the West and growing and blossoming – isn't it wonderful?"

And he said, "Well, it is wonderful, it's truly wonderful. There's just one thing."

"Well, what's that?"

"Sometimes," he said, "seeing people practice in the West reminds me of people sitting in a rowboat. They are rowing and rowing the boat with great ardency and effort and sincerity, but they also refuse to untie the boat from the dock."

What our teacher was saying was that he noticed people applying themselves with great sincerity and diligence; he saw them striving for powerful meditation experiences, wanting to go beyond time and space, beyond the body and the mind. They wanted to experience these wonderful transcendent or altered states of consciousness. But these very same people sometimes didn't seem to care so much about how they were relating to others day to day. They might not have much compassion when somebody was late, or when they were disappointed in a certain situation. Their capacity for kindness, presence, and awareness seemed to diminish when things weren't going so well. Sometimes, these people weren't paying attention to the ways they spoke to other people or how they related morally in their everyday working experience.

What our teacher was pointing out was that our lives are all of one, inseparable piece. We can't tell lies at work and then make an accomplished effort to seek the truth in formal meditation.

So we begin the process of meditation with the understanding that meditation is a life practice. It's not just a formal application of the mind in a certain unusual posture. It's really about how we live. We can honor that simple truth by making the mind quiet so that we can relate to our world as it is — not as we hope or fear it might be. In order to experience our deepest being, we need a life of integrity and wholeness. This is how we come to these answers, these truths, for ourselves.

The Pali word for "ethical conduct" is *sīla* (pronounced "shee-la"). Sīla is the foundation for liberation. It's the beginning of the path, and also one of the path's greatest outcomes. The Buddha taught moral conduct (or virtue, or ethical living) as the source of true beauty and happiness. It's the reflection of our deepest love and concern for ourselves and others.

Everything we do — the way we speak, the way we act — makes a difference. When we quiet our minds, we bring our lives into harmony, into spiritual truth. We see into the life of things. In order to do this, we need to pay attention to how we live, day to day.

Only dwelling in the present can make us free. We have to look into our suffering, our craving. And when we see its face we will smile: you cannot make me your prisoner any more.

— THICH NHAT HANH

Many of us feel that we're full of love and compassion when we're all alone, but as soon as we're with other people, we get frightened. Or we're fine as long as we're with other people, but we can't bear to be alone. Perhaps we're really expressing our highest values when we're working, but our family life is falling apart. Or things are going fine with the family, but we can barely keep it together at work.

The Buddha was an example of a fully integrated being. The threads of compassion and honesty and wisdom were true for him whether he was alone or among others; whether he was wandering or still; whether he was meditating or teaching. We also have the potential for that degree of wholeness and integrity. We begin with the practice of morality. The root of all moral behavior is said to be mindfulness, which is precisely what is cultivated through meditation.

THE FIVE PRECEPTS

Traditionally, Buddhists express their commitment to everyday morality by sub-scribing to five "precepts," or principles. The precepts are simply training tools that help us to keep out of trouble while our mindfulness is growing. The five precepts we undertake are expressions of our good-heartedness, our care for ourselves, and our care for others.

The first precept is a commitment to refrain from killing or physical violence. The idea is to use each day, each encounter, as an expression of our reverence for life. This approach counters the tendency to feel separate and apart, objectifying other living beings to the degree that we're actually capable of hurting them. The first precept includes bugs and animals, as well as people.

The second precept is a commitment to refrain from stealing – or literally, from the Pali, "to refrain from taking that which is not offered or not given." This means having a sense of contentment; being at peace with what we have; not stealing from the earth's natural resources; not taking more than we actually need; being grateful for what we have, and so on.

The third precept is refraining from committing sexual misconduct. This means that we resolve not to use our sexual energy in a way that causes harm or suffering to ourselves or others. Sexuality is a very powerful force in our lives; a mature spir-ituality demands that we can commit, without any self-righteousness, to not harming ourselves or others by means of this potent energy. When we don't know how to deal with our sexual desire in a skillful way, there are endless possibilities for abuse, exploitation, and obsession. That's a lot of suffering. So the third precept reminds us not to cause harm through sexuality. This includes not harming ourselves, in the sense that instead of being driven by our desires, we're able to make conscious choices.

The fourth precept is about using our power of speech in an ethical way. Traditionally, we commit to refrain from lying; but actually, this precept also covers harsh or idle speech and slander. We recognize that our speech does, in fact, have tremendous power. Words don't just come out of our mouths and disappear. Rather, they're a very important means of connecting. We need to take care with how we speak.

The last of the five precepts is a commitment to refrain from taking intoxicants that cloud the mind and cause heedlessness, meaning drugs and alcohol.

All of these precepts need to be understood in the context of training the mind. Following them is a process of getting more clearly in touch with our intentions and our degree of connection or separation from others. The precepts help us attain greater and greater awareness, and increased subtleties of understanding. They don't necessarily provide us with easy answers in every real-life situation – but what's really most important is that the precepts keep us from acting mechanically.

An example of how the precepts can wake us up comes from a spiritual community where we were invited to teach meditation. As we do when we lead retreats, we asked that the entire community – staff and retreatants – live by a form of the five precepts. When we arrived at this retreat center, we saw flypaper covered with dead flies hanging everywhere in the meditation room. We asked the staff to take the flypaper down, which they weren't very pleased about – it's true that this particular place had a bad fly problem. What was most telling about that experience, though, was that there was not a single screen on a window or door. No bug repellent was available anywhere. In our Western society, it's just so easy to kill. In fact, it's often the easiest thing to do.

Undertaking a strong and sincere commitment to the five precepts means that we're willing to forego the easy way, the convenient way, the conventional way. We're willing to really feel deeply into situations, and – using these precepts as a guideline – to see what's right and in harmony.

When you find that somehow you've broken a precept, the important thing is to take it again. Castigating yourself, or seeing the broken precept in the light of failure or an irredeemable character flaw, is pointless and counterproductive. Better to see the beauty and joy in living in harmony, and to use that inspiration to repair the fabric of wholeness in your life.

Many people ask if the first precept, to refrain from killing, means one should become a vegetarian. In terms of the Buddha's actual teaching, no. He defined killing as the intention to take the life of another being. In the Buddha's time, monks and nuns (to whom he was typically speaking) would go from door to door, begging for food. He told them that if someone offered them meat, they should take it. This was consistent with the monastic training to receive all that was offered, without discrimination. If a monk or nun knew, had heard, or even just suspected that the animal had been killed specifically for them, however, they were to refuse the meat.

It's up to you to decide how that translates into our culture, where we simply go to the supermarket and buy meat all nicely wrapped up. People work in different ways to resolve that issue for themselves. Again, the precepts aren't meant to be rigid rules that free you from the responsibility of thinking for yourself. It's good to keep experimenting with all of them, developing greater sensitivity to where your own edge lies. You can be heartened by the precepts, and find courage and simplicity of being in them — all with an attitude of love and compassion.

The purpose of the precepts isn't to feel better than anybody else, or to be self-righteous, or to feel somehow set apart and in a position to judge others. Rather, following them simplifies our lives so we can live in a straightforward manner. Have you ever had the experience of speaking badly about somebody and then having them come into the room maybe two minutes later? If you have, you know that queasy feeling: "I wonder if they heard me. What if they heard me?" That's an important feeling to notice, because this sense of shrinking, shame, embarrassment, and guilt is exactly what we don't need to be cultivating in our minds.

The point, again, is not to judge oneself: "What a nasty person I am to be slandering this person behind his back!" Instead, we ask ourselves how we could act the next time so as to cultivate clarity, directness, and consideration toward others. The Buddha said, "If you truly loved yourself, you would never harm another." So to explore our experience without judgment, but with curiosity and openness, is the greatest sign of love and compassion for others, as well. From that basis of self-respect, we can make tremendous progress in our spiritual endeavors.

The five precepts form the basis for being able to concentrate the mind in meditation. To try to concentrate the mind without following the precepts doesn't heal a certain separation or division within us. This separation is what sets us up to cause suffering for ourselves and others. Because our lives are of one piece, we can't cultivate strength of mind without strength of integrity — so the easiest way by far to meditate is to have this kind of ethical awareness as a base.

Another way to say this is that morality is taught for the purpose of concentration. If you sit down and try to meditate when your life is a mess, you're involved in deceit or a complicated set of relationships, or you've been abusing your body, you're going to find meditation difficult. When you try to concentrate, you'll encounter unsettledness, guilt, fear, and so on. There'll be a kind of fire burning in the mind. That doesn't make it impossible to meditate, but it does make it a lot more painful. We practice morality so that there's some serenity, ease, and balance in the mind right from the beginning.

From that basis, we begin to discover the power of concentration, which itself forms the basis for clear seeing. Concentration empowers us to practice mindfulness continually and effectively. Mindfulness brings wisdom, and wisdom helps us live with greater care, wholeness, and harmony – which bring us to a deeper relationship with the precepts.

So it's a unified process, where meditation helps us to see that with the full engagement of our activities, heart, intention, and mind, we can live a life of truth.

THE FIVE PRECEPTS
QUESTION AND ANSWER SESSION

Q: Most spiritually inclined people would agree that the five Buddhist precepts are all good ideas. Still, I find myself resisting the suggestion that I should follow a set of rules. It seems to imply that I'm basically a bad person who needs to be controlled.

A: Actually, the precepts aren't rules at all, but practices. The idea isn't to impose them on yourself as constraints, but to use them as supports to help you integrate the meditative state of mind into your entire life. Sometimes we need to step away from our normal way of doing things with a spirit of discovery and exploration – and also a feeling of compassion for ourselves and others. Morality isn't a question of defining ourselves as "bad" people or judging others. It's more about aspiration.

Q: I can see how maintaining the precepts can help sharpen my awareness – but how can adopting a moral code help me feel more connected with others?

A: The underlying principle of the precepts, and in fact of all Buddhist practice, is the idea of nonharming. Each of the five precepts describes a specific path that leads away from doing harm to oneself and others. When we do harm, it's because of a mistaken belief that we're separate from everyone else. Practicing the precepts gives us a very practical, everyday way to challenge that illusory separation. When we aspire not to steal, not to lie, and so forth, we're in effect acknowledging our interconnection with others, and committing to honor and cultivate that connection.

Q: Am I harming myself or others when I drink a beer with my friends on a Friday night?

A: You would have to answer that question for yourself. If you're an alcoholic, I would imagine so. If you notice that you become insensitive or muddled after a beer, that's also potentially harmful. The point here isn't to adopt an abstract idea of right and wrong, but to support your own awareness. If you've decided to meditate, you've already made a commitment to reduce the amount of delusion in your world. So the question you need to ask yourself is "Does drinking this beer support my efforts to live with less delusion? Does it sabotage my moment-to-moment awareness?"

Q: Would you clarify the precept about sexual misconduct?

A: Our sexual energy is a powerful force. The basis of the precept is an honest, sensitive awareness of what might be bringing harm to ourselves or others. This is an area that really needs our close attention, because desire can be so strong that it overpowers our aspirations.

Q: If I'm having an illicit affair with someone, should I even be learning to meditate? Is that situation canceling out the good I could otherwise derive from my practice?

A: It's always better to meditate than not to meditate, no matter what your situation. What you might find, over time, is that you become more conscious of your actions and their effects on others. This is because you can't separate your formal meditation practice from the rest of your life. You can't expect to see the truth of interconnectedness and touch your innate compassion on the meditation cushion if you're living the illusion of separation and doing things that harm others during the rest of the day.

Q: I can't shake this sense that vowing to keep these five precepts makes me some kind of mindless follower; that I'm bowing down to some external moral structure.

A: The Buddha said that morality – which basically comes down to the practice of caring and connectedness – is simply the outer manifestation of a heart filled with love and compassion. A good question to ask yourself might be, "What makes me truly happy?" Are you happier when you feel your connection with others, or when you feel isolated from others? Certain behaviors lead to happiness, while others lead to suffering. The precepts are like guideposts that point us in the direction of greater integrity, connectedness, simplicity, and compassion – all the qualities we need in order to be happy. You can use the precepts to experiment. How does it feel, for example, to not drink that beer? You could use that precept as a tool for exploring your experience. The more information you have about yourself, the more options are available to you. So instead of constraining you in some way, practicing the precepts can actually empower you.

Q: What should I do if I break a precept?

A: Just start again. That's the essence of all meditative practice: over and over and over, we're willing to start again.

POSTURE

In the Buddhist tradition, mind and body are considered interdependent facets of your experience. A relaxed body helps relax the mind. The traditional meditation posture presented here is designed to create a supportive physical structure for your awareness practice.

Many people experience some physical discomfort when they first begin sitting meditation. This is due partly to the unfamiliarity of the meditation posture, and partly to the practice of awareness revealing more deeply held tension. It's recommended that you sit comfortably and experiment until you find the posture that best supports your clarity and mindfulness.

Traditionally, Buddhist meditators have used a seven-point system to help them develop an optimal sitting posture. These suggestions apply to those who use a cushion as their meditation support. If you sit on a chair, try not to lean your back against the backrest. Keep your spine as erect as possible without straining, and your hands on your thighs. Your knees should bend at right angles, and your feet should be flat on the floor in front of you. All the instructions except those related to the legs apply if you sit on a bench.

However you choose to sit, consider these postural instructions as suggestions, rather than rigid requirements. It's better to shift your posture from time to time than to struggle against pain and stress.

1. Legs

Cross your legs loosely in front of you, just at or above the ankles. Your knees should be lower than your hips. If you use a *zafu,* your knees should be on the ground. If your legs "go to sleep" during meditation, try crossing them the other way around – or you can sit with one leg in front of the other without crossing them at all.

You can also kneel, turning your zafu on its side and placing it between your thighs and calves, as though you were sitting on a short bench.

2. Arms

Let your arms hang loosely at your sides. Now bend them at the elbows, and let your hands fall naturally onto your thighs. Don't use your arms to support the weight of your torso, or "hang on" to your knees to keep from falling backwards. Some meditators prefer the so-called "cosmic *mudra*" (gesture), which is formed by cupping your right hand in your left, palms up, with the second knuckles of your right hand roughly aligned with the first knuckles of your left. The tips of your thumbs should just barely touch one another, forming a triangle with your hands (see page 31). If you're feeling sleepy, it can be helpful to keep your thumbs very slightly apart, so that they warn you of an imminent nap attack by colliding with one another. In this mudra, your hands are resting loosely in your lap, close to your belly.

3. Back

How you hold your back is the most important element of your meditation posture. Imagine that your vertebrae are coins piled one on top of the other. Let your back find its natural erectness; don't strain. You'll find that the innate concave curvature at the small of your back helps to support your weight. As one teacher has suggested: "Imagine that your spine is a strong oak tree. Now lean against it."

4. Eyes

Let your eyelids fall closed, without squeezing them shut. If you find yourself dozing off, open your eyes slightly and let your gaze drop to the ground about six feet in front of you. Resist the temptation to let your eyes glaze – but at the same time, don't focus fiercely on whatever's in your field of vision. Let your gaze be soft.

5. Jaw

Relax your jaw and mouth, with your teeth slightly apart. It's said that your lips should be parted just enough to admit a grain of rice.

6. Tongue

Let the tip of your tongue rest behind your upper front teeth. This reduces the flow of saliva, and hence the urge to swallow. The late poet (and meditator) Allen Ginsberg called this "an old Buddhist trick."

7. Head and shoulders

When you first take your seat, position your head by gazing levelly in front of you. You'll find that this drops your neck very slightly forward. When you close your eyes (or drop your gaze), maintain this position. Be aware of your shoulders, and keep them relaxed.

These seven points have been used for centuries. You may find them difficult when you first begin to sit, but over time, you'll experience increasing ease. The first few guided meditations will teach you how to make your discomfort an object of meditation, drawing it into your field of awareness as part of the totality of your experience. With practice, you'll learn to cultivate a relaxed and attentive state of both mind and body.

GUIDED MEDITATION: BREATH

The guided meditation on awareness of the breath – the fundamental technique of insight meditation – can be found on CD 1, track 1. Use this printed version to review the instructions. As with any of the meditations in the course, you may want to record it yourself with longer silences, so that you can use it for extended meditation sessions.

Before listening to the guided meditation with each chapter, take the meditation posture on your chair, bench, or cushion. During the periods of silence, continue to practice the technique. Keep meditating as instructed until you hear the second gong, which signals the conclusion of the session. If you haven't already done so, prepare your meditation space and assume your meditation posture before beginning to listen.

You'll derive the greatest benefit from this course if you pursue each guided meditation daily for a minimum of one week. You may choose to move more slowly than that, but speeding up the process may weaken your practice and your understanding.

Each of these guided meditations lasts for about twenty minutes. After you get the hang of it, start increasing your sessions by five minutes every few days. Aim for a minimum of forty-five minutes a day – longer, if you can. If you can do this, you'll find it's a wonderful way to begin the day.

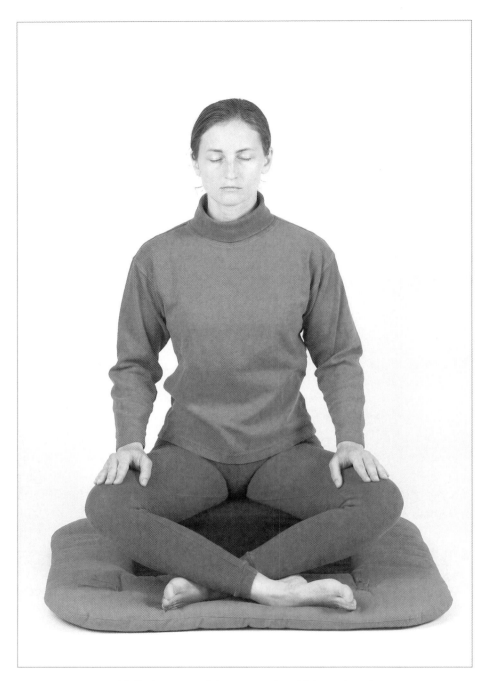

Meditation posture, sitting on a gomden with knees elevated

*Meditation posture on a zafu,
with knees lower*

*Kneeling posture, with
a meditation bench*

*When sitting on a chair,
keep the feet flat and back erect*

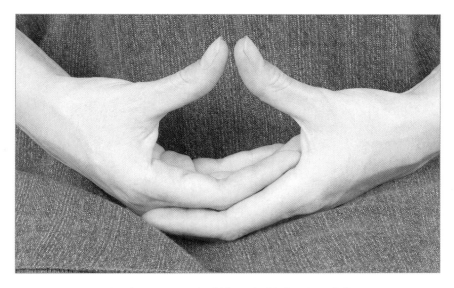

Hands may rest on the thighs, or in this "cosmic mudra"

Even if you can only sit for five minutes some days, it's more important that you sit daily. There's something very helpful about the "everydayness" of a committed practice, even if it's just for a few minutes each day. It brings you back to your intention on a very literal level. To sit regularly is to approach mind training pragmatically — not just thinking about it or admiring it, but actually putting it into practice. This is a very important point.

If it's not possible for you to meditate in the morning, it's perfectly fine to sit at any other time throughout the day. Whether or not you've sat earlier, you'll find it helpful to do so for just a few minutes before you go to sleep. The quality of your sleep will be much more peaceful and restful.

In developing a sitting practice, it helps to have a fairly comfortable posture. Find some way to sit so that your back can be erect without strain or rigidity. If you are sitting on a chair, it's best to have your feet flat on the ground in front of you. If you have a meditation bench, you might try that, or any combination of cushions. If you are sitting cross-legged on a zafu, you'll find it helpful to sit high enough so that your knees are actually touching the ground. You'll experience unnecessary discomfort if they're up in the air. On a gomden, just make sure that your knees are lower than your hips.

It's not necessary to force yourself into an uncomfortable, unfamiliar posture. In terms of developing awareness, how you sit doesn't really matter. It is helpful, though, if your back can be fairly straight, because then the breath will be more natural and you'll be more alert. Resist the temptation to lean up against something, since this, too, tends to contribute to sleepiness and other hindrances.

We sit in this tradition with our eyes closed, although this is not absolutely necessary. If you find you can stay more wakeful that way, feel free to sit with your eyes open. If you do keep your eyes open, don't look around. Just place your gaze some distance in front of you and relax. Relaxing in an alert way is the essence of the meditation.

The first instruction begins with simply hearing. As you sit comfortably, you may hear external sounds; you may hear internal sounds; you may hear a certain quality of silence. We begin with hearing because it points to something of the natural quality of mindfulness. We don't have to make the sounds come or go. We don't have to identify them; we don't have to manipulate them. We can hear sounds without having to make any effort to do so. The object of sound appears, and we're present … we're alert … we connect to it.

The mind can be relaxed, spacious; we don't have to fabricate anything. Simply hear, simply listen.

Now bring that same quality of relaxed, open, spacious awareness to feeling the breath. Take a few deep, easy breaths and release them.

Allow the breath to become natural, so you're not trying to force or control it in any way.

Notice the place where you feel the breath most distinctly. It may be the in-and-out movement of the air at the nostrils. You may feel tingling or vibration, or changes in temperature. You may feel the breath most distinctly with the rising and falling of the chest or the abdomen: stretching … pressure … tension … release.

Wherever you find it most natural, most easy, allow your mind to rest in that place and feel the breath.

As you feel the breath, you can make a silent mental note to sharpen the concentration: "in" as you feel the breath go in; "out" as you feel it leave your body. Or "rising, falling," with the sensations in your chest or belly. Very gently, very quietly in your mind, just support the awareness of the actual sensations … just note "in" and "out" … "rising" and "falling."

You don't need to make the breath special. It doesn't have to be deep or long or different from however it is and however it changes. It's happening anyway, so simply be aware of it … one breath at a time.

You may find your attention wandering. You may realize that you've been lost in thought, planning, remembering, whatever. Perhaps it's been quite some time since you last felt the breath consciously. It doesn't matter. You don't have to judge or analyze, or try to figure out how you got to where you got to. Don't worry. See if you can gently let go of whatever the distraction has been and simply begin again. Gently let go, and return the attention to the actual feeling of the breath.

This act of beginning again is the essential art of meditation practice ... over and over and over, we begin again.

You may find your attention wandering constantly. It doesn't matter. The mind has been trained to be distracted. In a very relaxed and patient manner, just let go ... reconnect ... come back to the feeling of the breath in this very moment ... the natural, uncontrived, normal breath.

You don't have to worry about even the very last breath or the very next one to come. There's no comparison, no anticipation ... it's the breath right in this moment, as it's happening. You can settle the mind there ... feel it.

If your attention feels tight or tense, go back to listening to sound ... simply hearing. Remind yourself of that effortless quality of mindfulness. We don't have to make anything happen. We don't have to make the sound happen, we don't have to make the breath happen. We don't have to perfect it; we don't have to change it. We're simply trying to be aware of it. Go back to listening to sound, simply hearing.

And then, once again, return to the sensation of the breath.

See if you can feel the beginning of this very breath, and the end of it ... or the beginning of the rising movement and the end of it ... the beginning of the outbreath and the end of it ... the beginning of the falling movement and the end of it. Just make a quiet mental note of "in, out" or "rising, falling" to support the experience, to help keep you more connected to it.

Don't try to hold on to the breath. If you find your attention has wandered, that's fine. See if you can practice being patient, being gentle, and beginning again.

You may discover that there's a pause or a gap between the inbreath and the outbreath, or between the outbreath and the next inbreath. If you find such a pause, you can allow the attention to settle in the body. Simply feel your body sitting there. Then allow the next breath to come naturally.

Notice the difference between feeling the breath and observing the breath from some distance. You're not struggling to see the breath or visualize it, but simply feeling it. Feel the tingling or the heat or the coolness at the nostrils … or the stretching, the pressure, the movement in the chest or abdomen.

There's nothing you need to do about it. You don't need to change it; you don't need to force it or perfect it.

A great teacher once said, "Be with each breath as though it were your first breath and as though it were your last breath." There's nothing to compare it with. There's a tremendous immediacy of attention. We're simply here. This is our life, right in this moment, this one breath.

Many, many distractions will arise. A torrent of thoughts and plans and images and aches and pains — it doesn't matter.

Recognize that you've lost touch with an awareness of the breath … and simply come back.

If you start to feel sleepy, try sitting up a little bit straighter. Maybe open your eyes if they've been closed. Take a few deep breaths consciously … and then again, allow the breath to become natural.

If you have to begin again and again and again in the course of one sitting, that's the practice. That's what meditation is.

Aim the attention toward the breath that's appearing right now. See if you can sustain attention through the course of one entire breath, either at the nostrils or at the chest or abdomen.

End the session by gently opening your eyes. Once again, listen to sounds … feel your body … and see if you can bring some of this quality of presence and connection to the next activity that you perform in this day.

BREATHING EXERCISES

Use the guided meditation above or on the CD to guide your practice every day for a week; then complete at least five of the following exercises.

Exercise 1

Technically, meditation can be defined as aiming the mind and sustaining attention upon an object. A common example is that of trying to pick up a piece of broccoli with a fork.

Imagine a piece of broccoli on a plate. You're holding a fork, with the obvious goal of spearing the broccoli just deeply enough so you can lift it and bring it to your mouth. To accomplish this, you need two things.

The first is called right aim. If you wave the fork around in the air, you won't get a lot to eat. Rather, you need to aim it directly at the food. The second quality you need is a careful modulation of energy. If you're too listless, the fork will just hang in your hand. If you're too forceful, you'll bash the fork through the broccoli and the plate. Everything will go flying – and again, you won't get much to eat.

In meditation, we rely on these same two qualities: aiming the mind directly at the object of the present moment, and connecting just deeply enough with our attention. Often the first object we use is the breath. We aim the mind toward just this very breath – not being concerned with what came before, or even with the next breath. In effect, we're saying: "Just this one breath."

Practice in this way for at least one meditation session of twenty minutes, and describe your experience.

_____

_____

_____

_____

_____

Exercise 2

What sensations do you feel with the in/out of the breath or the rising/falling of the chest or abdomen? Common sensations with the passage of the breath at the nostrils are coolness, warmth, tingling, vibration, pulsing, and itching. Common sensations when being with the rising and falling are movement, stretching, releasing, tension, pulsing, and pressure. Sometimes the sensations are experienced as a smooth flow, sometimes as staccato bursts. You may feel all of these, some of them, or sensations other than those described here. Spend at least twenty minutes observing your breath, and describe the sensations you feel.

_____

_____

_____

_____

_____

Exercise 3

There's no need to control the breath. Watch how outbreath just follows inbreath, without any imposition of your will. Take a few consciously full breaths, then let go. Describe how it feels to let the breath flow without directing or shaping it.

_____

_____

_____

_____

Exercise 4

Bring your awareness to the very beginning of the inbreath, either as the sensation at the nostrils or as a rising of the chest. See if you can catch the end of it. Then be aware of the very beginning of the outbreath, or of the falling movement. Briefly describe your experience.

_____

_____

_____

_____

Exercise 5

Do you use the technique of mental noting – rising, falling, in, out? What is your experience of the noting? Answer the following questions, briefly explaining each answer:

Is the mental noting too loud in your mind?

_____

Does it separate you from the actual experience of the breath?

_____

Does it help you sustain your attention?

_____

Does mental noting help you catch the beginning phase of each breath?

_____

Exercise 6

There's a difference between feeling and observing the breath. In this exercise, use a simple arm movement as a model. Move your arm slowly in front of you, back and forth. Observe it visually, as though from a distance. Now feel the sensations as though your consciousness were within the arm. Can you describe the difference?

_____

_____

_____

_____

_____

Exercise 7

Sometimes there are pauses between the in- and outbreaths, or between the outbreath and the next inbreath. If there's a pause or a gap, you can simply sit and listen to sounds, or feel touch points: areas where your body is in contact with a surface – e.g., your buttocks or knees touching the ground or chair, or your hands touching each other. Touch points are usually around the size of a quarter.

Spend approximately ten minutes bringing your awareness to the pauses between breaths, and describe the technique you use for maintaining attention at those times.

_____

_____

_____

_____

Exercise 8

Practice the gentle letting go of distracting thoughts. You don't have to judge yourself, or figure out why you were thinking or what you were thinking. Practice the simple but powerful act of always beginning again. What is your experience?

_____

_____

_____

_____

GETTING THE MOST FROM YOUR MEDITATION

- Practice breath meditation daily, using either CD 1, track 1, or your own voicing of the version above.

- Experiment with posture. Sometimes, very slight adjustments can ease discomfort.

- You might also want to try different types of meditation cushions and benches (see page 209 for resources); or see how it feels to sit in a chair.

- Use what might otherwise be considered "dead" time (e.g. in your car, or waiting for someone to show up for an appointment) to focus your awareness on your immediate experience. If you find it helpful, use your breath as the primary object of concentration. This practice will help you to expand the sense of presence and connection you're developing in formal meditation into your everyday activities.

LESSON ONE GLOSSARY REVIEW

bodhisattva: "enlightenment being" [Sanskrit]; a Buddhist saint; the Buddha's title before he became enlightened

mindfulness: the state of being fully present, without habitual reactions

mudra: "gesture" [Sanskrit]; usually refers to particular hand positions used in meditation practices

object of meditation: the activity (like the breath) or event (like sound) to which one directs attention during meditation

non-doing: meditation; the practice of refraining from reacting to internal and external events and situations

precept: a principle that defines a certain standard of conduct

right aim: mindful modulation of concentration, so that meditation is neither rigid nor sloppy; an aspect of the Noble Eightfold Path

sīla: "precepts" [Pali]; moral conduct

LESSON TWO

BARE ATTENTION

Bodhicitta is a Sanskrit word that means "awakened heart." Bodhi, as we've seen, means "awake," and *citta* means "heart" or "mind" (interestingly, "heart," "mind," and "essence" are all the same word in Sanskrit). The word bodhicitta is usually used in the sense of the heart/mind of enlightenment. Although we typically think of enlightenment as something very personal and specific to ourselves, bodhicitta actually refers to the motivation to practice for the benefit of all living beings. This is the motivation that has inspired all the *bodhisattvas* ("awakened ones") since the time of the Buddha himself.

When people first hear this teaching, they often ask, "How can I be helping others, just sitting by myself and meditating?" There are two answers to this question. First, when we meditate, we're experiencing the same basic sensations, emotions, and thought patterns that everyone experiences. The stories that go with them are our own, but the fundamental experience is no different from anyone else's. When you've been sitting for a few hours and your back aches, the sensation is the same as the backache any meditator might feel, anywhere in the world.

The more you open to that experience, the more you understand the common nature of suffering — and, by the same token, the common nature of freedom. Genuine compassion arises from this insight, because you recognize in your own suffering the suffering of everyone else on the planet. So amazingly enough, as you're sitting alone in silence, you begin to feel connected with a larger world. You recognize the depth of your own connection with every other living thing.

The second answer to the question, "How does my meditation help others?" lies in the personal transformation that always comes with sincere and continuous meditation practice. Perhaps you've seen the bumper sticker that reads, "Let peace begin with me." The only place peace, compassion, generosity, and love can begin is, in fact, with ourselves. The less selfish and judgmental we are, the more loving and accepting the world becomes. The world isn't something "out there"; it's made up of individuals like ourselves. We begin changing the world by cleaning up our little corner of it.

In the previous lesson, Sharon talked about the importance of ethical behavior both inside and outside the meditation hall. How you act inevitably affects everyone around you. Imagine, for example, that you're on a boat in the middle of a violent storm. Everyone is panicking – but it would only take one wise, calm person to get everybody working together to save the boat. That single person could save dozens of lives, just by being able to stay grounded when everyone else is too frightened to think clearly. You could say that our world is like a boat on a restless ocean. Each one of us has the potential to be the person who brings it safely home.

Solitude is the beginning of all freedom.

— WILLIAM ORVILLE DOUGLAS

Once we truly recognize the profound interconnectedness of all things, a powerful motivation arises to develop bodhicitta. That motivation deepens and strengthens our meditation, because now bodhicitta is not just some far-off goal; it's intrinsically involved in everything we do. By cultivating it, we open up our spiritual practice to include all the beings to whom we are connected. This can be a source of tremendous energy and compassion in our lives.

DEVELOPING BODHICITTA

There are many ways to cultivate bodhicitta. One that I have found useful is to begin and end my practice session or my day by reminding myself of my intention. When you wake up in the morning or as you begin your meditation, you can make the aspiration, "May I attain liberation, so that all sentient beings may be happy and free of suffering." You'll find that actually saying these words, or whatever words are meaningful to you, will help establish the intention in your heart. You can say them out loud or silently to yourself. The point is to bring your aspiration to consciousness.

Then, at the end of your practice session or your day, you can dedicate any merit you may have acquired to the benefit of all sentient beings. "Merit" refers to the benefits we gain by doing spiritual practices and living ethical lives. In the spirit of bodhicitta, we offer our merit to others. You might say, "May whatever merit I have gained today benefit all sentient beings"; or, again, you can use other words that better express your heartfelt intention.

PERSONAL TRANSFORMATION

Practices like stating your aspiration and dedicating the merit can be very helpful in developing bodhicitta. But in order to truly liberate our minds, we must go deeper. We begin by bringing awareness to our state of mind, just as it is.

If you were to ask your friends and colleagues whether their minds wander, most of them would probably say, "No – I'm pretty focused on what I'm doing." In meditation, though, we quickly come to see that our minds are engaged in fantastic voyages almost all the time. For this very reason, many people find their first meditation session disturbing. We think we have our minds pretty much under control, but as soon as we really look at them, we find that we're almost continuously lost in fantasies, judgments, and daydreams.

By now, you've probably experienced this for yourself. You sit on your cushion or your chair, and you begin to watch your mind. One breath; two breaths; and then you notice a thought sliding by and you jump aboard. Next thing you know, you're

Do not fear the arising of thoughts; only be concerned lest your awareness of them is tardy.

— CHINUL

reliving an argument or planning your vacation. Just as with the psychoanalytic technique of free association, one thought leads to another, and then another. Soon you're all tangled up in some hope or fear or drama – all centered around a very strong sense of "I" and "me." You've made a private little movie, and you're the star.

The Buddha said, "Your worst enemy cannot harm you as much as your own unguarded thoughts. But once mastered, not even your mother or father can help you as much as the mind that is tamed." That's a very strong statement, but you can see the truth of it all around us. War, injustice, exploitation, cruelty – all these originate in the mind. All of the suffering human beings inflict on one another begins with thoughts of greed or hatred or fear.

The alternative to violence and destruction is awareness. The Tibetan Buddhist teacher Pema Chödrön said, "It's impossible to harm yourself or others if you are aware." The thoughts we notice can be objects of observation, as in meditation practice – or they can be allowed to take over the mind, leading us to act out the causes of terrible suffering.

It's actually not difficult to be mindful of our experience. When we pay attention, awareness arises very naturally. The difficult part is remembering to be mindful. This is what meditation practice trains us to do.

The Nature of Meditation Training

How do we tame our minds? How do we train ourselves to stay open to our experience from moment to moment? The answer lies in a mind state called "bare attention." "Bare" means simple, direct, without trappings of judgment or interpretation. "Attention" means mindfulness, awareness; not forgetting to be present. A famous Zen haiku reads:

> The old pond.
> A frog jumps in.
> Plop.

This is a wonderful description of bare attention. The old pond is not necessarily beautiful or covered with lily pads or green or blue. The poet, Basho, goes directly to the essence of his experience: the pond, the frog, plop.

We could say that in meditation, we're developing "plop mind." We're stripping away everything extraneous to our immediate experience and simply being present with what's happening. This is bare attention: direct, essential, noninterfering.

In the previous lesson, Sharon discussed the balance between tranquility and alertness. This same balance applies to bare attention. It's similar to listening to a new piece of music: you're not straining to hear something in particular. You're attentive, but also relaxed. You're open to the way the music evolves. Bare attention works in much the same way.

Cultivating Bare Attention

There are four tools we use in meditation to support and strengthen the quality of bare attention. The first of these is called a *primary object of awareness*. It doesn't really matter what that object is. Traditionally, we use something that's already happening, so that our attention need not go to fabricating or maintaining anything. The most common objects of awareness are sound and breath – and in walking meditation, the walking itself.

The primary object of awareness is like a home ground that we return to every time we realize that the mind is wandering. It's not that we struggle to stay aware – awareness is a natural state of the mind. We simply practice to remain undistracted from this natural awareness, and we use the primary object of awareness as a reminder to come back to it. So you bring your attention to your breath, this breath, as it's happening; or to this step, or this sound.

It's also possible to cultivate something called "choiceless awareness." This is a state of great receptiveness, where we simply open up to whatever object arises from one moment to the next. Until the mind is somewhat stabilized through meditation practice, however, it's more helpful to use a primary object of awareness.

The second tool used in cultivating bare attention is *mental noting* or *labeling*. This is when, for example, we note the inbreath and the outbreath by saying silently to ourselves, "in," "out," "in," "out," and so on. You may sometimes find that noting in this way becomes mechanical: suddenly, you realize that you're labeling the outbreath "in" and the inbreath "out." This is not considered a problem. Just recognizing that you've slipped into automatic mode is, in itself, a return to awareness. If you hadn't been mentally noting, you might not have noticed it, at least as quickly.

It's very common to fall into the trap of judging yourself every time you realize your attention has wandered. Instead of judging yourself for getting lost in thoughts, you could celebrate the fact that you were able to recognize what was happening and use that recognition to wake up. Practicing delight is much more helpful than practicing judgment.

In the beginner's mind there are many possibilities, but in the expert's mind there are few.

— SHUNRYU SUZUKI ROSHI

Of course, breathing isn't the only thing that happens during meditation. You may use it as the primary object of awareness, but inevitably, other experiences arise: thoughts, sensations, emotions. We use mental noting to mark these experiences, too. When you recognize anger, for example, you can say to yourself, "anger, anger." At this point, the tone of the note can be very revealing. If you're judging yourself for being angry, your tone might be irritated or impatient. In that case, what is arising is irritation or impatience. So you note that. This technique can be very helpful in revealing the quality of your experience in any given moment of awareness.

Don't feel compelled to use mental noting all the time. Sometimes, you can simply rest in the awareness of whatever is going on — breaths or emotions or thoughts. That said, you will find that it's always helpful to bring in mental noting from time to time, because it can cut directly through to your immediate experience. Sometimes awareness can become superficial without you realizing it. At these times, mental noting takes you deeper. Experiment with this technique and see for yourself how you want to use it. Do work with it, though, so that it becomes a familiar and truly useful tool in your practice.

A third tool helpful in cultivating bare attention is *slowing down*. Say, for example, that you're eating your breakfast. You might be quite present in your body and aware that you're eating; but you could drop down to another level of awareness and feel the precise sensations of the food on your tongue, your hand holding the fork or spoon, and the movement of your arm as you bring the food to your mouth. In order to perceive clearly all these specific components of your experience, you'll find it very helpful to slow down. Try it for yourself. At any time during the day, bring your awareness to what you're doing – drinking a cup of tea, writing a note, walking from one place to another – and watch what happens when you slow down. As you do so, see how it feels to bring careful attention to the sensations in your body.

I have often regretted my speech, never my silence.

— PUBLIUS SYRUS

Slowing down isn't a contrived tensing or holding back. Rather, it's a settling back into the body; the opposite of rushing. When you're rushing, it's as though you're ahead of yourself. Your energy is being yanked forward by whatever goal you're rushing toward, and you're trying to keep up. To slow down is to regain your balance so that your energy is available for whatever is happening in this moment.

We all experience the feeling of rushing, every day. It's actually an excellent reminder that you're not present. In the same way that mental noting can bring you back into the moment, noticing that you're rushing automatically slows you down. As your attention grows more finely honed, you'll become aware of layers of experience you never knew were available to you. This is especially apparent during extended periods of meditation, whether in daily practice or – particularly – on retreat. As your mind grows still, everyday experience becomes somehow magically alive. You might notice a fallen leaf, the slow movement of clouds, the silhouette of a tree against the sky – all transformed through the lens of your deepened perception.

Your own experience is always the most reliable guideline in applying meditation techniques. When you slow down, notice what speed best supports your mind-fulness. Practice steadily and continuously, at a pace that allows you to be fully attentive to one thing at a time.

LIGHTENING UP

Sometimes, and particularly when they first begin meditating, people tend to confuse the effort involved in bare attention with rigidity. There's a perception that we have to be constantly vigilant in following certain rules to the letter. I like to use a contemporary Zen story to show the value of flexibility in your practice.

The Korean Zen master Seung Sahn Soen Sa Nim would tell his students, "When you eat, just eat. When you walk, just walk." In other words, you should keep your attention on one thing at a time. One morning, some of his students came upon the master reading a newspaper while eating his breakfast.

"How can you be doing this?" the students demanded. "Haven't you taught us that when you eat, you just eat, and when you read, you just read?"

Completely at ease, and without missing a beat, Soen Sa Nim said, "There's no problem here. When you eat and read, just eat and read."

So we can apply bare attention with some sense of ease and flexibility. We don't have to take ourselves so seriously.

There's one more tool we can use in both our meditation practice and our everyday lives. That tool is the very great gift of *silence.* Silence has been valued by all of the world's spiritual traditions throughout history. Isaac of Nineveh, a sixth-century Christian saint, said, "If you would be a lover of truth, be a lover of silence; for silence is the mother of truth."

For some of us, our first meditation session is our introduction to the revelation of silence. When the mind is free of the need to process speech – or music, for that matter – we perceive our minds, bodies, and experience at a level of clarity not typically available to us. Experiment with using periods of silence in your life. You could choose to be silent for an hour, a day, or even longer, when circumstances permit. Notice the quality of your thinking and feeling during these times.

LIVING IN THE MOMENT

One of the insights of meditation practice is that most of the time, our minds are caught up in thoughts of the past or future. We weave fantastic stories about things we remember or events we hope or fear will come to pass.

As our practice deepens, however, we realize that all these stories are simply thoughts in the mind. The only experience we have of the past is in the form of a thought that is happening right now. The same is true of our experience of the future. To recognize this in meditation – "Oh – this is just a thought" – is often a relief. You realize that the drama in which you've been lost, and which has consumed so much energy, is nothing more than a passing thought in the moment. Your experience immediately becomes more spacious, and you feel your body and mind relaxing again.

A very common misconception about meditation is that our goal is to stop thinking altogether. Thoughts are regarded as bad; as obstacles to meditation practice. But as long as we're conscious, thoughts will inevitably arise (although there are, of course, times when the thinking mind does quiet down). The function of meditation is to shine the light of awareness on our thinking. It's not that we shouldn't have thoughts, but rather that we train not to get lost in them.

Consciousness is selective, and the normal range of awareness is extremely narrow in the ordinary waking state. When consciousness begins to observe itself, however, it begins to expand.

— FRANCES VAUGHAN

The practice of bare attention opens up the claustrophobic world of our conditioning, revealing an array of options. Once we can see clearly what's going on in our minds, we can choose whether and how to act on what we're seeing. The faculty used to make those choices is called discriminating wisdom. "Discriminating," here, is not the same as the kind of discrimination involved in bigotry and prejudice. Rather, it's the ability to know skillful actions from unskillful actions. It's being able to see what leads to happiness, and what leads to suffering.

Henry David Thoreau made a very beautiful statement about bare attention and discriminating wisdom. He said, "I went to the woods because I wished to live deliberately, to front only the essential facts of life, and see if I could learn what it had to teach, and not, when I came to die, discover that I had not lived." This same aspiration sustains our meditation practice. We train to live deliberately, fronting only the essential facts of life, and we see if we can learn what these direct experiences have to teach. In this way, we truly live our lives, instead of ignoring them or waiting for them to happen.

Another common misconception about meditation is that one can only meditate successfully in an ideal environment — with perfect quiet, the right temperature, and so forth. In fact, nothing falls outside the sphere of meditation. Everything is subject to observation. Our minds are like the sky, in which the sun of awareness is always shining. We may experience hurricanes, ice storms, monsoons — but behind the clouds the sky remains spacious and open, and (as anyone who has flown above the clouds can attest) the sun continues to shine.

RIGHT EFFORT

It's possible – and, in fact, not uncommon – to be perfectly aware, but in the context of wanting something to happen. We could call this "in order to mind": "I'm watching the breath in order for a certain experience to arise." This can feel like "right effort" (the sixth step on the Buddha's Noble Eightfold Path – see page 10) but right effort actually refers to the effort to be aware of what's arising in the moment. Expecting some wonderful spiritual experience, or even just a time when your knee will stop hurting, is closer to a hindrance than it is to right effort.

Right effort is the energy we use to cultivate bare attention. When people hear the word "effort," they sometimes think of straining or struggling. But the effort we apply in meditation practice is more accurately described as perseverance. It's the energy of motivation, which brings us back again and again to our awareness. There are always ups and downs in meditation practice. Sometimes it's easy, even enjoyable. Sometimes it's irritating, difficult, or downright painful. We need right effort to keep returning to the moment, whatever it feels like.

The Pali word for "effort" is *viriya,* which can also be translated as "strong heart" or "courageous heart." Courage doesn't want or expect anything. It simply enters the situation with openness, determined to meet whatever arises with strength and integrity. What sustains this courageous heart is a sense of exploration. We take a strong interest in finding out the true nature of the body, the mind, the emotions, our experiences. We become curious: what is a breath? What is a thought? What actually happens, moment by moment, when the mind becomes drowsy?

After some practice, you may begin to feel that the breath is boring. It comes in, it goes out, it comes in – it seems so predictable. But there's another, more compelling way to look at the breath. Say, for instance, that someone was holding your head underwater. At that point, the breath would become more interesting than anything else. Breathing is not a metaphor for something else. Our lives depend on our ability to take the next breath. To watch the breath is to watch life happening. You can feel that vital energy entering and leaving your body. It only seems boring because we're not accustomed to bringing our full attention to each breath.

Nor is each breath the same as the last. As we watch, we discover nuances of temperature, texture, endurance, location in the body. Each breath is a separate event, with its own characteristics. The breath is not predictable at all. The flow of breathing is like a river: at first glance, it looks as though the water is flowing by in an unchanging pattern. But when you watch closely, you see that it's changing all the time. The currents, the colors, the texture of the water's surface – all are in con-stant flux. There's a whole world to be explored. The same is true of our breathing.

The same is true, in fact, of all our inner experience. When we bring a genuine spirit of exploration to our sensations, thoughts, emotions, and perceptions, we see that our lives are unfolding in all kinds of interesting ways. We just never noticed it before we discovered bare attention. This realization can provide powerful motivation for practice.

Investigating the nuances of our experience in this way also reminds us of the commonality of our human experience. As we delve deeper into the nature of being alive in this body, we come to a visceral understanding that we are never practicing just for ourselves, but for the benefit of everything that lives.

BARE ATTENTION: QUESTION AND ANSWER SESSION

Q: Am I supposed to clear my mind of thoughts during meditation?

A: One central function of the mind is to generate thoughts, and there are many situations in our lives where that's helpful – even indispensable. The point of meditation is to train ourselves to know the difference between thinking and being lost in thought. If we don't know that difference, we get trapped in worlds that exist only inside our minds, and miss the moment-to-moment immediacy of our lives.

Q: Does that mean that, at least when I'm meditating, thoughts are my enemy?

A: Not at all. Thoughts are no more and no less than fleeting images and im-pressions that pass through your mind. Watching them is enormously helpful, because this is the way you find out how insubstantial and ephemeral they actually are. When you start to investigate the thinking process, you come to understand more fully the difference between being lost in the stories of your thoughts and your direct experience. Without that understanding, it's very difficult to live in the present.

Q: Isn't the mental noting technique just another way of generating thought? I mean, here I am, thinking a thought, and then on top of that, I have to think "Oh, thinking."

A: The mental note is a thought, but it's a skillful use of the thinking process. It helps support your awareness of just what is arising. Not only does mental noting help you bring awareness to your thoughts, it cuts through the stories thoughts tend to spin. So for example, you might be thinking about how much you're attracted to someone, or how angry someone has made you, or you may be developing elaborate mental plans for the house you're going to build, but when you label these thoughts, they're all just "thinking, thinking."

When you don't get involved in them, all thoughts follow a natural life cycle of arising, dwelling, and passing away. Mental noting helps you to not take the contents of your thoughts too seriously.

Q: Some teachers stress focusing on positive thoughts and letting go of negative ones. Is that a good thing to do?

A: Certain practices work in this way and can be very helpful. In vipassana, we simply label all thoughts as "thinking," and let them go on their way. The result of that is that we can let go of negative thoughts because we see their impermanence and transparent nature, not because we're afraid of them or are condemning them.

Q: As I continue to meditate, will I find myself experiencing fewer thoughts?

A: Often, the mind does quiet down, and there may not be the usual flood of thoughts. Periods of great stillness might come more frequently. It's important to remember, though, that the goal of meditation isn't necessarily to stop all thought, but to become more present for your experience – including your experience of thinking – throughout every part of your life. The more we practice in this way, the less we find ourselves being driven by our mental constructions. So whether we have fewer thoughts than we did before, or thoughts continue to arise, our responses to our thoughts change. By becoming aware of the fact that we're thinking, we're better able to bring some discriminating wisdom to our choices. Do I want to act on this thought? Or just watch it pass on through?

> *It's not difficult to be mindful. It's difficult to* remember *to be mindful.*
>
> — JOSEPH GOLDSTEIN

Q: You've talked about emotions as one of the phenomena we pay attention to. But I typically can't feel my emotions. Do you have any advice for me?

A: A Japanese teacher was asked to write down the highest wisdom. He wrote, "Attention, attention, attention." When a student asked him what that meant, he simply said, "Attention means attention." It's actually very simple. The more you can bring your experience into the light of awareness, the more you'll begin to recognize that you do have feelings, and to track the ways those feelings inform your actions and behaviors.

Q: When I'm not paying attention, by definition, I don't know that I'm not paying attention. Is there any way to short-circuit my inattention before it blocks out my experience?

A: When you notice you have wandered, bring a closer attention to the primary object and simply begin again. If you sincerely bring mindfulness to the experience arising in the moment, you'll be able to be aware of what's happening. The trick is to keep coming back again and again to the practice of mindfulness.

Guided Meditation: Walking

Walking meditation is the application of bare attention in movement. It becomes a model, then, for being mindful in all the movements we make throughout the day. During this instruction period, please stand up. Stand comfortably, with your hands at your sides, or loosely holding them behind your back or in front. Your feet should be shoulder-width apart, so that there's a feeling of being at rest in this standing position.

For now, and for as much of this exercise as is practical, please close your eyes. Of course, in the actual walking practice, the eyes are open. Standing easily, eyes closed, bring your attention to the top of your head, and simply feel whatever sensations might be there.

Let your attention rest at the top of your head, feeling whatever's there … maybe it's the absence of sensation.

Very slowly, let your attention move down the front of your face. Feel your forehead, your eyes, nose, mouth … feel the cheeks, the jaw.

Now move the attention from the top of the head down the back, the back of the head, into the neck, noticing whatever sensations you might feel.

Let your attention move from the top of the head down the sides, feeling your ears as you do so.

Now feel the whole head, simply noticing whatever sensations are there … moving the awareness down into the neck and throat.

Feel the shoulders.

Slowly move the awareness down the upper arms ... feeling the elbows, the forearms. Feel your hands, the palms of your hands, the backs of your hands, the fingers, the fingertips.

See if you can feel each finger separately ... the sensations in each individual finger.

Let your attention rest for a moment in the feeling of the fingertips.

Now bring the attention back to the neck and throat, and slowly move the awareness down through the chest, feeling the whole chest area.

Feel the rib cage ... the abdomen ... being very receptive, very open, very gentle, not looking for anything in particular, but simply being open to whatever feelings might be there.

Bring the attention back to the neck and let your awareness slowly move down the back.

You can move straight down the back, or zigzag down ... feeling the different sensations as you move down the back.

You may feel areas of tightness or tension, tingling or vibration, warmth or cold. Simply be aware of whatever you feel as you move your attention down your back ... through the shoulder blades, mid-back, lower back.

Settle into the area of the pelvis ... opening to whatever sensations you might feel there.

Slowly move your awareness down your legs ... down through the thighs, feeling the knees ... feeling the calves ... slowly moving your awareness down through your legs, feeling your ankles ...

... bringing your attention into your feet ... the top part of your feet ... the soles of your feet.

See if you can feel each individual toe.

Become aware of the sensations of the foot making contact with the floor ... what are those sensations? Do you feel heaviness, or softness, or hardness? Do you feel warmth or coolness?

Feel the contact of your feet and the floor ... notice what those sensations may be ... hardness or softness ... pressure ... heaviness ... heat or cold ... simply opening to that experience, those sensations of contact, of feeling the feet touching the floor.

Now do a very quick scan of the body from top to bottom, from head to feet ... just as a way of getting centered in the body, getting centered in the awareness of body sensations.

Standing at ease, very slowly begin to shift your weight onto your left foot ... very slowly ... feeling the subtle sensations of movement as you shift your weight ...

... really bringing a microscopic attention to the subtleties of sensation in this very slow and careful movement.

Shift all your weight onto your left foot, and rest there for a moment.

Feel the difference between your experience of the left leg and foot and your experience of the right.

You might feel that the left leg and foot are heavy, there's more weight, there's more pressure, and the right foot is lighter ... or they may feel the same.

Again, very slowly, with a lot of care, begin to shift your weight back through center, all the way onto your right foot and leg ...

... moving very slowly ... noticing the nuances, the subtleties of the sensations in this movement.

Rest for a moment with all your weight on the right foot and leg.

Now with the same care, the same attentiveness, very slowly begin to lift the heel of your left foot.

Just lift the heel and feel the sensations of that movement ... feel the different sensations in the foot and leg as you lift the heel.

Very slowly, lift the foot ... and take a very careful and short step forward, moving forward, feeling the left foot and leg move through the air ...

... feeling that movement ... and then very slowly placing the foot on the floor.

Notice the sensation of the lifting of the heel, the moving forward of the leg, and the placing of the foot back on the ground.

Now bring your attention to the right foot ... very lowly lifting the heel, feeling the sensations of that movement ... moving the foot forward through the air ... placing it, noticing the sensations as you bring the foot down and let it come to rest on the floor.

Now, gently come back to center ... standing at ease.

This very slow movement is a model for the kind of care, the kind of attention that we can bring to our walking practice. If you're unable to walk for any reason, you can do this meditation in other ways and reap equal benefit. For example, if you're in a wheelchair, find a space where you can roll back and forth for some distance. Simply be aware of the movement of the arms as they're turning the wheels, or whatever movement you make in steering the wheelchair. Just stay very aware of the sensation of the movements. Stay aware of the touch sensation. When you come to the end of the path, be aware of the intention to stop. Notice the feeling of the whole body as you're sitting and stopping; notice what happens as you begin to turn.

Again, it's a question of being with the sensation of the movement, the sensation of touch, touching of the hands, the feeling of the whole body, the sense of touch contact with your seat and the chair; being aware of what's arising in this arena of sensation.

Even if you're bedridden, you can do the same movement meditation with your fingers or arms. Just raise your arms slowly up, feeling the sensation of that movement. Feel the arm move down, the sensation of touch on the bed ... Even as small a movement as curling the fingers could serve – so be creative and innovative in your application of this particular practice.

Now open your eyes. Find a place, inside or outside, about ten to twenty steps in length. It need not be a long distance. Stand at one end of this path for a moment and do a body scan as a way of getting centered, settling the attention in the body.

We'll divide the walking period into three sections. During the first ten minutes, walk back and forth at a slightly slower-than-normal speed. As you're doing this part of the walking practice, you can use a very simple mental label with each step. Note "left, right, left, right" or "stepping, stepping" each time the foot touches the ground. Or perhaps "touching, touching."

The primary emphasis in the practice is to stay centered in the body, feeling the actual sensations of movement. The mental noting should be very soft, in the background. Use it simply as a way of helping to keep the mind connected to what's going on.

The essence of the practice is bare attention. What we're practicing is bare awareness of the feeling or the sensations when we walk or move.

As you're walking at a near-normal speed, feel the movement of your body. Feel the movement of the legs and the feet.

Feel the sensation of the foot touching the ground, and make a simple mental note of "left, right, left, right," "stepping, stepping," or "touching, touching."

Be relaxed in your body with that quality of bare attention. It's alert, it's receptive, it's noticing the sensations in the movement of walking.

Notice when your mind wanders. Notice when you get lost in a thought.

Whenever you notice that the mind has wandered, simply be aware of this and come back to the step … come back to the movement.

After walking back and forth at a speed just a little slower than normal for about ten minutes, begin to slow down. Now we'll divide the step into two parts. Begin to note the lifting and placing, lifting and placing. Feel the specific sensations associated with each of those parts of the step.

As you lift, what is it that you feel in the foot and leg?

As you place, what sensations are arising?

See how carefully you can notice what is going on – "lift, place, lift, place." Or you might use the note of "up, down, up, down."

When you begin to slow the movement down, you can bring your awareness to the two distinct parts of the step: "lifting, placing" or "up, down," feeling the specific sensations with each part of those steps.

What does it feel like as you lift the heel, as you lift the foot? What does it feel like as you place the foot on the ground – the lowering movement, the actual sensation of touching?

After some time, slow the walking practice down even further. Now you can divide the step into three parts: "lift, move, place" or "up, forward, down." Finish one step completely before lifting the other foot.

Settle back into the very slow and easy rhythm, with careful attention to the sensations of lifting, the sensations of moving forward, the sensations of lowering the foot and touching.

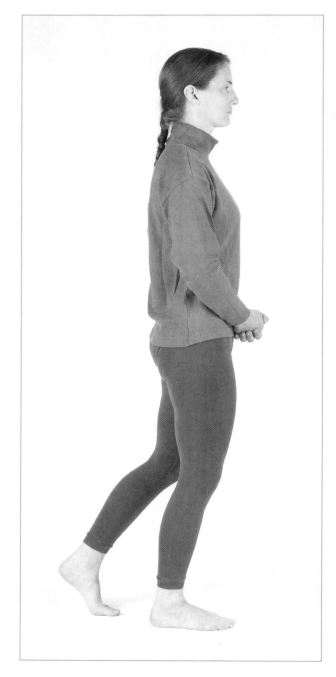

Walking as meditation in motion

The walking meditation principles can be used with any repetitive movement, such as raising and lowering an arm

Lifting   *Stepping*   *Placing*

The rhythm of this slow walking is quite different from the way we usually move. It may take a short while for you to get used to this rhythm, where you finish one step completely before lifting the other foot. Lift, move, place, come to rest … and then lift the other foot, move it forward, and place it.

Continue at this speed, settling back into the movement, settling into your body with bare attention, feeling the subtlety of sensations with each part of the step. Try to keep the mind and body relaxed. There need not be any kind of struggle or forcing.

The walking meditation can be as graceful as a slow movement in a martial art, or perhaps a slow movement in a classical dance. "Lift, move, place; lift, move, place." Keep the noting very soft.

The noting is simply an aid to help us stay connected to the actual feeling, the actual sensations we're experiencing.

How slowly should you walk or move? At the speed that keeps you most mindful. For most people, this means starting at a somewhat faster pace, and then gradually slowing down as the mind becomes more focused and concentrated. But at times, you might find it helpful to begin with very slow walking. If you find that the mind is wandering a lot, that you're not connected, you can change the speed at that point to a faster pace.

Feel free to experiment with the speed at which you move, keeping in mind that the guideline is mindfulness. Walk at the speed that keeps you most attentive, most mindful.

Generally, you place the emphasis on the sensations in the foot and leg as you move. At times, though, you can also be with the sensations of the whole body. Feel the whole body as it's moving through space ...

... and then come back again to the specific sensations in the foot and leg. Notice when the mind wanders, when you get lost in thought ... and come back again to the feeling of movement, the feeling of touch.

Doing this walking practice at different speeds is a useful model for how we can be attentive in movement throughout the day. You can take the experience of this exercise into your daily life, and remember to feel what it is you're doing as you stand, as you sit, as you turn, as you reach. It's very simply being in the body with awareness, with the quality of bare attention. Through this awareness, we begin to understand the nature of the body on deeper and deeper levels.

It's very helpful to do this walking meditation every day, either before your sitting practice or at some other time in the day. If you have time to do both the sitting and walking practices during the same session, you'll find that doing the walking first will help you be more concentrated when you sit down to practice. If you don't have time to do the two together, find any other time in the day where you can do the walking for twenty minutes, half an hour, forty minutes – whatever is convenient.

Sometimes in the evening, if you're feeling full of energy or restless or tired, you might find that the walking practice is actually more helpful than the sitting. Because the movement is quite obvious and tangible, people often find it easier to focus the attention in the walking.

WALKING EXERCISES

Practice along with the instructions for walking meditation on CD 1, track 2, or use the version above. For a visual sense of how to do walking meditation, review the photographs on pages 58-59. If you are unable to walk, practice some other repetitive movement, such as curling and uncurling your fingers or bending and straightening your arm. After practicing in this way for a week, respond to at least five of the following exercise questions in the spaces provided.

Exercise 1

Slowly lift, move forward, and place your foot as you take a single step. What sensations do you notice? What do you feel as the weight shifts to the other foot? Go through the same three-part movement again, noticing what sensations you feel in each part of the step.

_____

_____

_____

Exercise 2

Practice walking back and forth without any destination. Now walk for a few minutes with a destination. How do you experience the difference between these two approaches?

_____

_____

_____

Exercise 3 – Standing Meditation

Stand (or sit, if necessary) in a relaxed position, and notice the difference between your concepts or image of the body and the reality of bodily sensations. What do you actually feel in your foot, your leg, your body? Do you feel any sensations?

_____

_____

_____

Exercise 4

Practice walking meditation as though your consciousness resided in your head. Now walk as though your consciousness were within the physical sensations of movement. Describe the difference.

_____

_____

_____

Exercise 5

Practice mental noting as you walk. Try to time your noting so that you label "lifting" at the very beginning of the lifting movement, "placing" at the very beginning of the placing movement, and so on. How did you do?

_____

_____

_____

Exercise 6

Do you feel the shifting of your weight between steps? What is your full body experience as you turn?

_____

_____

_____

Exercise 7

Practice walking meditation with your senses as wide open as you can make them. Hear, see, and feel everything in your field. Describe your experience.

_____

_____

_____

_____

GETTING THE MOST FROM YOUR MEDITATION

- Practice walking meditation regularly – either before or after your daily sitting meditation, or during a separate walking meditation session each day.

- Apply the techniques of walking meditation to your routine activities during the day. For example, try bringing your awareness to the movements you make when you open your front door, or the ways you hold your fork when eating.

- Be especially aware of the added distractions that may arise when you practice with your eyes open (as during walking meditation). Use mental noting to renew your awareness of the movement of your foot and leg.

- Experiment with pace. Try walking a little faster, then a little slower. This will help you find the pace that best supports awareness. Give yourself permission to change your pace as necessary.

- Regard walking meditation as a practice in its own right, rather than a break from sitting meditation. Although it can provide physical relief through movement during lengthy sitting sessions, walking meditation is equally effective for practicing awareness. Try to stay continuously mindful as you move from one practice to the next.

LESSON TWO GLOSSARY

bare attention: the awareness of direct experience (see "plop" mind, below)

bodhicitta: "awakened heart"; the state of mind that motivates us to help alleviate others' suffering

discriminating wisdom: the capacity to distinguish between direct and conceptual experience; sometimes used to distinguish wholesome or beneficial thoughts and actions from unwholesome or harmful ones

"in order to" mind: a goal-oriented motivation; a mind filled with expectation

mental noting: a technique used in meditation to help direct the mind to the object of meditation

merit: the spiritual benefits we derive from practicing generosity, ethical conduct, and meditation

"plop" mind: immediate awareness, like the sound of a frog plopping into a pond

retreat: an extended period of meditation

right effort: the energy to undertake the spiritual journey; an aspect of the Noble Eightfold Path

viriya: the strong, courageous heart of energy

LESSON THREE
DESIRE AND AVERSION

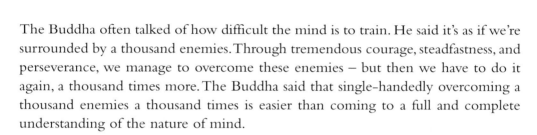

The Buddha often talked of how difficult the mind is to train. He said it's as if we're surrounded by a thousand enemies. Through tremendous courage, steadfastness, and perseverance, we manage to overcome these enemies — but then we have to do it again, a thousand times more. The Buddha said that single-handedly overcoming a thousand enemies a thousand times is easier than coming to a full and complete understanding of the nature of mind.

So we've undertaken a very difficult task. It's not surprising that problems or difficulties arise in the course of our practice. These are very much part of the path. What we're learning to do is to recognize and work skillfully with whatever obstacles and hindrances arise. In this way, we can actually free the mind in the midst of difficult inner or outer situations.

The mind itself is clear, lucid, and unobstructed. Its nature is to simply know whatever is arising. We don't recognize this empty, open nature of awareness because we get distracted and seduced. We get caught up in long-established habit patterns of thoughts and feelings. Often these conditioned tendencies are so familiar to us, so much a part of who we take ourselves to be, that they remain invisible until we illuminate them with the power of mindfulness and investigation.

We all have our own particular conditioned stories and dramas that we get caught up in again and again. The Buddha singled out a few of these very strong tendencies that lie at the root of distraction in the mind. He called them the "hindrances," and he named five of them. In this lesson, we'll discuss the first two: desire and aversion.

Desire

We begin with the hindrance of desire. In English, the word "desire" has several meanings: the simple motivation to do something; our basic needs for food and shelter; greed; lust. When we talk of desire as a hindrance, we're referring to a force of craving, clinging, or grasping. Desire, in this context, means a quality of attachment or holding on in the mind. Our strongest attachments (and therefore our strongest desires) are to our bodies, to other people, and to the things we crave. The intensity of desire has a huge range. It can manifest as an obsessive passion that dominates our lives, or some addictive craving that we get caught up in again and again. It can be the recurrent fantasies that play through the mind repeatedly, or even just a passing thought. Desire surfaces many times through the day, in the form of a passing want for chocolate, or a new car, or an athletic body.

In meditation practice the field of desire narrows considerably, because meditation involves a significant level of renunciation. In our culture, we tend to think of renunciation as a burden. "I don't want to do it," we say, "but I will because it's good for me" – like a child eating spinach. But when we begin to understand the power, joy, and meaning of renunciation, our point of view changes. Now we can see that addiction is the real burden, and that not buying into desire is the greatest freedom. Yet even in the renunciation of the meditative state, the mind finds many opportunities for wanting to arise. One simple example involves the desire for food. For many people, how we relate to food and eating is a major issue. The desire for excitement or stimulation is another common occurrence in our culture, and one that advertisers do their best to encourage.

A good time to practice recognizing desire is during walking meditation, when you have the urge to look around. You catch something out of the corner of your eye, and when you're not mindful, not aware – before you know it, you turn, you look, and you start thinking about what you see. You can get lost in pleasant or unpleasant fantasies, either about the people around you or about situations outside the meditation hall.

A very common phenomenon, especially on retreats, is the vipassana romance. We may have anywhere from 50 to 150 people practicing in silence; not speaking to one another; supposedly not looking around. Yet it doesn't take long before somehow, you've managed to scope out the entire room and find that one person to whom you feel this amazing attraction. You may never have spoken to them; you may know nothing about them. And yet the mind starts building this fantasy of meeting them; getting together after the retreat; going off someplace together;

getting married; having kids … a whole fantasy arises through the power of desire in the mind. These internal dramas can be very enjoyable.

We can also get attached to the calm and peaceful states we sometimes experience in meditation. As the practice deepens and progresses, it can get very, very peaceful. You might feel a kind of calm you've never experienced before, and it's a delightful feeling. If you're not aware of what's happening, it's easy for the mind to get attached to that sensation. At that point, it becomes simply another object of desire.

DESIRE VERSUS REALITY

Another way desire arises in meditation is in the form of expectation: a desire for results. Sometimes expectation comes masked as effort, but it's really the wanting mind. Expectations can come when you're bored and start wanting something to happen, or when the mind gets attached to the excitement that comes with some interesting experience. The comparing mind also fuels expectation. You compare this sitting with the last sitting, and maybe it's different or more difficult, so an expectation arises to regain something you've felt before.

If we gain something, it was there from the beginning. If we lose anything, it is hidden nearby.

— RYOKAN

I had an experience with this form of expectation – a very difficult situation that turned out to be a great lesson for me in my practice. I was in India at the time, and practicing quite intensively. I went through a period where the energy flowed easily and my body felt completely open whenever I meditated. It was as if I had a body of light. Every time I sat down, this fluid, light energy circulated through my entire body. I was blissful. It was wonderful. I thought, "Oh, this is it. I have it. This is what it's going to be like now, for the rest of my life."

I came back to America to work and earn some money, but I couldn't wait to get back to India and my body of light. After several months I did return to resume my intensive practice – but instead of a body of light, I felt as though I had a body of twisted steel. Every part of my body felt contracted and twisted. I practiced diligently, but with a wanting; an expectation of pushing through the pain and contraction to find the body of light I had experienced before.

Practicing in that way was tremendously painful and frustrating. It took me two years to fully understand that that's not what the practice is about. It's not about getting anything back. It's not about having any particular experience. The practice is about opening to whatever presents itself. When I finally let go of my desire and relaxed into how things were, my whole practice started moving again. So I received a very important lesson about expectation and wanting.

This is a graphic example of how desire (and aversion, for that matter) can undermine our confidence in the spiritual journey. The habit of grasping on to pleasure and trying to evade pain sets us up in opposition to the simple truth of the present moment. In trying to manipulate events, we lose our sense of trust in the direct, immediate experience of the now. We're locked in a struggle with reality – a struggle that erodes the "beautiful mind state" of faith and our devotion to the path of liberation.

It makes no difference whether the thing we're craving is an external object or an internal state. The force of desire or addiction in the mind to a particular outcome hinders concentration and obscures our natural wisdom. We become entranced and seduced by the object of our wanting. It's as if we're living in a world of enchantment, and then we get lost in the force of that wanting. We're no longer clearly seeing the true nature of phenomena, being simply present with just what is. Instead, we get further and further entangled in our thoughts and reflections. We get bound by the force of attachment.

To defend one's self against fear is simply to ensure that one will, one day, be conquered by it; fears must be faced.

— JAMES ARTHUR BALDWIN

One of my particular addictions is reading spy novels. Often, I'll stay up till all hours, totally immersed in some exciting story. It gets later and later, and I know I need to go to sleep – and yet somehow the mind is caught up in that wanting: in this case, wanting to know what happens. Finally, at one or two o'clock in the morning, I gather enough mindfulness to say "enough" and put the book down. Then it's as if I'm being released from the grip of some force. There's a sense of relief. This is how the force of wanting, of desire, grabs and controls the mind.

Not only does unnoticed desire hinder concentration and obscure clear seeing – in the final analysis, it doesn't deliver on its promise of happiness. An ad I came across in a magazine reads: "It can take several lifetimes to reach a state of inner peace and tranquility. Or it can take a couple of weeks. Concentrate deeply. Think about a fourteen-day ocean voyage to Singapore or Bali, Thailand or China. Days when your every whim is anticipated, instantly met. Places where the sights, smells, lights are a sensual feast imagination can't do justice. Now, a flash of insight – Royal Caribbean® will soon take you to the Far East. It's a vacation that until now simply did not exist, but you can believe. Call this number for a free brochure or ask your travel agent about the *nirvana* you have coming. Don't put it off another lifetime."

This is a message we often get: "Fulfill this desire, buy this product, have this experience, and you will achieve everlasting happiness." The gift of meditation is that it helps us see through this illusion. We go after different sense pleasures, including the pleasures of the mind, because of the enjoyable feelings they give us. The problem is that these pleasant feelings, like everything else, are impermanent. We always need another and another and another to feel satisfied.

It's said that the hardest disease to cure is the kind that's caused by the medicine you're taking. The same principle applies to desire: endlessly trying to satisfy the wanting mind only leads to more wanting. Naturally, this doesn't mean we should never enjoy ourselves. That's not the point of understanding desire. The point is simply to realize the very transitory nature of enjoyment, and that it's not capable of finally satisfying us. Meditation practice opens up the possibility of much greater happiness in our lives.

UNDERSTANDING DESIRE

How can we come to understand the deep, powerful conditioning of desire in the mind? The first and most important step is to make it the object of mindfulness: recognize desire when it appears, noting it carefully without getting caught up or lost in it. We don't judge the desire, the fact that it arises, or ourselves for having it. We simply notice that it's appearing. If enjoyment is associated with the desire, we notice the enjoyment, too. All we're doing is seeing clearly whatever is happening. From this foundation of mindfulness, we investigate more deeply and see that desire is born out of pleasant feeling. It's because an experience is pleasurable that we desire it. And so we begin to notice, to be aware of, the pleasantness itself.

This doesn't mean that we should not enjoy whatever pleasant experiences do arise. Rather, we should be mindful of the pleasure so that it doesn't unknowingly lead to more wanting. Our aspiration is to not be so lost in, or driven by, the force of desire.

It's helpful, as we practice, to reflect on where this desire is leading. Where is it taking us? Do we want to go there? The recollection of impermanence is also very helpful in freeing the mind from the grip of desire or addiction – impermanence on the momentary level, where things arise and pass away constantly, and also on the level of life itself. Life is going by so quickly. Looking back at the time of your death, what will have really been important for you? What will have been of greatest value? What would you have wanted to do in your life? Reflecting on these questions now helps prioritize where we put our energy.

Try this experiment the next time you watch television. Imagine, for a moment, that you desire everything you see in the endless stream of commercials. One after another – "I want this, I want this, I want this." It's easy to see that this would be an awful, hellish state of mind. The great peace is in letting it all pass by. There's no need to want it all. Of course, TV commercials are easy to deal with. The commercials in the mind are more difficult.

Most important in all this is appreciating the depth of our conditioning around desire and not judging it. We don't judge ourselves or the meditation. Instead, we become interested in understanding how our mental habits arise and pass away. In other words, we become interested in freedom. Can we look deeply and really see the workings of our minds and our lives?

Learning about desire in our meditation practice helps us see this same tendency more clearly in our everyday lives. Seeing it more clearly gives us more choices. It clears the space we need to practice discriminating wisdom. When should we act on desire? When is fulfillment of the desire appropriate? When is it not? When is it simply leading to more suffering? Seeing clearly gives us the freedom to ask these questions and to make choices based on understanding, rather than on unconscious habits. This is the great power of meditation.

AVERSION

The second major hindrance or obscuration of understanding is aversion. We experience it in many ways: as anger or hatred, fear, irritation, annoyance, or sorrow. Just as the untrained mind becomes entranced by pleasant feelings, we become dissatisfied with, angry at, or fearful of unpleasant ones. Aversion is the expression of the condemning mind.

In meditation, it is very common to experience pain or discomfort at times – and with it, aversion in the form of frustration or depression. You might have pain in the knee, or pain in the back. If you're not mindful of those sensations, it's very easy for the mind to get caught up in a fear of them. You become afraid they may get worse, and you begin obsessing: "How will I last for an hour?" Or you might start feeling sorry for yourself: "Poor me, I'm sitting here in so much pain! My practice isn't going anywhere, while everybody else who meditates is sitting in bliss."

Aversion also comes up in the form of bargaining. Without necessarily being conscious of it, you may promise to be "good" by watching the pain in exchange for relief: "Here's the deal: I'll stay aware of you if you'll go away." But experience is not subject to bargaining. Awareness requires complete and genuine acceptance of whatever conditions you're observing. Bargaining is conditional, and as such, a subtle variety of aversion. Like all other strategies, it doesn't work, either to relieve pain or to increase awareness.

A similar strategy comes up as the "in order to mind," which we discussed in the previous lesson. This happens when we open to pain, but still interpret it as a problem to be gotten rid of: "I'll be with this in order to release it." I had this experience sitting in Burma with my teacher U Pandita. My body felt quite open, except for one strong knot of tension. I reported it as a block in my practice. I said, "My whole body is clear, but there's this one block." My teacher pointed out that my interpretation of it as a block reflected a quality of aversion. If it's a block, I need to do something to unblock it. His point was that I could simply be with the heaviness, tightness, or pressure, just as it is.

There is never enough of what does not satisfy.

— NIRMALA

In the same way as it arises with physical pain, aversion can surface with certain emotions. These are the emotions we consider not okay: despair, hopelessness, unworthiness, or perhaps even anger itself. How much of our lives are spent avoiding certain feelings?

Thoughts of past situations are also fertile grounds for aversion. We think about things that have happened and then get angry or sad or frightened by them. One of my teachers had a very insightful and helpful aphorism about this phenomenon. He said, "The thought of your mother is not your mother." In other words, the thought of a person is not the same thing as the actual person. Yet so often in reliving old difficulties or problems, the thought of the person assumes some kind of substance in the mind. When this happens, it can trigger all sorts of stories and emotions. Sometimes we even start to experience aversion to things that we imagine might happen. They haven't happened yet, but we play them out in our minds and get upset or angry.

Aversion can happen, too, when we're thinking about situations that arise in our practice. A good example is a retreat phenomenon called the vipassana vendetta: the other side of the vipassana romance. In this scenario, you find one person in the group whom you just can't stand. You don't like the way this person walks, eats, or dresses. You may never have seen your nemesis before, or have had any interaction with him or her — and yet the force of aversion plays itself out in your mental projections.

Meditation is invaluable for unraveling these stories and getting down to the original thought or emotion that triggered them. Practicing doesn't help us avoid feelings of frustration or aversion, of course. Rather, it helps us be with these emotions in a way that creates spaciousness, and this in turn creates a certain lightness of heart in the face of difficulty.

WORKING WITH AVERSION

Just as with desire, we need not judge our fear, anger, frustration, contraction, irritation, annoyance, or the many other forms of aversion we experience. We simply notice the moments of ill will, disappointment, or indignation as they arise. We keep noting these feelings, even labeling them – "anger, anger" – and watching our tone so that we're not noting in an angry way. We simply take note of our experience as a means of recognition and acceptance.

As an experiment, you might see how many notes it takes until the feelings of anger or aversion dissipate. Five notes, ten notes, a hundred notes? As you investigate, you'll begin to reinforce the understanding that these feelings, like all others, are impermanent. They're going to change. You don't need to be caught up in them. You don't need to be driven by them. You can create the space in yourself to simply be aware.

Recognition without judgment – that's the first way of working. The second way of working is to look at the associated feelings that may be feeding the anger or the ill will. For example, anger is often associated with a feeling of self-righteousness, which feeds it like an underground spring. You might find yourself saying, "Well, I'm perfectly right and I should be angry." You may notice the anger, but if you're not also noticing the self-righteousness, the anger will continue to grow. It's being fed in a way that you're not seeing. Remember to investigate the associated feelings in just the same way as before, without judgment or condemnation. We simply see, simply notice.

Not to be attached to something is to be aware of its absolute value.
— SHUNRYU SUZUKI ROSHI

In the case of anger, people sometimes feel that to give it up is to relinquish a source of power and energy for changing the world. But there is a greater source of power that harms neither ourselves nor others, and this is the power of compassion. Later, we'll discuss and investigate the nature of compassion, and how it works in our practice and our lives.

DESIRE AND AVERSION:
QUESTION AND ANSWER SESSION

Q: When I practice I notice some boredom – and an even greater fear of boredom. What should I do?

A: Boredom is actually a form of aversion. When we truly experience it with the power of mindfulness, we discover that boredom comes from lack of attention. We don't like what's happening, so we withdraw our attention, which leads to boredom. Fritz Perls said, "Boredom is lack of attention." If we recognize boredom, it becomes a useful signal to pay closer attention. We break through to a whole new level of understanding. By focusing your awareness on boredom as an object of meditation, you can open your mind and heart to include the fullness of your experience – including your sense of dissatisfaction and flavorlessness. Then you may find that even the repetitive sensation of breathing can be an amazingly interesting and wonderful experience.

Q: My knees and back hurt quite a lot when I sit for any length of time. Isn't pain my body's way of telling me that I'm doing something that could damage it?

A: There are definitely signals that, like the smoke and heat of a fire, tell us when action is needed. But there's also a type of discomfort known as *"dharma* pain": sensations we carry with us all the time but don't notice until the mind is stilled through meditation (dharma is a term used to identify the Buddha's teachings). Becoming aware of this type of pain is actually a sign of progress. When we make it an object of meditation, we can see past our fear and avoidance. A good guideline for distinguishing between dangerous pain and dharma pain is to notice whether the pain goes away when you stand up and walk. If not, it may be a sign that your posture is too strained or forced.

Q: Is having strong desire or aversion always a bad idea? Doesn't what we're grasping or pushing away make any difference?

A: The difficulties that arise in our meditation practice come, not from the object of desire or aversion, but from the energy of desire or aversion itself. The energy of desire keeps us moving, looking for that one thing that will finally bring us irreversible contentment. The energy of aversion makes us want to separate ourselves from our experience, making it impossible for us to explore the present moment with a spirit of discovery. So it doesn't matter what the object of your desire or aversion may be. The next time these mind states arise, take the opportunity to explore their nature and the relationships they create to the experiences of your life. Then we act in the world with greater wisdom and less reactivity.

GUIDED MEDITATION:
WORKING WITH DESIRE AND AVERSION

Begin by listening. Establish a feeling sense within you of the relaxed, natural state of mindfulness. Sounds are simply coming and going; you don't have to do anything about them. There's no struggle, no fight, no conflict … just a very immediate and present connection to what the experience is.

Bring that same quality of relaxed and spacious awareness to the sensation of the breath at the nostrils, or to the rising and falling movement of the chest or abdomen, whichever is most clear. Make a quiet mental note of "in, out" or "rising, falling" to help establish the attention on the actual experience of the breath.

As you sit, feeling the breath, you may find that sensations arise in the body in a way that is strong enough to take your attention away from the breath. You may find that the sensations have become the predominant experience of the moment. If this is your experience, don't struggle or try to push away the sensation to get back to the breath. Just let go of the awareness of breath and allow your attention to settle fully on the experience of the sensation. This becomes the new meditation object.

You can make a quiet mental note of what you're experiencing in this moment: pain … itching … vibration … tingling. There's no need to struggle in any way to find the right word. If a word comes to you that is truthful, that bears a relationship to what you're actually experiencing, you can use it in the same way you've used the mental note for the breath. You can use that word to help support your awareness, to bring the mind more directly into contact with the actual experience.

It's the same quality of awareness as you've used to note the breath – relaxed, spacious, open, free, not trying to control what's going on, not trying to change it, allowing things to come and go on their own.

If the sensation that arises in the body is very pleasant, you may feel a conditioned tendency to try to cling to it, to possess it, to keep it. If you feel that tendency arise, relax, open up, and see if you can be with the sensation of pleasure without clinging to it.

If the experience arising in the body is unpleasant or painful, you may feel a reflexive tendency to push it away. You may feel angry about it, or afraid of it. You may experience mental and physical tension in relationship to it. Once again, if you see any of these reactions, see if you can note them and come back to the direct experience of the moment. What is the actual sensation of the pain?

Resist the tendency to get lost in speculation, asking yourself questions like, "What's it going to feel like in forty-five minutes?" Resist the urge to compare this sensation to what you think ought to be there.

Feel it directly, without interpretation or judgment. What is the actual experience? Is it burning? Is it twisting? Is it cold?

Whether it's pleasurable or painful, note the sensation for a few moments. Observe it to see if it changes in any way. Does it grow stronger? Does it grow weaker? Does it break apart? Does it disappear? Or does it stay exactly the same?

Once you've made this observation, see if you can bring the attention back to the breath.

Perhaps the sensation is still quite strong, and it's pulling your attention. That's fine. You can focus fully on the sensation, periodically returning to the anchor of the breath.

Stay relaxed. You don't have to fight. You don't have to struggle. It's an exploration. You're taking an interest in the arising and passing away of this phenomenon you call "my body," and the tremendous changing flow of sensations that it actually is.

If you find that you're fighting against the pain, that you're hating it, that you're growing more tense, it's better just to change your posture, and then begin again…

… but see what happens when you don't relate to the pain according to your conditioning.

Be open to exploring it. What is it that is actually happening in this moment?

If a painful sensation arises in the body, and you add to it a fearful anticipation of the future, or terrible self-judgment, then your painful physical sensation will change into great mental suffering.

What happens when you don't add any of these things, when you're with the direct experience as it appears? Relaxed ... observing ... learning.

If pain does arise, look at just one small area within it. Don't try to take in every sensation that's happening in your back or your knee, or wherever the pain is. Look at the most intense point. Observe it ... see if it changes ... see how it changes as you watch it.

Don't try to stay with painful sensation uninterruptedly for a sustained period of time. Keep bringing your attention back to the breath or back to hearing. Remember that felt sense of being relaxed, being mindful in a very natural, easeful way, not needing to be in control.

Notice the difference between the physical sensation when it's experienced directly, and when you experience it adding the future: "This is the way it's going to be forever." Notice whether the feeling is pleasant or painful.

See the difference between experiencing the pain directly in this moment or adding the past, saying, "Oh, my last sitting was much better." See the difference between experiencing it directly in this moment and a story: "Oh, this sensation means that I am the greatest meditator in the world, or the worst meditator in the world." Can you open to the experience in the moment as it is, constantly changing?

Allow the attention to move between hearing, the breath, and the sensations in the body. The breath becomes the primary object of awareness. It's the anchor for your attention. When sensations are strong enough to take your attention away from the breath, then those sensations become the primary object. You may spend much of a sitting simply with the breath; you may spend very little of a sitting with the breath, because sensations are very strong. Just allow the attention to move freely, according to what's most natural.

Being relaxed, being at ease is the key.

Allow the waves of pleasure and pain to come and go. Rest the attention in the awareness of all of these different changing experiences.

Notice that you can be aware of both pleasure and pain in the body. Notice that awareness, the quality of mindfulness itself, can go anywhere.

Mindfulness remains free and open and relaxed and spacious no matter what it's looking at.

You can't hold on to the pleasure, and you can't keep the pain from coming, but you can be aware.

Use the mental noting to support your awareness. If you're noting "tingling, tingling" or "pain, pain" in a quiet way, it directs the attention more to the direct experience in the moment and away from the elaboration of some story or interpretation about it.

The goal is not to struggle against the pain. Rather, it's to have a clear and open awareness that can go anywhere ... not to be lost in your conditioning or habits of mind, but rather to see for yourself directly. What is the nature of pleasure? What is the nature of pain? What is the nature of awareness?

If you feel a strong sensation somewhere in your body, scan the rest of your body briefly. If the sensation is painful, are you tensing up against it? Are you trying to push it away by contracting the rest of your body? Is there a pleasant sensation somewhere that you're trying to hold on to?

In either case, once again, relax. Relax your body ... take a deep breath. Relax your mind.

As you end the meditation, see if you can bring the sense of being within your body into the rest of your day. See if you can continue to feel the incredible world of sensation and all of its changes, moment by moment, as you move into the activities of your daily life.

EXERCISES FOR WORKING WITH SENSATIONS AND PAIN

Use the guided meditation on CD 1, track 3 (or the version above) in your meditation practice for at least a week. During meditation, avoid allowing pain or discomfort to spark a struggle with yourself. Move or change your posture as necessary. At the end of your week of concentrated practice with desire and aversion, complete at least five of the following exercises.

Exercise 1

Bring your awareness to a small area of your body, such as a hand or knee. Name the sensations you discover there.

_____

_____

_____

Exercise 2

Identify a part of your body that's experiencing pain. What sensations make up the pain? Name your mental reaction to it.

_____

_____

_____

_____

Exercise 3

What conclusions are you drawing about yourself because of the pain?

_____

_____

Exercise 4

How does the past figure in to your mental attitude to pain? How does the future figure in to it? Describe your experience during meditation when you separate pain or discomfort from thoughts of past and future.

_____

_____

_____

Exercise 5

Can you open to pleasant sensation? What is your mental attitude to pleasure?

_____

_____

_____

Exercise 6

Explore the relationship between your body and your mind. What is the connection between your mental state and the degree of physical pain?

_____

_____

_____

Exercise 7

Relax your body. Move your attention from a one-pointed perspective (i.e., focused on the physical discomfort) to a big perspective (i.e., an awareness of your entire body and all the sounds, smells, sensations, and so on arising from your environment). Describe how it feels to shift your awareness in this way.

_____

_____

_____

_____

GETTING THE MOST FROM YOUR MEDITATION:

Working with Desire

- Recognize what you can control, and practice letting go of those things you can't. Ending the futile struggle against inevitable change releases our energy for more effective and realistic activities.

- Practice generosity. Generosity reverses the energy of desire, freeing us from the endless self-absorption involved in trying to draw satisfaction inward. Instead, the energetic flow of giving moves outward, toward others. You may find, paradoxically, that this natural outflow yields the greatest satisfaction of all.

- Cultivate gratitude. Instead of seeing our lives in terms of what we aren't getting, we can open our hearts with joy to all those things we continually receive from our world.

- Simplify your life. Ask yourself the question, "What do I truly need in order to be happy?" The practice of meditation is very helpful in learning to see what is really essential to our happiness, and what is simply a web of illusion spun by the force of desire.

Working with Aversion

- Shift your focus from your anger to the suffering of the situation – both your own and that of others. The Buddhist texts teach that all aggression arises from pain. Your own angry response will diminish if you can remember that others' anger points to a sense of helplessness that keeps them from pursuing a more effective course of action.

- Free yourself from the role of avenger. If someone has caused harm, they will inevitably suffer – this is the law of karma (see Lesson Seven). The Buddha said, "Hatred can never cease by hatred." By meeting aversion with love, you can cut the cycle of escalating anger and change the momentum of painful situations.

- Practice forgiveness. This is not an abstract, altruistic concept, but a practical self-help strategy. When your mind is full of anger and hatred, you're the one who's suffering the most. Pema Chödrön teaches that fueling our own hatred is like eating rat poison and expecting the rat to die. Forgiving those who have hurt you releases you from a great burden of unhappiness.

- Notice your response to pain that arises during your everyday activities. Practice bringing close, loving attention to it as soon as you're aware of its presence.

- Learn to recognize anger, fear, disappointment, and guilt as states of aversion. In this way, you can see and understand your responses in the light of awareness. Although all these forms of aversion may continue to arise, you can find a place of clarity where they need no longer control you.

- Learn confidence in the power of lovingkindness (see Lesson Nine). This isn't a state of weakness or complacency, but a source of tremendous strength that is more powerful and effective than anger.

LESSON THREE GLOSSARY

aversion: hatred; anger; the tendency to push away unpleasant experiences

desire: greed; addiction; the tendency to grasp at and try to prolong pleasurable experiences

dharma: "carrying, holding"; "that which supports" [Sanskrit]; the teachings of Sakyamuni Buddha

nirvana: "extinction of suffering" [Sanskrit]; a state of bliss that is attained through fully apprehending the nature of reality

samsara: "journeying" [Sanskrit]; the ocean of worldly suffering; the state of being governed by the five hindrances

LESSON FOUR

SLEEPINESS, RESTLESSNESS, AND DOUBT

We've discussed two of the five classical hindrances to concentration: desire, or grasping; and aversion, with its manifestations of anger and fear. Now we'll turn to the remaining three.

SLOTH OR SLEEPINESS

The third of the hindrances is the state of sloth or sleepiness – a heaviness or dullness in the mind. Perhaps you sit down to meditate and suddenly, your eyes get heavy and you just want to go to sleep, even if you had perfect rest all night long. Everything is murky, confused; you feel disconnected.

Sloth or sleepiness has many causes. Sometimes it's simply an energetic imbalance. We've talked about finding the delicate balance between tranquility and alertness that is the essence of the meditation practice. It's not uncommon for the tranquil side of things – relaxing, letting go, yielding, surrendering, being at peace – to develop faster than the alert, energizing, interested, inspired aspects of the mind. When tranquility isn't balanced with an equal measure of alertness, it's easy to fall into a dreamy, drifty state. You just ooze along, sometimes quite pleasantly, enjoying the many images that pass through the mind. Sometimes this state is so pleasant that it's difficult to rouse yourself.

This happened to me once at a retreat, when I was leading a sitting. I sat down in front of about a hundred people to give that day's meditation instruction. Then I closed my eyes and immediately fell into this state – it's called "sinking mind" in classical practice. I was drifting pleasantly along, dreaming, with no clear definition of objects, no precise sense of thoughts arising and passing away, and no real awareness of what was happening.

I quite enjoyed myself in this way for twenty minutes or so when I suddenly thought, "Maybe I should try mental noting." I began actually noting the breath — not just feeling it, but noting it as "in, out" or "rising, falling." As soon as I did that, the clouds began to clear away, and I realized that I was sitting in front of a hundred people who had been waiting patiently for me to give some meditation instruction. I didn't say anything until the end of the sitting. When I rang the bell, I described what had happened to me — and I gave a strong plug for mental noting.

So sometimes this dullness of mind is an energetic imbalance. At other times, it can be a way of shrinking away from difficulty. Something emerges from the unconscious: perhaps a painful memory or an uncomfortable state of mind. Our habit, at times like this, is to resist or avoid the experience, so we pull away.

Actually, this pulling away can be an expression of wisdom coming from our intuition. The point of practice isn't to suffer. The point is to develop a mind so completely open that it can experience great pleasure and great pain with spaciousness, compassion, awareness, and energy. So when you become drowsy, you may be intuitively stepping back a little from a state of suffering that you aren't yet practiced enough to experience with equanimity.

We had a wonderful teacher named Dipa Ma, who died a few years ago. She was an extraordinary being who had suffered a lot in her life. She had been placed in an arranged marriage at the age of twelve. She and her husband actually fell deeply in love and had three children. Then two of the children died, followed quite unexpectedly by her husband.

There lives more faith in honest doubt, believe me, than in half the creeds.

— ALFRED, LORD TENNYSON

Dipa Ma went into a state of massive grief. She was bedridden, ill, unable to sleep or find inner peace. Finally a doctor told her, "You've got to do something about your mind state. You still have one daughter. You need to raise her; you need to be strong. You should learn how to meditate."

So Dipa Ma went to a meditation center.

"When I started doing the meditation," she told us, "I was crying all the time because I wanted to follow the instructions with full regard, but I couldn't do it because of sleepiness. Even standing and walking I would get sleepy; I needed to sleep. So I cried, because for five years I had tried to sleep but couldn't sleep; now I was trying to meditate and all I could do was sleep. The sleep was obstructing me from doing the meditation. I was giving my full energy to not sleeping, but still I couldn't accomplish it. Then one day, all of a sudden, I came to a state where all of my old sleepiness disappeared. No more sleepiness came to me, even when I sat for many hours."

Going even more deeply into her experience of anguish was more than Dipa Ma could do. After having meditated long enough to create more space in her mind, she no longer needed the sleepiness that had been protecting her.

Sometimes you may experience sleepiness or sloth because your basic experience is neutral. The sights, sounds, physical sensations, feelings, and memories that arise as you practice are not very exciting. They're not tremendously pleasant – it's not that you're intoxicated with pleasure. They're not terribly painful – you don't have to struggle to face pain. Everything is ordinary, featureless. You're bored. Boredom can be difficult for us to welcome in to our experience. We're constantly seduced into seeking progressive levels of stimulation. We forget about the refined awareness that is the real basis for our fulfillment, happiness, and sense of completion.

This neutral mind state often arises when you do ordinary, everyday things that you've done many times before – say, eating an apple. If you're not really paying attention to how the apple smells and tastes in that moment, you're only half present (if even half). Maybe you're lost in thought about a career change, or contemplating reading a new book. Whatever it is, eating the apple is not going to be a very fulfilling experience. You're not even there.

It's rare, in that moment, to recognize the crucial role of attention in attaining fulfillment or happiness. Mostly, we tend to blame the apple. We get lost in "if only" mind. "If only I had an orange, then I would be happy." So we get an orange, and perhaps we eat it in exactly the same way we ate the apple: not really paying attention, not experiencing it fully. So once again, it's not a very fulfilling experience.

Then we say, "The problem with my life is that it's so conventional. I'm too bound by the ordinary. What I need is something really exotic, really special, really unusual. I need a mango – that's what I need." And so, perhaps at great expense and effort, we go out and get a mango. But if we eat that mango in the same way that we ate the apple and the orange, it's still not going to satisfy us. So in an attempt to feel alive, awake, and connected to what's going on, we get lost in addiction to ever-increasing levels of stimulation.

In fact, many of our experiences are just neutral. They're repetitive. They're not strikingly pleasant or strikingly unpleasant – but they're part of life. If you look at the quality of your attention, you can wake up to them and connect fully to them. It isn't necessary to fall asleep in neutral experience.

In Lesson Two, Joseph talked about the difference between being present uncon-ditionally and being present in the hope of cultivating some kind of spiritual insight. I had a direct experience of this teaching, early on in my practice. I was living and meditating in a compound in India. I had been instructed to make a mental note of the predominant experience going on in my body, mind, and world as I was perceiving it. I began to see that, as I walked around the compound, the single most common mental note I was making was "waiting." I was going around saying to myself, "Waiting, waiting, waiting, waiting, waiting, waiting."

Finally, one day I asked myself, "What are you waiting for?" I realized that I was waiting for something exciting enough or spiritual enough or significant enough to happen so that I could note it; so I could be aware of it. I was living my life like a tape recorder with the pause button on – very disconnected. This is one example of how not fully accepting our neutral experience can separate us from the immediacy of what's actually happening now.

Probably the sleepiest times I have ever had in my practice happened in the monasteries and meditation centers of Burma. There, we were expected to strictly follow the Eight Precepts – the five precepts of basic ethical conduct we discussed earlier, plus three more. The most significant of these was the precept not to take food after the noon meal. This meant no milk, no tea, no coffee.

Breakfast in a Burmese monastery is served at about 5 A.M. Lunch is at 10 A.M., and it takes about half an hour to eat. At 10:30, after lunch, I would walk back to my room, and with every step my mind would get more dull, more heavy, more sleepy. It took me a while to realize that the sleepiness wasn't due to having eaten too much, or even the extremely hot weather. I was sleepy because I knew there was very little distraction to look forward to for the rest of the day. No more tea, no more coffee, no more food: just hot water, sitting, and walking. And so my mind became dull and bored. I couldn't connect strongly to what was happening in the moment.

Working with Sleepiness

Whatever the cause, it's important not to make sleepiness or sloth the enemy. The point is to be as aware of it as possible. You can actually make it the object of your meditation, explore it, and come to know it in a different way through mindfulness and compassion.

It's also possible to gently correct the energetic imbalances. If you feel sleepy while meditating, you can open your eyes. You can stand up – it's much more difficult to fall asleep standing up than it is sitting down. You can try very careful mental noting, as I did when I was leading that retreat session. When I began actually making a mental note of the breath — not just feeling it, but noting it as "in, out" or "rising, falling" — my energy became more balanced.

You can move your attention from object to object very consciously. When you're feeling drowsy, staying with the breath can begin to feel like a kind of lullaby. But you can move your attention from hearing to the breath, to sensation in the body, back to hearing, in an ordered or patterned way.

One of the most significant ways of working with sleepiness is "right aim," which was discussed earlier. Right aim is expressed through the understanding or mind state that says, in effect, "Just this one breath. Just this one sound. Just this one step." In fact, you can only be aware of one moment at a time. Your attention gets dispersed and disempowered if you try to take in too much at once. If you say, "Just this one breath, just this one moment," your energy comes together and you're empowered. You're awake. You're connected and present in that moment.

Right aim is very precise. I saw its effect in walking meditation. I often would notice the place at the other end of the room where I knew I'd soon be turning around. I would say to myself, "Okay, be mindful from now until you reach that wall and turn around." But nobody can really do that. You can only be mindful of one step at a time. My resolve, well-intentioned as it was, essentially spread my energy out to the end of the room, rather than applying it completely, wholly, fully — just this one moment, just this one step. The power you get from concentrating your energy in that way helps tremendously in dealing with sleepiness or sluggishness.

RESTLESSNESS

The fourth hindrance is the opposite of sleepiness: restlessness. Like sleepiness, restlessness can come from an energetic imbalance. In this case, there might be a lot of alertness, energy, enthusiasm, inspiration, and interest; but not nearly the same level of tranquility, peace, surrender, and calm.

Sometimes we experience restlessness very physically. A friend of mine once had this happen to her in a large meditation center. She got so incredibly restless, she felt as though she was jumping out of her skin. Maybe ten times in the course of a one-hour sitting, she felt compelled to pick up her cushion, move to the other end of the meditation room, put it down, sit, and try again — and again and again. This is an extreme example of restlessness in action, but not an uncommon one.

We can also experience restlessness emotionally, mentally, or psychologically.

Sometimes it arises through worry or insecurity. Typically, we try to find security by imagining that we can control the outcome of a certain situation – but we sense that in reality, there is no possibility of control. It's difficult to be with the resulting feeling of insecurity, so we block it. We try to fight it. Our minds move faster and faster to try to overcome it.

One way this process manifests is in obsessive planning. When I was first meditating in India, I decided that I was going to spend the entire rest of my life living in that country. Having made that decision, I felt anxious about whether I could accomplish it. So I began obsessively planning my strategy. As soon as I sat down to meditate, I'd start thinking, "Okay, when my visa expires next year, I'll go to this particular visa office, because I've heard that the people there are sympathetic to meditators, and they'll definitely give me an extension. Then the year after that, I'll go to this other office, because I've heard that the officials there will accept bribes. Then the year after that, I'll go to this third visa office, because it's in a remote place where very few Westerners go, so they'll probably give me an extension. Then the year after that..."

And so it would go. I would do that for an hour; I would get up to walk; I'd come back to sit down, and I'd have to start all over again, trying to reassure myself that somehow I was going to spend the rest of my life in India – which, of course, I didn't. I finally had to say to myself, "You're not even really in India while you're in India! All you're doing is scheming about how to stay here. Why not just be here while you're here?" That was how I was able to cut through some of that obsessive energy.

Another way restlessness can arise is in the form of guilt. It's natural, in the course of practice, to find yourself doing a kind of moral inventory. Without intending to direct your mind there, you begin recalling past actions and words that you aren't particularly proud of: things you've said that hurt others; behaviors that were harmful to yourself or others; things you've omitted to say or do. All of this comes tumbling into your mind, unbidden. What's actually happening is a kind of spontaneous purification of your being. Having these types of memories is not a problem, but the discomfort they generate can make you feel very restless.

This brings up a very interesting distinction that is implied in the Buddhist system of psychology, the Abhidhamma. According to these teachings, there is a distinction that can be made between guilt and remorse. Remorse is considered a wholesome or skillful state of mind, in which you genuinely feel the pain of what you've said or done. You're able to forgive yourself and let go of that situation. Then, with renewed energy and determination, you can move on.

Guilt, on the other hand, is considered a kind of lacerating self-hatred. This occurs when you go over and over and over what you did, becoming completely identified with it. Your whole sense of who you are may collapse around this single event. "I am that person," you tell yourself. "I'm the kind of person who did that. That is all of who I am, and always will be." There's tremendous restlessness in that guilt. It leaves you devastated, debilitated, without the energy to go on or the determination to change. This is why guilt is considered unskillful or unwholesome.

The first time I ever meditated with my Burmese teacher, Sayadaw U Pandita, I entered a period of practice where uncomfortable memories started coming up. I was so embarrassed and caught up in them that I didn't even want to tell him about it. But we were seeing U Pandita for meditation interviews six days a week, to talk about whatever our primary experience was. So I finally had to disclose what was happening.

I told my teacher, "I'm seeing all these really negative things I've done, and what a bad person I am." He looked at me and teasingly said, "Well, I guess you're finally seeing the truth about yourself." That was exactly what I'd been thinking, but somehow when he said it, clear seeing rose up in me and I said, "No, I'm not." He just laughed and told me, "Stop thinking so much."

Working with Restlessness

There are several ways to work with restlessness. Sometimes you just need to simplify your experience and cool out the mind by literally coming back to your senses. Feel the breath; immerse your attention in the breath. Feel one step in the walking. If you're walking outside, feel the breeze as you move. If you're drinking a cup of tea, feel the heat of the teacup. Don't worry about elaborate or grandiose meditative experiences. Just get present.

Restlessness is a highly energized state. Our goal is not to dissipate the energy, but to try to harness it somehow. All that energy can be quite uncomfortable, so the temptation is to burn it off, to make it go away. But if you were to ground it, channel it, that energy could be available to you. Sometimes it's better to walk than to sit; better to move quickly rather than slowly. There's a difference between moving in order to burn off unwanted energy and moving in order to feel into the body. Moving mindfully when you're restless can help you get grounded.

One can also bring a very large, open awareness to the state of restlessness. Rather than trying to pinpoint sensations in the body, try looking at them as if through a wide-angle lens. Step back and take in the big picture, the wild movements of energy through your body. Don't try to get a narrow focus anywhere. Just feel the chaos of it. Feel the quality of restlessness itself.

Ultimately, our goal is to make the restlessness an object of mindfulness. When you can look at it clearly and say, "This is restlessness," you can accept it, have compassion for yourself, and cultivate a powerful awareness of your experience. At this point, the restlessness is no longer controlling you. Instead, you're directing it in ways that support your mindfulness practice.

DOUBT

The last of the five hindrances is the state of doubt, which is defined as "great indecision." The doubting mind is one that runs all over the place. We're considering possibilities, we're looking for answers, we're trying to figure things out. In the Buddhist texts, doubt is often likened to a person who's standing at a fork in the road and can't decide which direction to take.

Doubt is an inability to make a commitment, or to take the risk of finding out for yourself where a certain path might lead. Doubt is especially detrimental when it keeps us from truly listening. Our experience often needs a little time in order to reveal its complexities and subtleties, so that we can understand more deeply what is true. When we let doubt hold us back from meeting the consequences of our choices, we never learn to make better ones.

First you have to accept doubt completely — not indulge it, but go on with it. This is essentially an experience of faith. It is not a feeling, it's a willingness.

— ANDO MUELLER ROSHI

There is an aspect of doubt that is wholesome and positive. The Buddha, of course, is famous for having taught that you should not believe anything just because a great teacher, including himself, has told you it's true. You should take the teaching and put it into practice. You should test it for yourself. If you find it leads to greater love, compassion, insight, and awareness, you can call it a true teaching. If you find that it leads to more suffering, more grasping, more hindrances in the mind, you can see for yourself that it's not a useful teaching.

Other types of doubt can be very unwholesome and unskillful. One of these is called "skeptical doubt." Because we're unable to commit or take a risk, we remove ourselves from the process of discovery. We stay at a safe distance. Instead of letting something speak to us, we obsessively analyze it; perhaps we disparage or judge it. We haven't actually experienced it fully or deeply because we haven't allowed ourselves to. That is how doubt functions in the mind: we remain immobilized at the fork in the road.

I experienced a great period of doubt early on in my practice. I didn't question the benefit or the efficacy of meditation, but I couldn't decide which set of techniques to follow. My very first teacher taught in the Burmese tradition. I did this for some months – and then somebody showed me a picture of a particular Tibetan lama. I was so struck by his picture that I took a train to the other end of India to study and practice under this lama's guidance. He became my second teacher.

The Tibetan teacher offered a different way of practice. I simply couldn't decide which to follow. For a while, I effectively did neither. Every time I tried to meditate, I would sit and think, "Should I do this, or should I do that? I bet that's faster; but maybe this is faster. Which is better? Look at the people who do that one – what do I think of them? What about the people who do this one? Are they progressing faster?"

Rather than practicing mindfulness, I was completely lost in my doubts. Finally, I had to say to myself, "Just do something. It doesn't have to be a lifetime commitment. It can be for a defined, short period of time, but do something. Do a practice for six months, or a year – whatever." I had to bring something to life, actually try it, take the risk. I had to get unstuck and then see what happened. Doubt is a kind of stuckness that doesn't allow the truth to be revealed. That's why we need to disentangle our doubt for the process to continue unfolding. It was a great realization for me to understand this at last.

Sometimes we feel doubt about our own ability. We sit and think, "Am I doing it right? Am I doing it perfectly right? Is it worth doing? What am I doing here?" The mind just can't settle. We're separating from the process in order to compare, judge, and assess. When the mind gets caught in this state, it's quite difficult to get anywhere in practice, because we believe strongly that the doubt is speaking the ultimate truth. We give it a lot of power.

Looking at our experience, however, we see that regular practice does progressively create more spaciousness and peace in our lives. This recognition gives rise to faith, which acts as an antidote to doubt.

From the viewpoint of doubt, you might see your own daily routine as repetitive and unproductive. You wake up, eat breakfast, go to work, and engage with colleagues. Then you leave work, come home or go out, engage in relationships, maybe run or do yoga or work out, go home, and go to bed. The next day is some variation on the same theme, and meanwhile, each of us is moving inexorably toward death.

What's the Point?

Only when we approach our lives with a sense of progressive understanding does any of it make sense. With confidence in our own capacity to awaken and devotion to the process of cultivating that capacity, everything in our lives becomes a potential step on the path of freedom. In every situation, at every moment, we can ask ourselves, "Am I awake? Am I present? Is there suffering here? What is its cause? How can it end?" Questions like these open the possibilities and lead to deeper understanding. Doubt, by contrast, keeps us fixed in the same old cycles.

Doubt sometimes reflects a kind of frivolousness – an indulgence of the mind. The Buddha described this state when he gave the example of a man who had been struck by a poisoned arrow. Somebody ran up to pull the arrow out and save his life, but the man said, "Wait a minute. Before you pull this out, I have to know who shot the arrow. I have to know what part of the country he was from; what the bow was made of; what the arrow was made of; what the poison actually is," and so on. The man would have died before his questions had run out.

> *There is more to life than increasing its speed.*
>
> — MAHATMA GANDHI

Many of our questions and doubts are like the poisoned arrow. It's not that questioning is bad; questioning is very good. In fact, it's essential. Sincere questioning opens us to deeper understanding. Skeptical doubt closes us off, removes us from experience, and keeps us from actually practicing, from actually living. This state of stuckness is the kind of doubt we must release in order to be free.

WORKING WITH DOUBT

The antidote to doubt is called "sustaining attention," which means being able to connect to what's going on. Doubt is a very jumpy state. You hop from one thing to the next, considering and wondering and judging and assessing. The power of doubt is diminished when the mind can settle – even on a simple object in the moment. You can make that effort very gently; it doesn't have to be harsh. Instead of allowing yourself to become enchanted by the state of doubt, you can see the suffering in it and have some compassion for yourself. You can give yourself a time frame, as I did when I told myself, "Well, I need to do a certain practice, even if it only lasts for six months. Let me actually try. Let the practice reveal itself to me." Rather than fearing a lifetime commitment to a particular way of being, I saw that I could take it in manageable chunks. Then, when I was able to open my heart and mind and explore each practice fully, I could see what each had to teach me.

It's important to recognize doubt as doubt, because it's very seductive. When doubt is governing your experience, it provides distance, and this gives you a sense of mastery. But when you feel how limited this mind state truly is, you can very gently let go of it, reconnect, and settle the mind. Then you can bring the attention back to what's actually happening, with a willingness to learn.

BRINGING AWARENESS TO THE HINDRANCES

An old Chinese saying goes, "To understand the nature of the water, look at the waves." Grasping is a wave; anger is a wave; sleepiness, restlessness, doubt – they're all waves in the mind. To understand the true nature of your experience, your mind, your life, you look at the waves. You don't have to flatten them out – you couldn't if you tried. You can't possibly control their arising, and you don't need to despair at their strength or frequency. That's all quite out of your hands; it's an impersonal arising due to the fact that various conditions have come together to create these events.

But if you work carefully and openly with all of these qualities, they will actually enrich your understanding of who you are. You can see right through the different states to their more essential nature. You realize that however intrusive or trouble-some the hindrances may seem, they're ultimately impermanent. They have no substance. As conditions arise, the mind states come into being; then they pass away as the conditions subside.

With meditation practice, you begin to see the ephemeral nature of the hindran-ces – and you realize that when you are lost in them, you're suffering in some way. With this realization comes compassion, tenderness, and open-heartedness toward yourself. Then compassion for others begins to arise, because you see them getting lost in the same hindrances and suffering in the same ways.

The poet T.S. Eliot wrote a wonderful line: "For us there is only the trying. The rest is not our business." For us as meditators, there is only the trying to be aware. Whether what we're aware of is the hindrances or something else, the pristine quality of awareness is untouched. So we don't need to judge or scorn our desire, aversion, and the other hindrances; nor do we need to condemn ourselves for expe-riencing them. They're like waves in the mind – challenging, sometimes terribly difficult, and full of potential for greater understanding.

ENCOUNTERING MARA

In various spiritual traditions, destructive energies are personified as demons or other unfriendly spirits. The Buddhist tradition embodies these hindrances in the form of a legendary figure called Mara, the Tempter. Mara represents all the habits of mind – such as greed, hatred, and denial – that keep us from experiencing what is actually happening.

Each of us encounters the metaphorical Mara when we meditate. He may arise initially as temptation and desire. When you find yourself thinking, "Why am I sitting on this cushion doing nothing? I'd so much rather be doing something else instead," you know Mara is at work.

If you aren't seduced by these temptations, Mara may become more aggressive. It's at this point that you might feel anger, irritability, and doubt. If you continue to meditate past these hindrances, Mara grows more subtle. This is when you're likely to begin feeling flushed with pride in your accomplishment. "What a good meditator I am! I didn't give in to temptation. I've gotten past my anger." You find a little clarity and try to hold on to it.

When the Buddha – then known as the Bodhisattva, or aspiring Buddha – sat down under the Bodhi tree, he vowed not to arise until he became fully awakened, free of all suffering. It's said that Mara came and tempted him with desirable sense objects, threatened him with fearful objects, then questioned him scornfully. "Who do you think you are? What makes you believe you can attain enlightenment?"

The Bodhisattva responded with a gesture that has since been replicated in countless works of art. He calmly reached down and touched the ground, calling on the earth itself to bear witness to his many lifetimes of diligent, sincere effort to wake up completely. The earth trembled in response, Mara was vanquished, and the Bodhisattva sat on through the night. As dawn broke the next morning, he attained enlightenment.

The Buddha was a human being who dedicated himself completely to seeing clearly, without delusion. The fact that he succeeded means that we can follow his example and achieve the freedom of clear seeing. Like the Buddha, we can learn to remain balanced in the face of Mara. Meditation practice can help us to see that even these most challenging assaults on our equilibrium and compassion are merely impermanent phenomena, plays of light and shadow that arise and vanish in the vast space of mind.

Sleepiness, Restlessness, and Doubt: Question and Answer Session

Q: My sleepiness is stronger than my mindfulness. No matter how wholeheartedly I try to watch my breath, the next thing I know I'm falling off my cushion.

A: After having noted and directly investigated the feeling of sleepiness itself, there are a few practical things you can do to feel more wakeful. One is to change your posture. Get up off your cushion and take a short, brisk walk. If you're sitting indoors, go outside for some fresh air. Another thing you can do is to look at light: electric light, sunlight, moonlight, whatever you have available. This has the effect of awakening the system. You can also splash cold water on your face to wake yourself up.

If, after all these efforts, you're still falling asleep, then it's time to take a nap. But it's important to make a sincere effort before coming to that conclusion. Every time you give in to drowsiness, you're strengthening the hindrance. Bringing some kind of energy and resolve to the situation, without being harsh or angry, is much more helpful in the long run.

Q: Are there any specific techniques, like those you just described for sleepiness, that apply to restlessness and doubt?

A: In every case, the antidote to the hindrances is mindfulness. When you penetrate the feelings and perceptions to simply experience what is, these qualities cease to be hindrances and become objects of meditation instead.

More specifically, though, you can work with restlessness by focusing the awareness on a single object, such as the breath. Because a restless mind tends to hop from one object to another, this technique produces serenity by declining to feed the feelings of agitation. We can also make the mind more spacious by focusing on sounds or the whole body, for example. By making the container larger, we can often more skillfully hold and be aware of the energy of restlessness.

In the case of doubt, you can support yourself by having a good conceptual understanding of the path of insight. Then, when doubts arise, you can draw on your intellectual resources and match them to your experience to produce what is traditionally called "verified faith."

Q: I know I'm not supposed to judge, but I often become impatient with myself when I realize I'm caught up in one of the hindrances. Then it's as though the judgment is a whole new hindrance in itself. How should I work with it?

A: Actually, judgment is an aspect of the hindrance of aversion. When you fall into self-condemnation, you strengthen the body of hindrances altogether. Try going back to Lesson Three, and see how much of the material on working with aversion you can apply to this situation.

Ultimately, the most useful technique in working with any of the hindrances is to refrain from identifying with them. When you examine your experience of judgment, you discover that there is in fact no "me" to blame for this condemning mind. The recognition of impermanence is another powerful ally. Like all other thoughts, these judgments arise and pass away. They don't define the unchanging truth of who you are.

Guided Meditation: Working with Hindrances

One of the keys to a skillful relationship with the five hindrances is being able to name them or to make a mental note of them. We practice noting very softly, giving about ninety-five percent of our attention to actually being with the experience; to sensing it completely. Only five percent of our energy goes into the soft, gentle naming of it.

We use mental noting with the hindrances to bring us into a direct relationship with them, as opposed to elaborating or judging or creating a story about what's going on. If anger were to arise, for example, we would note it as "anger, anger." This brings us close to the exploration of anger itself. What is anger? What does it feel like? What is its nature?

Mental noting takes us in a very different direction from getting lost in a story: "Oh, this anger is so miserable; I am such a terrible person because I'm always angry; I am the worst person in the world; this is just how I always will be," and so on. Instead, we simply say to ourselves, "anger, anger" – and cut through all of that elaboration, the story, the judgment, the interpretation.

"What's happening right now? It's anger." It's not good or bad or right or wrong. You don't have to bring in the past; you don't have to bring in the future. You don't have to create a sense of who you are around this momentary and transitory experience. You don't have to create a self around it. And so we use mental noting to bring us into direct relationship with what's happening right now.

With the hindrances, the mental note often serves as a wonderful feedback system. Hear the tone in which you are using the mental note. If you find yourself, in effect, shouting silently at yourself, that is a hint that you are not in a relationship of clear acceptance. You're judging, you're disliking. Perhaps you're even hating the anger. If you find that happening, adjust. Once again, make a gentle, easy, simple mental note – "There's anger."

When we say, "Make a mental note," we're also alluding to a whole set of feelings and understandings that is implicit in that one note. By naming anger as anger, gently, easily, we are in effect saying, "This is okay. This is the truth of the present moment. This is how things are right now."

We're also saying, "I cannot control what arises in my mind. Forces come and go in the mind, not due to my invitation or my wish, but as conditions arise." We are saying, "I don't have to feel responsible for the arising of this anger or this hindrance. I don't have to blame myself, I don't have to hate myself." We're also saying, "Everything changes. This is the truth right now. It will pass." We're bringing forth all of the force of our love and compassion and wisdom and understanding, expressing it in that single word: "Anger. This is anger."

You don't have to create long and elaborate discourses. You don't have to lecture yourself. Instead, you allow wisdom and compassion to come forth in the naming process and just recognize that this is what's happening right now.

As you note the particular hindrance, you can also be conscious of what happens to it. How does it behave? Does it intensify? Does it fade away? Pay particular attention to whether or not it manifests in the body. If so, how does it feel? What parts of the body are affected by the arising of this force in the mind? The chest, the stomach, the head, the eyes, the breath – where are you feeling it?

What does it feel like in the mind, in the heart, as a mood, as a coloration, as an experience? Do you feel open or do you feel contracted when this hindrance is present? Do you feel closed off and separate or do you feel connected? Whatever it is, explore and discover without judgment. Simply pay attention. Watch to see the nature of the hindrance in the moment and observe how it changes. Is it growing stronger? Is it growing weaker? Is it changing into something else?

Listen to the voices that come along with the hindrances. What are they saying to you? What are they saying about you, and what you're capable of? Very often with the hindrances, and especially with the forces of desire and anger, we get so lost in the object that we forget to pay any attention to the feeling itself. We fixate so much on what we want, or what we want to keep, or what we hate and want to push away, that we don't spend much time feeling the nature of desire or of anger itself. So ask yourself now: what do they feel like? See if you can let go of that fixation on the object of the feeling. Relax. Abide in the feeling. It's an exploration. It's an act of discovery. It's as though somebody were to say to you, "What is desire? What is anger?" Not "Why are you feeling it?" or "Is it right or is it wrong?" Just "What is it?"

You don't have to hurl a lot of questions at these experiences or try to investigate them analytically. Instead, just get quiet with them. Let go of judgment. Feel them without interpretation, without conclusion. Learn who they are, what they are. Desire or attachment; aversion, with its manifestations of anger and fear and impatience; sleepiness or sloth and torpor; restlessness; doubt – which of these are you feeling? What is its nature?

Be aware of how the body feels when any of the hindrances are present. Be aware of how the mind feels. See the various components of the experience. See how impersonal it is, and that it's not within your power to wish it away. As it comes and goes, all by itself, see how impermanent it all is.

The hindrances we've been discussing will very commonly arise. We don't have to be upset or afraid about that. We don't have to feel disappointed because of it. We can come to understand a great deal about our experience – about our own suffering and our release from suffering – just from coming to understand these hindrances better.

You can begin sitting now. Once again, sit comfortably and close your eyes. Be at ease. Listen to sounds as they appear naturally.

———

Feel the natural state of mindfulness. You don't have to struggle to create the sound or make it go away. Simply be present. Listen.

———

Feel the breath in that same way. Feel the normal, natural breath, without trying to control it or make it better or make it deeper. Bring your awareness to whatever area of the body you feel it most distinctly.

———

The in and out movement at the area of the nostrils … or the rising and falling movement of the chest or the abdomen.

———

Let your mind rest there. There's nothing you need to do. Simply be aware. You can make a quiet mental note of "in, out" or "rising, falling" to support the experience of the breath.

———

If a sensation arises in the body that is strong enough to take your attention away from the breath, focus fully on that sensation. It becomes the object of meditation.

You can name it, you can note it. Be with it without fear, without resistance, without adding anything to it.

Observe it to see if it changes.

At times as you sit, one or a combination of the five hindrances will arise and be the most predominant experience. Maybe it's desire or grasping.

See if you can note it, name it. Acknowledge it. Recognize it.

You have the capacity to touch and be open to the most difficult places within yourself. Note the grasping or desire as "grasping" or "desire." Be with it, observe it. What is it? What do you feel? Do you feel that leaning-forward nature, the vulnerability, the unease, the insecurity that is part of grasping, trying to hold on?

Can you experience it without judging it?

Maybe it's anger or dislike. Again, can you name it? Can you be with it without judging or condemning it? Without wanting to prolong it? Simply be with it. What does it feel like?

How does it color your mind? What mood does it create? How long does it last? Does it change into something else?

What happens in your body? Does it get tense? Does it get rigid?

Does it affect your temperature? Does it affect your breath? How painful is it?

Again, it's a quiet investigation. Be with the feeling of anger without preconceptions, without judgments, without interpretations, and it will reveal all these things to you, because you're interested, you're exploring.

Perhaps the hindrance is sleepiness or dullness or sloth or torpor. Is it like tendrils of fog? Is your mind scattered? Do you feel depleted? Can you name what you're feeling – the heaviness in the body, the heaviness in the eyes?

Can you sense any of the conditions that helped create the sleepiness? Is it tiredness? Is it resistance?

Bring an interested awareness to the nature of sleepiness itself.

Try to note very carefully, to sharpen the sense of what is called "right aim." Being with just this one breath, just this one moment, will empower your practice and help clear away the clouds of sleepiness.

If your attention gets too diffuse, if you try to take in too much at once, sleepiness will deepen. What happens when you say, "Just this one breath," and then feel it?

Perhaps the hindrance you're feeling is restlessness. Like everything, restlessness is a series of thoughts and feelings and sensations. It's not something solid; it's not something substantial and permanent. It's a composite.

With mindful attention, see if you can let go of that false sense of a solid entity called "restlessness," that can be so overwhelming. Experience the different strands of thoughts and feelings and sensations that, when woven together, create what we call "restlessness."

Once again, try to name it. Look at it carefully. Look at the various strands that make it up. There might be a feeling of fear; there might be a feeling of conceit; there might be a feeling of resistance.

With doubt, the most important thing is to recognize it as doubt, because it's so seductive. When you don't become involved in the story, a wonderful transformation can happen. Doubt itself becomes the object of your awareness.

When you're not identified with and caught up in the moods of your mind, you can see with clarity and acceptance: "This is doubt; this is its nature. This is how it affects my body. This is how it affects my energy." You don't need to get uncentered, unsettled, or tossed about as doubt comes and goes.

See if you can make a mental note of the hindrance or the combination of hindrances arising.

Feel it. Observe it with compassion, with awareness … and periodically come back to the breath. Bring your attention back to the breath.

As you come back to the breath, you return to a basically neutral object: something that isn't strikingly pleasant or unpleasant; something you're not trying to improve upon or make go away.

And it reminds you; it helps you touch that quality of mindfulness in which you're not reacting to what your experience is. You're with it, closely connected to it, fully aware of it, and not trying to control it.

Be particularly aware as the hindrances arise.

You can open your eyes now. Feel your sitting posture. Notice the world around you, and see if you can bring an awareness of these hindrances – desire and aversion, sleepiness, restlessness and doubt – into your day. The arising of the hindrances is outside of our control, but the way in which we relate to them can determine our degree of being trapped or of being free.

EXERCISES FOR WORKING WITH HINDRANCES

Listen to the guided meditation on CD 2, track 1, or record the version above yourself. Use it in your meditation practice daily for at least a week; then respond to the following exercise questions in the space provided.

Exercise 1

The classical list of the hindrances includes grasping, aversion, sleepiness, restlessness, and doubt. Can you recognize, acknowledge, and note each of these as you experience them? Describe your experience.

_____

_____

_____

_____

_____

Exercise 2

Make an effort to surround each hindrance with acceptance. Do you find this harder to do with one of them than with the others?

_____

_____

_____

Exercise 3

The Buddhist teachings say that being lost in the hindrances is a state of suffering, rather than a sign of being "bad" (as we might say in the West). What happens when you revise your relationship to these states in this way?

_____

_____

_____

_____

Exercise 4

Classically, each hindrance is said to be transformed by a particular factor of the concentrated mind. A list of the hindrances and their antidotes follows. Practice with each of these tools and describe your experience.

Grasping or desire is said to be transformed by one-pointedness or steadiness of mind. Desire makes the mind jump to consider each new possibility for pleasure: "Should I do this next?" "Do I need that?" If you sit like a mountain, you can let the desires arise but not be swayed by them.

Aversion, or striking out at the truth of the present moment, is transformed by interest. You can't push away what's happening and take an interest in it at the same time.

Sleepiness is transformed by right aim – that is, not letting the attention become diffuse. Aim it at the experience of this very moment: "Just this one breath. Just this one step." Don't be concerned with what's already gone by, and don't anticipate what has not yet come.

Restlessness is transformed by happiness, or comfort of mind. Notice that awareness can go anywhere. You can look at a painful experience with an awareness that is open and free, even though the object may be painful. This insight is empowering, and is useful in overcoming the sense of desperation that can accompany restlessness.

Doubt is transformed by sustained attention in the moment. The mind filled with doubt is a mind that hovers, uncertain of what to do or commit to. If you allow your attention to sink into the object of the present moment – to really connect with that object, even if it's just a breath – that attention will energetically transform the quality of doubt.

- Recognize sleepiness as something we experience in parts of every day. We practice meditation in order to wake up. By bringing awareness to the state of torpor, you can gain glimpses into those parts of your world you may be excluding from the totality of your awareness.

- If you find yourself losing interest in your surroundings, wherever you are, focus on just one thing. "Just this sentence." "Just this step." Bring yourself back into the present moment by becoming mindful of those objects and events that are actually arising.

- Surrender. Let your mind be as restless as it wants to, but stay with it. As with any conditioned phenomenon, the restlessness will change shape as you watch it.

- Recognize doubt as a thought process. It takes form as a string of words. Drop below the words to your actual experience, and you're likely to encounter the subtle fear and resistance from which doubt can arise.

- If possible, read the lessons on the five hindrances in *Seeking the Heart of Wisdom: The Path of Insight Meditation* and *The Experience of Insight: A Simple and Direct Guide to Buddhist Meditation* (see resource list, page 224).

LESSON FOUR GLOSSARY

sinking mind: a dreamlike state in which mindfulness is not in balance with concentration.

skeptical doubt: doubt whose function is to undermine faith

sustaining attention: a gentle concentration of the mind on a single, present object; antidote to the hindrance of doubt

LESSON FIVE

CONCEPTS AND REALITY

When we speak of "insight" meditation, we're actually using a loose translation of the Pali word vipassana. The literal meaning of vipassana is "to see clearly" – specifically, to see our experience clearly. This refers to our inner experiences, such as physical sensations, thoughts, and emotions; and also to the natural laws, like impermanence, that we experience all around us as well.

One of the natural laws that we seek to see clearly is the selfless nature of all our experience (in the Buddhist context, "selfless" means "empty of self," rather than its more common meaning of "unselfish"). Many students of Buddhism find this teaching difficult to understand at first. After all, if there's no self, who is reading this page? Who is practicing meditation? Whose back is aching? To say that there is no self sounds like nonsense. Yet selflessness – *anatta* in Pali – is considered the Buddha's greatest realization.

An ancient Greek tale tells of King Gordius, who created a very complicated knot with which to test his warriors. He promised to give a large portion of his kingdom to anyone who could undo the knot. Many strong and clever men tried, but none of them could disentangle it. Finally, Alexander the Great arrived. When King Gordius took him to the famous knot, Alexander unsheathed his sword and sliced it in half. In the same way, it is possible to circumvent the notion of self – the ego – and cut directly through to an understanding of selflessness.

One of the functions of meditation is to bring us to this understanding. After a while, we begin to see that everything we think of as "me" is insubstantial and impermanent. The pain in my knee; my anger at a friend or coworker; my dinner plans – none of these is "me." In fact, nothing I experience lasts long enough to qualify as a solid, consistent self. I begin to realize that this entity I've called "myself" is nothing more than a mental construct. (It's actually quite a relief to come to this understanding. Imagine if you really were everything you thought and felt!)

THE MYTH OF SELF

The concept of "me" arises in the mind. But what is the mind, if not "me"? The mind is simply the ability to know. It is the faculty of cognizance. When we try to look for the mind, it's nowhere to be found. It's the basic consciousness that arises before we can label things "good" or "bad"; "right" or "wrong."

Nonetheless, the mind is the crucial link between our senses and our understanding. A corpse still has a nose, but cannot know perfume. What's missing is the consciousness that knows "I am experiencing an aroma." That element of consciousness is the mind. And because there are no obstacles of interpretation between mind and its objects — such as sights, sounds, or sensations — the mind in its natural state is pure and clear.

The capacity of mind goes beyond just knowing, however. Shadings of experience called "mental factors" are also functions of the mind. Hatred, cruelty, and greed are some of the mental factors considered unwholesome, because they cause suffering. Among the wholesome mental factors that bring happiness are loving-kindness, compassion, joy, and mindfulness itself.

One mental factor, in particular, keeps us trapped in the illusion of "self." This factor is perception: the function that recognizes different experiences, attaches concepts to them, and stores them in our memories.

You might see a tree, for example. The mental factor of perception will register the tree and hold it at the surface level of consciousness so that you can examine it more closely. But without mindfulness, perception doesn't go any deeper than that surface impression. Your understanding of "tree" is frozen at that superficial level and fed, as is, to your memory banks. The next time you see a tree, this unexamined concept comes instantly to mind. "Tree" has become a monolithic entity, its characteristics and relationship to you unvarying from one encounter to the next.

We can cut through this Gordian knot of illusion with the sword of mental noting. At the moment perception registers "tree," if we're awake, we can illuminate that moment with the light of awareness. Instead of leaving perception on autopilot to define our experience, we can now look more deeply into what that particular tree is to us in that particular moment.

There's nothing wrong with the faculty of perception in itself. We use it continually, to tell a car from a bus or a girl from a boy. Perception becomes a problem at the point where we depend on unexamined impressions to tell us the meaning of "car" or "girl" and let them direct how we respond to our notions of these phenomena.

THE NATURE OF PERCEPTION

Most of us have had the experience of running into someone we once knew and feeling like or dislike, warmth or caution, before we consciously register who the person is. This is one example of how perception puts blinders on us. Even the people we do recognize are usually coupled, in our minds, with pleasant or unpleasant experiences. Based on these memories, concepts arise. We often don't even have to know a person well in order to develop fixed ideas about her. This makes it very difficult to open to new possibilities and experiences.

A friend of mine had a son in third or fourth grade. His teacher asked the class, "What color are apples?" The students responded with answers like "red," "green," and "gold." But my friend's son raised his hand and said, "Apples are white."

"No," the teacher told him, "that's incorrect. There are no white apples." But the boy insisted, until his teacher became quite impatient.

Finally the boy asked her, "When you cut an apple open, what color is it inside?" Of course, the answer is white. This young child had a mind free enough to look beyond superficial perceptions and respond to the question directly from his experience.

A similar principle is at work in the so-called "trick" questions that sometimes appear in magazines or circulate on the Internet. "Does Canada have a fourth of July?" Many of us Americans would immediately say no. Yet, on closer reflection, Canadians don't skip right from July 3rd to July 5th. Canada does have a fourth of July, but not the annual event we've come to picture when we hear that term in the United States. We're so identified with our own context that the fourth of July can cease to exist for us in any other.

In this example, a neutral date on the calendar has acquired a single narrow, inflexible meaning in our minds. This is how we approach reality in general when our perception is stronger than our mindfulness. We believe that people, things, and sometimes even ideas are solid, unchanging. We see ourselves as solid, too, which is the source of much of our suffering.

> We should take care not to make the intellect our god; it has, of course, powerful muscles, but no personality.
>
> — ALBERT EINSTEIN

In Lesson Three, I introduced the notion of impermanence: the fact that everything in our experience is constantly changing. Material objects, relationships, systems of government – no matter how long any of these seems to last, in human terms, every one of them arises, dwells in a state of constant flux for a period of time, and then passes away. We witness the impermanent nature of the world and everything in it from one moment to the next.

Why, then, have we come to believe so strongly that everything is solid? One reason is that our perception is unable to keep up with the rapid pace of events. We can understand how this happens by looking at how movies work. The film comprises millions of frames, each one capturing a fraction of a second in time. When these frames are run rapidly through the projector, they create an illusion of continuous movement. We watch the stories they tell and get completely lost in them. It all seems so real – but if you slowed down the film, you'd see that each frame tells its own story. The illusion of motion depends entirely on the rapidity with which each frame is replaced by the next.

Meanwhile, the light passing through the film and projecting it onto the screen appears entirely stable. Yet it's driven by an alternating electrical current. The alternation happens at such great speed that we perceive the light as steady and continuous.

Distance is another phenomenon that protects the illusion of solidity. Typically, we don't look at things very closely. If you take something seemingly very solid – say, a fragment of gravel – and look at it under a microscope, you'll see an extraordinary display of movement and change. The way we think of gravel is entirely at odds with this evident reality.

You don't need a microscope to experiment with this phenomenon. Just look at something in the distance: perhaps a house. At first, you'll see it as a shape of a certain color or colors. As you move closer, you'll begin to see the different elements of the house. The windows are quite distinct from the roof, for example. The closer you get, the more clearly you see that the house is composed of countless elements. If you get close enough, you'll cease to perceive it as a house. It will have become a field of texture and color. By this time you'll know a great deal more about the house than you did at first glance.

The same is true of every "solid" object we perceive around us: airplanes, highways, furniture, other people. Without mindfulness, our experience of these things remains at surface level. We don't see the incredibly complex interplay of changing elements that goes to make up that chair or that person.

Who Am "I"?

We typically apply the same superficial understanding to what we call the "self." Since the body is our most visible evidence that we seem to exist, we often equate this self with it. Sure, the body is going to get old and die sometime, but until then it seems pretty substantial.

Here's how we use the body to construct a self. I perceive an appearance we call "Joseph." This "Joseph" has certain attributes, like height and weight and shape. When I see myself in a mirror, there's a moment of instant recognition: "Yes, that's me, the same person I saw here yesterday." Yet this "Joseph" is no more substantial or enduring than a rainbow. Just as we recognize the rainbow's attributes of red, orange, yellow, and so forth in their predictable pattern, we see a particular constellation of elements — mind, body, energy — and call it "Joseph." Then we believe that it exists as an independent reality. (Perhaps we could think of ourselves as rainbows: beautiful, vivid, ephemeral, and selfless.)

We identify with thoughts in the same way. As soon as a thought arises, I have the sense that "I'm thinking." "I" and the thought become two separate, self-existing entities. Then I get lost in the thought, and go on to identify with it. In a matter of seconds, I've created an entire mental cosmology. The thought acquires an independent existence. Without realizing it, I've given it the power to limit my possibilities.

All we are is the result of what we have thought.

— THE DHAMMAPADA

We're also in the habit of taking our emotions personally. Rather than watching anger arise and change, I say, "I'm angry." Then I solidify the sense of self still further: "I'm an angry person." From there, I can create all kinds of scenarios about my life, my practice, my relationships, my future: a massive superstructure resting on a single, simple moment of experience.

In fact, there is no "I" to be angry. Anger is what angers; love is what loves. A writing teacher at the Buddhist-inspired Naropa University kept a sign up over his desk that read, "I make something" — except the "I" and the "something" were crossed out, leaving only "make." No creator behind the writing, and no product. Just the experience of making.

In meditation practice, we sometimes find ourselves identifying with awareness itself. I may be observing sensations, thoughts, and emotions diligently, even recognizing their impersonal nature, but I still solidify myself as the observer: "I'm watching my experience." Yet awareness itself is selfless. A good way to investigate this more deeply is to do your mental noting in the passive voice: "Sounds being heard"; "The breath being known"; "Fear being felt." In this way, you eliminate the "I" from the experience of knowing.

Regular meditation helps us begin to form a more accurate picture of both inner and outer phenomena. Our minds begin to see past superficial perceptions, and we realize that we and everything around us are constantly changing energy fields.

It's possible to refine our practice to the point where the perception of "body" completely disappears. We see how the breath involves the mouth, throat, chest, and abdomen (often, particularly if you've never watched it before, breathing can involve the shoulders, too). We see that it is none of these things, but a constantly changing experience that may be engaging any combination of them at any given moment.

The same is true in walking meditation. Is it the foot that's walking? Is it the leg? When we ask ourselves these questions over a period of time, we see that the concepts of "foot" and "leg" are just that – concepts. They have no real existence. All that exists is the experience of walking – and then it's gone.

Of course, we don't want to lose our sense of the whole. You need the concept of "body" so that you can buy clothes that fit and eat nourishing food. You need the concept of "car" so that you drive it rather than try to take a shower in it. The point is not to throw out these perceptions, but to understand that your immediate experience of "body" and "car" is the result of numerous conditions that happen to come together for one brief moment. All conditioned things – everything that arises out of conditions – are, by their very nature, impermanent. That understanding helps us to see through the illusion of a solid world.

So pervasive is the urge to solidify our experience that we even try to freeze vast intangibles, like time and space. Most of us have formed pretty fixed ideas about these concepts – and they impact very powerfully on our relationships to our lives and the world.

Take, for example, the notions of "past" and "future." You may be sitting in meditation when a memory arises. In an instant, you've solidified the memory and tossed it back into an area you label "the past." Now there's a solid reality somewhere out there called "my past." All that's really happened, though, is that a thought arose in your mind.

The same goes for the future. You don't have to be meditating; fantasies about the future come up all the time. You see yourself landing your dream job or losing your car; you pack that thought into a solid little form, like a snowball, and you toss it forward into the place you've called "my future."

The Buddha actually cites our concepts of past and future as direct obstacles to concentration. So not only are these thoughts misleading, in that we tend to believe they reflect solid realities – on a practical level, they interfere with our meditation.

"ME" AND "MINE"

The belief in a self naturally gives rise to the concept of ownership. Once we accept that the body is solid, we imagine that it's the property of the imagined solid self. Then we go on to think of ourselves as possessing other people, animals, objects, and even experiences.

Mark Twain tells a story about horse traders in Russia. What makes this story especially interesting is that it's told from the horses' point of view. In their minds, they're involved in certain relationships with the various people in the story – some nurturing and some destructive. But they never see themselves as owned. The humans are the ones who think they own the horses.

Much of the misunderstanding that exists between the world's indigenous peoples and their "civilized" colonizers has its roots in their radically different relationships with land. Typically, colonizers in the Americas, Africa, and Australia assumed that all land belonged to somebody. The indigenous people didn't think of land as something that could be owned. So to the colonizers, these new worlds were theirs for the taking. The indigenous people, on the other hand, were quite distressed to find themselves suddenly denied access to their ancestral hunting and grazing grounds, because somebody else now "owned" them.

This concept of ownership is very deeply ingrained in us. You've probably had the experience of enjoying a conversation with someone at a party. You get up to fill your glass or go to the bathroom, and when you return someone else is sitting in "your" chair. It's not uncommon to feel a flash of frustration and even indignation in this kind of situation. I have sometimes asked retreat participants to imagine how they would feel if they came into the meditation hall and found someone else sitting on their cushion. For some people, the sense of ownership is so pervasive that an incident like this can trigger considerable agitation.

By not quite accepting, because they do not please us, things that are so, we spend our entire lives making meaningless gestures somewhere next door to reality.

— NAN SHIN

Another concept to which many of us are attached is that of self-image. We imagine that we have certain defined roles to play in our families, at work, and in society in general. We have expectations about what it means to play these roles, and we limit our thoughts, words, and actions to conform to those concepts. Living in this way prepares the ground for great resentment, rigidity, and potential disruption when you realize that the role you're playing isn't, after all, what you want for your life.

Some time ago, when I was living in India, I needed to submit a particular government form related to my status as a nonworking tourist. I went to the appropriate office, fully prepared to wait (you spend a lot of time waiting in India). Sure enough, when I asked the man behind the desk for the form, he said, "Please wait." I sat and watched my breath – "rising, falling, rising, falling." After nearly an hour, I went back to the desk and asked the man, "What am I waiting for?" He said, "The forms are locked in the cabinet behind me."

I went back to my seat and sat a little longer. Then a bright idea struck me. I went back to the man and asked, "Where's the key to the cabinet?"

He pointed. "In that drawer."

"Well, why can't you get the key from the drawer, open the cabinet, and give me the form?"

"It's not my job," he shrugged.

This is an extreme example of someone identifying with his role – but to some extent, we all do the same thing. I might see myself as male, American, a son, a Buddhist, or a teacher. All of these are accurate descriptions, but to the extent I become identified with any of them at a given moment, I'm freezing myself in that role. I can't be open to experiences that, in my mind, a man or a Buddhist or whatever wouldn't have. I'm trapped in the prison of ego: a claustrophobic place that admits very little opportunity for insight, new understandings, or healthy relationships.

We see the results of this kind of thinking throughout our society. People identify powerfully with their race, gender, political affiliation, or religion, which then serves as a point of separation from everyone else. Yet in meditation, we quickly discover that the mind has no politics. The breath is neither male nor female. The sensation of walking has no opinion about the nature of God.

Reality is that which, when you stop believing in it, doesn't go away.

— PHILIP K. DICK

All these concepts – body, time, self-image, and the rest – spring from the belief in a solid self. That "self" guards the gate where all my experience enters. Everything I see, hear, taste, touch, smell, and think is instantly processed through this construct, which then accepts, rejects, or modifies the information to support the illusion of its own existence. The Wizard of Oz said, "Pay no attention to the man behind the curtain!" But as we know, the man behind the curtain was creating the entire show. That's how it is with this illusory self to which we give so much power. As one Sri Lankan monk expressed it, "no self, no problem."

THE MECHANISMS OF ILLUSION

Early on in my practice, a teacher told me that experience is "empty phenomena rolling on." "Empty," in this case, means empty of self. Neither I nor anything I encounter has a separate, substantial existence. There is no one to experience, and nothing I can point to and say, "That is the experience." Everything – including this "me" around which the whole world seems to revolve – is simply a reflection of the conditions arising in this moment.

Clearly, then, the self is a mental fabrication. So why do we believe in it so strongly? Most of us never question it. If you were to ask someone in the street, "Do you exist?" the response would almost certainly be, "Of course! Here I am, right in front of your eyes!"

But superficial impressions, as we've seen, cannot reveal the true nature of what we perceive. In order to see into the composite nature of this changing experience we call "self," we have to examine it closely. One central reason we fixate on the notion of a solid self is that we don't look past our initial impression. We rely on our surface perception as an accurate reflection of reality.

Most of us are familiar with the constellation of stars known as the Big Dipper. Once you've identified it, it's very hard to look at the night sky without perceiving that shape. Yet we all know that there's no such a thing as the Big Dipper. It's simply a random arrangement of stars that happens to conform to a recognizable pattern. To perceive that shape, we have to bring it to the foreground – we stop paying attention to all the other stars around it. We attach ourselves to the concept, "the Big Dipper," thereby separating it from ourselves and from the other stars.

In ancient times, mariners used the Big Dipper to find the North Star. That's how they navigated the oceans. So again, it's not that there's anything wrong with perceiving the Big Dipper. The point is to recognize the perception as a mental construct, rather than believing it actually exists as a solid entity.

CUTTING THE KNOT

The belief in a separate self is so habitual and deep-rooted that it may seem impossible to cut it with even the sharpest sword. Through the millennia, however, countless meditators have discovered that the sustained practice of mindfulness and awareness gradually reveals the true nature of experience. We begin to see all the constantly shifting elements and conditions that give rise to the objects and events we perceive, and in time, the notion of self is worn away.

It is said that a man once traveled from one end of India to the other to hear the Buddha's teaching. When he arrived, he found the Buddha and his monks gathering alms. Right there in the middle of the street, the man said, "Please give me your teachings." The Buddha said, "Certainly. Wait until we're done with our alms round. We'll eat our lunch, and then I'll give you the teachings." But the man couldn't wait. "No, no!" he cried. "I must hear the teachings right this minute!" Again, the Buddha tried to hold him off, but after the man had begged him three times to teach, he finally agreed.

How to transmit something so profound in just a few short minutes? The Buddha pondered briefly, then told the man, "In the seen, there is only what is seen. In the heard, there is only what is heard. In the sensed (i.e., what is smelled, tasted, and touched), there is only what is sensed. In thoughts, there is only what is thought."

When you are not thinking about who you are, who are you?

— SONJA MARGULIES

It's said that the man attained enlightenment on the spot. He understood what the Buddha was saying: what we perceive with our senses is just that, and nothing more. The only reality is our direct experience right in this moment, free of concepts and interpretations. This understanding is the beginning of the end of our addiction to "me" and "mine."

A famous Tibetan meditation master named Kalu Rinpoche died just a few years ago. One particular teaching of his summarizes everything we've been discussing here. He said:

We live in illusion and the appearance of things.
We live in the world of concepts.
There is a reality; we are that reality.
When we understand this, we see we are nothing
And being nothing, we are everything. That is all.

CONCEPTS AND REALITY: QUESTION AND ANSWER SESSION

Q: You've said that concepts aren't bad; that they're actually useful in many senses. Yet you seem to come down heavily in favor of reality. How can I use concepts without letting them distort my perception of reality?

A: Reality occurs on many different levels. One of them is the conventional level on which we function as a "man" or a "woman," in which we differentiate the green traffic light from the red. We need to use concepts like these, but it is helpful to recognize that there's another level of reality that arises directly out of our experience. Often concepts arise so quickly and seem so solid that we miss our direct experience. When this happens, we take as unchanging that which is always in flux; as desirable that which is actually bringing dissatisfaction; and as "self" that which is insubstantial and empty of self. That is ignorance.

Q: If the notion of a foot or a leg is a mental fabrication, then what is it that causes pain when it's broken, that develops blisters if I wear shoes that are too small?

A: In the Buddhist tradition, there are four so-called "ultimate realities" – ultimate, not in a metaphysical sense, but simply because they can be experienced directly. These are physical, material elements; consciousness, or our capacity to know the object of our awareness; mental factors, which are defined as the qualities of mind that determine our relationships to the objects of consciousness; and nirvana, or the experience of freedom.

The more we practice careful attention, the more it becomes our habit of mind. We then find that awareness comes into our activities at whatever speed we are doing them. Slowing down is simply a training that helps us get into the habit of mindful attention.

— JOSEPH GOLDSTEIN

The words we use descriptively (including "foot" and "leg") are concepts we use to point to the reality. There's no sensation called "foot." But language or concepts can direct us to experience, in the same way that a finger pointing to the moon can lead us to look at the moon. We just don't want to confuse the finger with the moon.

Q: How did we get so far away from seeing the "ultimate realities" you describe? How did we get so entangled in conceptual thinking?

A: We're driven by the forces of ignorance and desire. Ignorance is that mind state in which the reality of experience is obscured; and desire, as we've discussed, is the tendency to abandon the reality of experience in favor of an imaginary world. The Buddha taught that ignorance and desire have been driving us since beginningless time. The antidote is to pay attention to the truth of our experience in this moment. That's the direct link to the real truth of existence.

Q: If I have opinions about injustice or violence, should I consider them concepts that block my experience of reality? Isn't it important to declare sometimes that something is wrong or unjust?

A: The idea here is not to become wishy-washy, or to shrink from taking right action when appropriate. Rather, the danger is of becoming lost in our point of view without seeing distinctly what it is. If you see clearly that a situation is unjust, you should definitely respond to it as skillfully as you can. But your response comes from an open and loving heart and a full sense of what's happening — not from a mind bent by rigid opinions, that's disconnected from what's actually going on.

Guided Meditation: Eating

Record the following guided meditation, have a friend record it, or trade off reading it out loud with your friend. Procure some raisins, nuts, or some other small food items. Bring them to your meditation space and have them within reach as you prepare to sit.

Eating is a common daily activity that provides a very good opportunity for us to practice bare attention, free from the many concepts that may arise around it. Typically, the mind is quite heavily conditioned in various ways around food. Our conditioning may include desire, greed, fear, or anxiety — perhaps even revulsion. So it's very helpful to learn how to be with this essential aspect of our lives simply and directly, free of the conditioning or habituated concepts that may cause us suffering.

Take the food you've brought into your meditation space and put it on some surface in front of you. Sit comfortably. Now, to begin with, simply look at the food. Look at it, see it ... so it becomes a meditation of seeing.

You could make the soft mental note, "seeing, seeing." Be very gentle, very receptive.

Notice the color of the food. Notice the form.

Now, very slowly, begin reaching for the food. Be aware of the sensation of movement of the hand, of the arm. Do it very slowly, with care, with enjoyment.

See the food, aware of seeing. Reach for the food, aware of reaching.

With the same kind of care, touch a piece of food. Bring your awareness to the touch sensations.

Feel the texture: is it rough? Is it smooth? Is it warm? Is it cool?

Is it hard? Is it soft?

See the color and form ... feel the sensation of the movement ... notice the touch sensations that may arise as you hold the food in your fingers.

Very slowly, begin to lift the food to your mouth. Feel the sensation of the movement.

See if you can be aware of the very subtle sensations as you lift your arm.

Lift very slowly; then be aware of opening the mouth. Feeling the sensations of the opening. Still moving very slowly, place the food on the tongue. Notice the placing movement and then the feeling of the food as it rests on the tongue.

Notice the closing of the mouth and then the lowering of the arm to a resting position.

Very slowly, begin chewing. Notice the movement of the jaws, the tongue, the teeth, the food interacting with the teeth. Be aware, if you can, of the very first sensation of taste that may arise. Notice the taste, the sweetness or the saltiness, whatever it may be.

There's chewing, and at a certain point, there's a little explosion of taste in the mouth. Notice that, and notice how the taste fades away while the chewing may still be continuing.

Chewing, tasting, chewing, tasting, chewing, chewing ...

... and then when you're ready to swallow, be aware of the swallowing. Feel the sensations at the back of the tongue, in the throat. Sometimes people can feel the food as it goes down into the stomach.

Then sit for a moment, maybe being with the breath or the feeling of the whole body sitting.

And you can repeat this exercise several times.

Notice that when you see the food, there might be an immediate tendency to name the kind of food it is. "Seeing raisins, seeing peanuts." But these are concepts – the eye doesn't see "raisin" – the eye sees color and form. And then the mind will think "raisin, peanut," whatever it may be.

So right in this meditation on eating, we begin to see the difference between our concepts of things and the direct experience of them.

Now begin again with seeing ... and then reaching for the food ... feeling the sensation of the movement of reaching ...

... touching the food ... holding it ... feeling the sensation of touch.

Raising the arm, feel that movement. Opening the mouth, feel that movement.

Notice how it feels to place the food in the mouth. At every stage, remain very relaxed and very attentive.

Place the food in the mouth, close the mouth, lower the arm, noticing the sensations throughout; and again, begin to chew.

Feel the whole mechanism of chewing.

Notice the taste as it arises; notice the response to the taste. You may like it, you may dislike it; it's pleasant, it's unpleasant. All of this can be noticed with every mouthful.

You chew; taste arises; taste diminishes. Finish chewing that particular mouthful and feel the sensations of swallowing.

And again, sit for a moment with the breath, with the body.

When we're on retreat, this meditation on eating can be done for the entire meal. In the busyness of our daily lives, we might not have sufficient time to do that, but we can still reconnect with the depth of this practice even if we take only a few minutes of every meal. You could perhaps either have a single piece of fruit mindfully, or one part of the meal mindfully. Or you might take the first few minutes of each meal to eat in this way.

The more we practice careful attention, the more it becomes our habit of mind, and we find that then the awareness comes into our activities at whatever speed we're doing them. The slowing down is simply a training that helps us get into the habit of mindful attention.

So please continue this mindfulness meditation on eating with the food that you brought out for this exercise, doing it slowly, carefully, attentive to each part of the process. When you're finished, sit for a few minutes, feeling the body sitting, being with the breath. Then slowly getting up, taking your mindfulness with you in whatever your next activity may be.

EATING EXERCISES

Practice while listening to your recording of the guided meditation above. Incorporate the following exercises into your practice at least three times during the next week; then respond to at least five exercises in the space provided.

Exercise 1

Place a small handful of raisins or nuts on a surface in front of you. Describe how it looks and smells.

_____

_____

_____

_____

Exercise 2

Pick up a raisin or nut. Feel the sensations associated with lifting your arm. What do you experience?

_____

_____

_____

_____

Exercise 3

Bring the piece of food to your mouth and begin to chew it. How do you experience feelings of pleasantness and unpleasantness as you do so?

_____

_____

_____

Exercise 4

Notice the impulse to take another mouthful before the first is done, if that arises. What is your experience of this?

_____

_____

_____

Exercise 5

What mental and/or emotional states are you experiencing?

_____

_____

_____

Exercise 6

What thoughts, self-images, and judgments arise as you do these exercises? Briefly describe each of these three phenomena.

_____

_____

_____

GETTING THE MOST FROM YOUR MEDITATION

- When you find yourself confused by any situation, return to your immediate experience. What are your physical sensations? What can you see, hear, smell, touch? Practice recognizing the difference between this awareness and interpretations or judgments arising in your mind.

- The Buddha taught that three mental factors are the roots of all unwholesome activities: greed, hatred, and delusion. Happily, there are also three wholesome roots of mind: generosity, love, and wisdom. Cultivating these qualities helps to bring clarity to our minds, drawing us closer to a fuller understanding of the truth. Display the card listing the six wholesome and unwholesome roots of mind where you can see it every day. Whenever it catches your eye, notice the state of your mind in relation to the factors.

- "Wrong view" is the mental factor that wrongly identifies with the changing elements of mind and body as being self; as belonging to "me."

Work with diffusing the energy of this false concept by practicing mindfulness in every moment, with every experience. You can return to mindfulness any time you realize you've been lost in concepts.

- Experiment with how it feels to not be attached to opinions. For one day, resolve to let go of judgments and conclusions. Recognize when your point of view is not resting on an actual experience, but is simply an opinion. Pay attention to the quality of this day, and to the ways in which it differs from other days.

LESSON FIVE GLOSSARY

anatta: "selflessness" [Pali]; insubstantiality

beginner's mind: a mind that is open to the experience of the moment, free of conceptual overlays (coined by Suzuki Roshi — see resource list, page 226)

ego: the pattern of conditioned habits that we mistake for a solid self

wrong view: the tendency of the mind to cling to concepts at the expense of reality; taking what is impermanent to be permanent, what is dissatisfying to be satisfying, what is selfless to be self

SHARON SALZBERG

LESSON SIX

SUFFERING

In the last lesson, we contrasted living our lives behind a veil of illusion and concept with directly perceiving the truth of things. But what is "the truth of things"? What do we perceive when we step out of an illusory, conceptual vision of the world?

A primary truth that the Buddha taught — a law of nature, in fact — is *dukkha*. This Pali word is typically translated as "suffering." It means sorrow, discontent, dis-ease, unsatisfactoriness, that which is difficult to bear. It also means hollowness, insecurity.

Once, just before my book, *Lovingkindness,* was released, a newspaper reporter interviewed me. Every question she asked started with, "Do you believe in …?"

I said, "No."

"Well, do you believe in …?"

"No."

Finally she asked, "Well, what do you believe in?"

Much to my surprise, I heard myself say, "I believe in suffering." I don't know who was more shocked, her or me. But it was a true statement.

The Buddha said, "I teach one thing, and one thing only — that is suffering and the end of suffering." While suffering is certainly not all there is in life, it is a thread that needs to be recognized clearly if we're going to be fully awake, completely present with all of our experience, and truly compassionate toward ourselves and others.

Dukkha — suffering — doesn't necessarily mean grave pain. It also refers to a sense of the fleetingness of things. It is that queasy recognition that the events in our lives are ungovernable; that we can't control them. Things are insubstantial. They change whether we want them to or not. This is what the Buddha was referring to when he said, "I teach one thing and one thing only — that is suffering and the end of suffering."

123

Probably this statement, more than any other, has given the Buddha's teachings a reputation for pessimism. But it's not meant to be depressing or disturbing at all. It simply affirms what, in fact, we already suspect to be true.

In conventional life, we receive very little support for trusting our own vision of the truth. This is why many people, upon hearing that statement – "I teach one thing and one thing only – that is suffering and the end of suffering" – find themselves breathing a sigh of relief. Finally, somebody is saying it directly: "There's suffering in this life." It's not all fun and games. It's not all pleasure – and it's not my fault if I don't experience it to be all pleasure.

When we look truthfully at our own experience, it's no big surprise that suffering exists. We have our ups and downs; we feel pain or loss or sorrow as things change. We all experience this pattern. We know this experience is real, yet often we don't receive external confirmation of our perception. This denial, in the long run, is far more painful than a frank acknowledgment of the truth. We're brought up to believe that suffering is somehow wrong and to be avoided. Suffering, in the conventional view, is unbearable and shouldn't even be faced. As a result, we've created a society that continually accommodates our need to deny and avoid pain.

When a friend of mine received a terminal diagnosis, the first thing he said was, "I'm not going to make an enemy of my own death." That's a very beautiful statement, and my friend lived up to it. Most of us, though, have learned to make an enemy of our own death. We've learned to make an enemy of our mental and physical suffering. In other words, we've learned to make an enemy of our own perceptions; of our own vision of what's true. The logical conclusion of this world view is that we make an enemy of life itself.

Why Is the Truth So Hard to See?

Our conditioning begins very early in life. Often, families try to shield their children from the difficulties, conflict, and fear that inevitably arise in any human situation. A great and ignoble silence descends. This is not the silence of clear seeing: the silence we use in meditation to discover, nurture, and honor our own vision of what is true. It's the silence of denial and avoidance. Terrible abuse or violence may be going on, but they're just not spoken about – or if they are spoken about, they're repackaged and manipulated so as to cloak the pain of the actual experience.

Almost always, in these situations, the child knows exactly what's going on. But because there's no external affirmation of the truth she clearly sees, she learns not to trust her own perceptions. Most of us live like children growing up in a dysfunctional family. All the pain is being denied, but inside, we know what's really happening.

One of my favorite examples of the denial practiced in our culture dates back to when Ronald Reagan was first running for president. Around that time, images of the American family started popping up all over the media. The concept of "family" began ascending, almost to the level of the sacred. According to the social mythology of the era, the family was going to take care of every issue. The courts would no longer need to adjudicate, and the legislatures would no longer need to mandate. The family was going to address all injustices and conflict, and everyone was going to be happy again.

Ye shall know the truth, and the truth shall make you free.

— JOHN 8:36

In this picture of the American family, there was no suffering, no anger, no fear. Everybody was talking to one another and respecting one another and communicating perfectly. There was so much respect and closeness within the family that the government would no longer need to intervene at all.

Seeing or hearing these impossibly perfect depictions in the media, I would think, "Who are they talking about?" They weren't talking about any family that I'd ever encountered. They weren't talking about the family dealing with violence or alcoholism. They weren't talking about the family where people hadn't spoken to one another in twenty years.

I don't mean to imply that all families are miserable; great happiness can be found in family life. But how often is it so very, very perfect — as immaculate as this political vision was implying? When models like these are being held up as the truth, it's no wonder people feel bad about their own situations. By comparison, our own families look like terrible failures.

You don't have to come from a wounded family to feel confused. No matter how healthy and supportive your surroundings, pain is always part of the human condition. Life is full of moments of dissatisfaction, insecurity, uncertainty, and loss. To the extent that these aren't acknowledged and recognized as integral to our human reality, we experience a disparity between our inner sense of what is real and what our families and society are telling us. This is why the Buddha's teaching — "suffering and the end of suffering" — represents enormous liberation. "Here it is:" he's saying, "the truth of things. Suffering exists."

Needless to say, there's also great pleasure in this world. There are wonderful arisings; times of people coming together; countless beautiful things to enjoy and celebrate. And by the same token, there are partings, loss, and separation. There's birth and there's also death. That's the truth of things. Even just this one teaching, apart from anything else the Buddha taught, is an extraordinary gift. Without this realization, we feel terribly alone when we're in pain.

In the great Hindu epic, the *Mahabharata,* someone is asked, "What is the most wondrous thing in the entire universe?" The reply is, "The most wondrous thing in the entire universe is that all around us people are dying and we don't believe it will happen to us." It's as though there's this big surprise at the end of our lives. We feel we've been made fools of. It embarrasses us that we were unable to control this shocking event. This kind of thinking can make us feel terribly alone.

Another good example of widespread cultural denial shows up in the supermarket tabloids. It seems that people are constantly catching sight of Elvis Presley. "Elvis Spotted in Florida"; "Elvis Spotted in California" – or even, once, "Elvis Spotted on Mars." Why can't he just have died? People do die.

When there's this much denial of our own experience, we're moving away from something real to something fabricated. To live by this web of legend, of myth, of unreality, will always harm us. The truth may be difficult to face, but it will never harm us.

> *Acting out and repressing are the main ways that we shield our hearts, the main ways that we never really connect with our vulnerability, our compassion, our sense of the open, fresh dimension of our being. By acting out or repressing we invite suffering, bewilderment, or confusion to intensify.*
>
> — PEMA CHÖDRÖN

Sometimes the truth that we open to is painful. The poet Rumi said, "Pain will be borne from that look cast inside yourself, and this pain will make you go behind the veil." It's natural, in our commitment to open to everything, that at times we will encounter pain, suffering, uneasiness, loneliness.

In the late eighties, *The New Yorker* magazine ran an article about Buddhism. Someone interviewed for this piece said that according to Buddhism, the purpose of life was to suffer. No wonder Buddhism has such a bad reputation as pessimistic and depressing. The reality, of course, is that it's not at all the purpose of life to suffer. What the Buddha actually taught is that it is neither wise nor compassionate to pretend that suffering's not there. We only learn to be free of it by first recognizing its existence and pervasiveness in our experience.

Suffering and Motivation

When the Buddha's father decided to keep his son inside the palace walls (see "The Story of the Buddha," page 5), he did it by eliminating all evidence of suffering and impermanence. He knew that unhappiness often prompts deep questioning, so he provided every conceivable pleasure: food, drink, entertainment, exquisite works of art. According to legend, the king even employed a team of gardeners to pluck out any withering blossoms in the palace gardens at night. The prince was shown only life's enjoyments, and none of its pain.

In our endless search for pleasure and ease, we're trying to do for ourselves what the Buddha's father did for his son. But the spiritual quest requires that we question everything: who we are; what our lives are about; all our assumptions about happiness. We question everything we've always believed in. We even question the value of belief itself, as compared to a direct and intimate experience of what's happening in the moment. It takes a very powerful motivation to give up the quest for pleasure and open ourselves to that level of questioning.

At the age of twenty-nine, the Bodhisattva finally did leave the palace grounds. Only then did he see an old person, a sick person, and a corpse. When he saw a renunciate – a spiritual seeker who had renounced worldly pleasure in order to look for the truth – he heard his call to awakening.

Imagine the shock this pampered, protected young man must have experienced at encountering overt suffering for the first time in his life. It can take that much to unstick us, to turn us away from our habitual patterns.

It's hard to leave home. It was hard for the Bodhisattva; it's hard for all of us. But when we do, we discover a very different meaning of "home." Uneasiness propels us to question, and the questions propel us to a living reality. We come home to a vital sense of being in harmony with the truth.

The Suffering of Pain

The Buddha taught that there are three kinds of suffering. The first is the most obvious: that is, painful experiences that are easy to acknowledge as painful. These include being sick, having physical pain, and being in a state of grief or rage. Despite their directness, these kinds of pain can still be quite difficult to look at. Seeing clearly the extent of this kind of suffering is not the same as being depressed or enraged. As the poet William Butler Yeats said, "We are fastened to a dying animal." Just to be in a body implies physical suffering, at least some of the time. It means inevitable decay, aging, sickness, and death, whether we want that or not. We don't die because we've done something wrong. This is simply how things are.

Coming to understand this truth can be distressing, because we can confuse it with self-denigration. But to see that we're "fastened to a dying animal" isn't an expression or admission of self-hatred. In fact, we're not even talking about ourselves. We're talking about the nature of the body. To the extent that we don't see it truthfully, we get lost in the world of "Elvis Lives On." Why would we choose to spend our lives in this delusion? Seeing truth will never harm us — it will only free us.

THE SUFFERING OF CHANGE

The second kind of suffering arises when we see that everything in life changes. All the pleasant feelings that come up in the body or the mind — they are transitory. There's pleasure, and then there's pain. We have what we want, and then it goes away, breaks, or changes. When we're unable to understand and accept that this is the way things are, we add an enormous amount of suffering to the fundamental truth of change. It's actually possible to experience this fundamental truth without getting stuck in it.

The suffering of change really came home to me once when I was expecting a visit from a friend in California. She had never been to the East Coast, and she was planning to come in the fall. Of course, the autumn leaves in Massachusetts are glorious. For two weeks before my friend was due to arrive, I walked around looking at the beautiful leaves and willing them to stick on the trees so that my friend could enjoy the display when she came. I felt an intense, visceral demand that those leaves stay on the trees.

As it turned out, my friend didn't come at all. When I heard that she'd cancelled her trip, I felt a great relief. It was as if I thought, "Now I can let the leaves fall off the trees." It was a ludicrous fantasy, of course — but the fact is that we spend much of our lives trying to keep the leaves on the trees. We imagine that we can defy the laws of nature and manipulate events that are entirely beyond our control. Blinded by our thirst for pleasure and our flight from pain, we try to freeze the world in place so that it conforms to our own notions of how things should be.

When our culture denies the inevitability of change and the reality of suffering, we're more likely to feel alone when we experience loss or pain or sorrow. Our conditioning keeps telling us that suffering is an aberration. After all, you should have been able to control events, to make them turn out right. Why couldn't you keep those leaves on the trees? This is the message we hear all the time. Living this way gives rise to terrible suffering.

Once we realize how impermanent and insubstantial our world is, it can be tempting to see our lives as meaningless. If we can't control reality, events can start to look haphazard or disconnected. But the opposite of control isn't chaos. It's freedom. To let go of the illusion that we can keep things from changing, or control the way they change, frees us to connect deeply with both pleasure and pain as they evolve and change, and to learn from both.

Pain multiplied by resistance equals suffering.

— SHINZEN YOUNG

The purpose of opening to pain is not to make ourselves feel bad, but to be available for what the pain or the suffering has to teach us. It can teach us to see things in a different way. It can teach us to have the courage to let go. It can teach us that we're not alone; that we could never be all alone in this kind of experience. Suffering can teach us the faith and determination to keep on growing – not to get lost in a swamp of judgments about our experience.

THE SUFFERING OF CONDITIONALITY

The third kind of suffering the Buddha taught is very subtle. In some texts, it's defined as the suffering that remains after the other two kinds have been described. More directly, it's called the suffering of conditionality.

Nothing stands apart from the conditions bringing it about – no entity, experience, or action. Say, for example, that you want to eat a meal. That probably means you have to have a job, so that you have the money to buy food. You might need a car so you can get to the store; and then you have to buy the food, bring it home, and cook it. Finally, you get to eat the meal. There's no such thing as a meal in and of itself. Rather, a combination of conditions comes together in a certain way at a certain time, and we call it a meal.

Our world is like a house of cards. Everything is dependent. Nothing can ever just be on its own in a state of rest. In a very subtle way, we find this oppressive. There's a quality of restlessness in the continual arising and disintegrating of all our experience. This is the suffering of conditioned existence itself: what it is to be alive, with a body and a mind.

What's important here, as with every kind of suffering, is to recognize that we are not alone in the truth of things. Someone once told me something very beautiful when I was teaching a *metta,* or lovingkindness, retreat. In metta practice, we direct the power of lovingkindness and compassion to all beings, everywhere. This person said that she'd been in a lot of emotional pain all year long. The one thought that had given her the strength to go on was the recognition that somewhere in the world, someone was doing metta practice, directing unconditional lovingkindness to all that lives – including herself. Never having met her, without any particular connection to her, and not because she did something special to deserve it, some-body was sending her lovingkindness, simply by virtue of the fact that she existed. She felt included in the family of life and that helped her realize she wasn't alone in her suffering.

THE ORDINARINESS OF DUKKHA

Sometimes we experience dukkha quite directly and graphically in our meditation: our knees hurt and our backs hurt and our minds hurt. At other times, it's more subtle. We can't seem to concentrate; we feel restless; we don't think we're doing very well. Then our perception of suffering comes from seeing that we can't control things. The mind is ungovernable. We say, "I will never fall asleep in meditation again," and then we fall asleep.

That's dukkha.

Many, many times I told my teacher, Sayadaw U Pandita, "Things are going very badly. My head hurts and I have uncontrollable movement in my body and my mind is all over the place and I can't practice. Things are really bad."

He would just say, "That's dukkha, isn't it?" I would look at him expectantly, waiting for him to tell me the magic trick, that one little technique that would make all the suffering go away. I wanted him to say, "Walk a little more. Sit a little more. Sit in a chair. Don't sit in a chair. Count your breaths," or whatever. But all he would say was, "Well, that's dukkha, isn't it?" After a while, I began to hear what he was saying. "This is a rightful perception," he was telling me. "This isn't just a personal drama. This is an opening into one aspect of life. This is part of how it is. This experience has to be seen and acknowledged." You don't have to immerse yourself in suffering or get lost in it; but in order to be fully open, you have to let the truth of dukkha in as well.

This is a very refined teaching, easy to misunderstand. It doesn't mean that we should be passive, or that taking action is never appropriate. Rather, it means that we hurt ourselves the most by fervently trying to control things so that we never have to suffer. That's what U Pandita was talking about.

Aristotle said, "Suffering becomes beautiful when anyone bears great calamities with cheerfulness, not through insensibility, but through greatness of mind." I don't know if I personally would use the word "cheerfulness"; but what makes sense to me is that suffering can become beautiful when we work to bear great calamities with faith, mindfulness, awareness, and understanding. That's how real trust and compassion arise – and that truly is greatness of mind.

Everybody suffers, but it's a sad fact that not everybody is made noble by suffering. It takes great courage and mindfulness to open to the truth of things as they are. But when we do, we're terrifically empowered. We have the potential to experience things as they are.

That's freedom.

The Four Noble Truths

The very first teaching the Buddha ever gave, considered the central gem of the dharma, is known as the Four Noble Truths. These four axioms are:

- the existence of suffering
- the origin of suffering
- the end of suffering
- the path to the end of suffering

The Existence of Suffering

The world is full of hunger, illness, loss, and change. Yet somehow, we manage to live much of our lives denying these facts. Like children playing in a blazing house, we distract ourselves with momentary pleasures and ignore the heat and smoke surrounding us.

The Buddha's first noble truth is that pretending in this way doesn't help us. No matter how we try to whitewash our experience, the body will age, decay, and die. Meanwhile, we continue to endure the pain of greed, hatred, and delusion. Essentially, the first noble truth encourages us to face the reality of our existence.

The Origin of Suffering

Why do we continue to increase our suffering by avoiding the truth? The Buddha taught that four attachments keep us bound to our own pain. These are:

- attachment to sense pleasures
- attachment to opinions and views

- attachment to rites and rituals, at the expense of genuine spiritual experience
- attachment to the belief that one exists as a solid, permanent self

Thus, the origin of our suffering is our desire for pleasure and our attachment to a set of concepts designed to boost our sense of security.

The End of Suffering

Lest the first two noble truths discourage us, the Buddha also taught that we are definitely capable of putting an end to our suffering. He described two levels of nirvana, or freedom: momentary nirvana, in which we're able to tame the forces of greed, hatred, and delusion in the moment; and a more ultimate form of nirvana — a state described as the complete ending of the burden of suffering.

According to the Buddha, there is no higher happiness than peace. This is the meaning of the third noble truth.

The Path to the End of Suffering

The method for ending our suffering isn't a mysterious rite. It involves neither self-mortification nor self-indulgence. The Buddha's path is not one of extremes; it's the Middle Way.

The teaching of how to release ourselves from the burden of suffering is the Noble Eightfold Path (see page 10). Following this path requires mindfulness and awareness — qualities we cultivate daily through our practice of meditation.

Suffering:
Question and Answer Session

Q: I get pretty depressed when I contemplate the truth of suffering. Most of the time, I prefer not to read or watch the news, because it makes me feel unhappy and helpless. Are you saying that I should force myself to look at all the mayhem in the world around me?

A: You don't have to watch the news to be aware of suffering. The pain of existence presents itself to you every day, in the form of illness, losses of all kinds, frustrations, unfulfilled longings … the list goes on and on. There's plenty of suffering right in front of us, without having to go looking for it. And that's where we start: by recognizing and acknowledging the unhappiness and dissatisfaction in our own lives and those of the people and other beings around us. As for getting depressed by it – the Buddha pointed out to us the cause of suffering and how to release ourselves from it. There actually is a path to freedom, and we can walk that path right this minute. So with that perspective, the recognition of suffering can motivate us to explore the means to ending it.

Q: As a hospice worker, I spend most of my time trying to relieve suffering – not just in my patients, but also in their family members and other loved ones. Am I interfering with their spiritual development by somehow protecting them from the truth of suffering?

A: The Buddha never said that we had to be lost in our suffering; just that we should understand and accept the fact of its existence. The appropriate response to suffering is awareness and compassion, always. If you're trying to convince your patients that they aren't dying, or encouraging family members to avoid the truth, that might interfere with your own practice of truthfulness and courage. But to offer compassion and empathy to those who are suffering expresses the fact of our shared experience, our interconnectedness.

Q: Why do we suffer? I understand what you've said about the origin of suffering being attachment, but I'm wondering what the purpose of pain is in the grand scheme of things.

A: I once heard a story about a Tibetan teacher who visited San Francisco in 1987, soon after the earthquake that hit during the World Series. His Holiness the Dalai Lama had also just been in the Bay Area. A student asked this teacher what the message was in all these momentous happenings. The teacher said, "If a vase falls off a table and breaks, the message is: it's breakable." The point is that maybe we can't know the "grand scheme of things." All we know, for sure, is that suffering does exist in this moment; and our job is to bring as much wisdom and compassion as we can to all that we encounter.

Guided Meditation: Emotional States

We've talked about working with the mind states of the hindrances as they arise in meditation and in our lives. We also want to become aware of the entire range of our emotional life. The different emotions that arise in sitting practice, in walking meditation, in the eating meditation — we want to bring this awareness to all of these, and then beyond that, to the emotions we experience in the world every day. As you sit, feeling the breath, feeling sensations, noticing the hindrances as they arise, be aware of different emotions as they appear in your experience. There might be the feeling of happiness or sadness; there might be the feeling of joy or depression. You might feel quite light and buoyant. You might feel heavy or despairing.

Each one of these states can be opened to, noticed, and noted. The practice is to be aware of them without identifying with them; not taking them to be "I" or "self" or "mine," but seeing them as a constellation of experience arising out of conditions. We see them lasting for some time, changing, disappearing, in the form of sensations in the body; particular thoughts or images associated with the emotion; or a certain texture or coloration of the mind. Each emotion has its own particular flavor. We want to investigate all of these aspects.

The first step in working with an emotion is to recognize what it is. It's very helpful to use mental noting to bring forth clear recognition: "This is happiness, this is sadness, this is loneliness, this is excitement, this is interest, this is boredom." Clear recognition can be very helpful.

When an emotion is arising strongly in your experience, it's useful to notice the different aspects or constituents of the emotion. Feel the specific sensations in the body. Is there heat? Is the body contracted? Is it open? Is it soft? Notice whether there are particular images or thoughts associated with the emotion, and notice the mind flavor of the particular feeling. Each emotion has its own flavor, of sadness or happiness or joy or love or anger. Open to the subtleties in the mind and body as each of these feelings arises.

Sometimes, you may not be able to recognize exactly what the emotion is. There's no need to spend a long time trying to analyze it; you can simply open to the feeling with the general note of "feeling" or "emotion" until what it is becomes clearer to you.

So the first step is recognition. The second step is acceptance. There's often a tendency to resist or deny certain emotions, particularly if they're unpleasant. There are certain emotions that we don't like to feel. These can be different for each of us. For some people, there is a resistance to feeling anger or sadness or unworthiness.

In our meditation practice, we want to recognize what's arising and be accepting of whatever it is.

Acceptance is the key to the third step, which is nonidentification with the emotion. The understanding is that this constellation of experiences is arising out of conditions and then passing away. It is nonpersonal. There's no one behind them to whom they are happening.

This may take some practice to understand. It's a very subtle and difficult point, because often what we most personalize, what we most identify with, are the emotions. They're what we're most likely to take ourselves to be.

Take a comfortable meditative posture ... settle into the awareness of your body, awareness of the breath ...

... aware of sounds as they're appearing ...

... feeling each breath carefully ...

... using the mental label of "in, out" or "rising, falling" if it is helpful.

Observe what feeling tone is in the mind.

Is the mind calm? Is it peaceful? Is it bored?

It there happiness? Is there sadness? Is the mind neutral?

Does the mind feel steady, calm?

See if you can open to and recognize the emotional background as you would with the breath and physical sensations.

Be aware of any predominant emotions that may arise – emotions that come into the foreground of experience, perhaps associated with memories or plans.

You might notice anticipation or anxiety or excitement.

A common emotion that arises in meditation is boredom. Sometimes as people are being with the breath for some time, there's a certain lack of interest. This boredom should be noted as simply another arising state, not to be identified with, not taking it to be "I," not taking it to be "self."

Emotions also frequently arise around the experience of bodily pain.

We might feel impatience or irritation or aversion.

Notice the emotions that arise around particularly painful or pleasant experiences.

Feelings of delight ... feelings of aversion.

Work with this range of emotions in the same way that we worked with the hindrances. This is simply an expansion of the field, so that you become aware of the entire range of your emotional life.

At first, you notice the very obvious emotions. As the practice continues, you begin to notice the subtle emotions that appear.

Through recognition, acceptance, and nonidentification, you can experience these feelings and emotions from a place of freedom.

Awareness has the capacity to be with whatever arises.

Our practice brings us to the edge of what we're willing to be with, what we're comfortable with. The challenge then is to open at that edge.

Can you feel this emotion? Can you be with this sensation? It's important to open in a soft and relaxed way so that you're not struggling with experience, but taking an interest in what it is that's arising.

As you gently open your eyes, see if you can carry the momentum of this exploration into the rest of your day.

EXERCISES FOR WORKING WITH EMOTIONAL STATES

After practicing the guided meditation on CD 2, track 2 (or the version above) for a week, answer at least five of the following exercise questions.

Exercise 1

When you scan your inner emotional landscape, what feelings do you notice? Do you feel happy? Sad? Peaceful? Excited?

_____

_____

Exercise 2

Choose the feeling that seems strongest and investigate it. What bodily sensations accompany this feeling? Do you sense a tightness in the throat or chest? Warmth or pressure in the stomach? Sensations elsewhere in your body? Describe your experience.

_____

_____

_____

_____

Exercise 3

What is the energetic nature of the feeling? Does it bring with it a sense of aloneness or isolation? Does it bring with it a sense of connection to others?

_____

_____

_____

Exercise 4

Do you notice any resistance to this emotional state? Is there any condemnation or pushing away associated with it? Do you notice a tendency to cling to it, wanting it to stay?

_____

_____

_____

Exercise 5

Choose any emotion that arises during meditation. Notice how it began and what preceded it. Was there a thought or image that triggered this particular state?

_____

_____

_____

Exercise 6

Most feelings pass or alter in a minute or two. Sometimes they grow stronger; sometimes they dissolve, or change into different feelings. Anger, for example, may dissolve into sadness, then into regret, then into resolve. Follow an emotion that arises in your sitting practice and observe what happens to it.

_____

_____

_____

Exercise 7

Practice exercises 2-6 above with at least three different feelings. Describe your experiences.

_____

_____

_____

_____

_____

GETTING THE MOST FROM YOUR MEDITATION

- Practice maintaining your awareness of suffering. We're typically conditioned to brush discomfort under the rug; to trivialize or ignore the pain in the world, lest it penetrate and wound our hearts. Developing the discipline of awareness in this difficult area opens up a realm of insights and choices that aren't available to us otherwise.

- It's been said that pain is inevitable, but suffering is optional. This week, watch your responses to suffering and try to distinguish between the inevitable pain of the human condition and the optional suffering that comes from trying to avoid pain.

- When you do something that creates suffering for yourself or another, acknowledge what you're doing. The pervasive myth that "ignorance is bliss" is not supported by Buddhist teaching, which holds that even a harmful act is mitigated by awareness. When we cause suffering without understanding what we're doing, our ignorance actually compounds the damage.

- Recognize your limits. Awareness is never cultivated through force. Sometimes you may find yourself backing off from painful experiences for a while. Practice being gentle with yourself, never ceasing to watch what happens as you approach and withdraw from the source of suffering. As with any object of awareness, it will inevitably change as you work with it.

◗ Display the card showing the three kinds of suffering where you can see it every day. Use it as a reminder whenever you experience emotions that feel threatening, challenging, or seductive.

LESSON SIX GLOSSARY

dukkha: "suffering" [Pali]; the pain that arises out of the ungovernable nature of events

metta: "kindness" [Pali]; unlimited friendliness; lovingkindness

JOSEPH GOLDSTEIN

LESSON SEVEN

KARMA

Earlier, we discussed the Buddha's Noble Eightfold Path. The first step on this path is right understanding – and this, in fact, is the foundation of the entire spiritual journey. Right understanding directs all our actions appropriately, it leads us further on the path of liberation, and it harmonizes in every way with the dharma. Without right understanding, we're left with basic misdirection, confusion, alienation, and unease.

Central to right understanding is the realization that every act of body, speech, and mind has the power to generate consequences. Wholesome acts lead to wholesome results, while unwholesome acts lead to unwholesome results. The Buddha called this principle the law of karma.

The Sanskrit word *karma* literally means "action" or "deed." It refers to the universal law of cause and effect. The Buddha taught that every action has a consequence. Thus, happiness and unhappiness are the consequences of previous actions, not only from this life, but according to Buddhist understanding, from past lives as well. The law governing this process is karma. This is not an esoteric teaching, or a belief requiring an act of faith. Karma reflects the simple fact that every action leads to a result that reflects the nature of that action. With this realization comes the possibility of making wise choices in our lives.

THE MECHANICS OF KARMA

The Buddha taught that karma is volitional activity: that is, it consists of intentional or willed actions. These are the seeds in our minds that ultimately and inevitably bear fruit. When you observe a seed, it's easy to overlook the enormous power it holds. Yet, as we know, a tiny acorn will grow into an enormous tree. This little seed contains both the potential and the blueprint for tallest, strongest oaks that ever existed. In exactly the same way, each of our intentional actions contains the potential and the blueprint for its inevitable consequences. The nature of the results is determined by the nature of the seed.

Intention is a neutral factor of mind. It's neither wholesome nor unwholesome. What determines the karmic fruit of an action is the motivation associated with the intention. Our motives are what drive an action in a wholesome or unwholesome direction. This is why the Buddha laid so much emphasis on explaining wholesome and unwholesome roots in the mind. The motivating forces of greed, hatred, and ignorance are the roots of our suffering. When these forces motivate our actions, disharmony, sorrow, and afflictions follow.

The roots of happiness, on the other hand, are generosity, love, compassion, and wisdom. To understand karma is to know what leads to happiness and what leads to suffering. If we're committed to moving away from suffering and toward happiness, we must pay close attention to the motives that drive all of our actions. This requires a great deal of courage, honesty, and mindfulness.

How can we experience the law of karma directly, not just as an abstract theory? The answer lies in awareness, or being present for the consequences of our thoughts, words, and deeds. "Present karma" is the practice of noticing the immediate effect of different states of mind and actions. How do you feel in a moment of lying? How do you feel when you're being truthful? What's your experience when your mind is angry? How about when it's filled with love? How does it feel to be miserly? Generous?

Show up. Pay attention. Tell the truth. Stay open to the outcome.

— THE FOURFOLD PATH TO ENLIGHTENMENT OF THE ZUNI PEOPLE

You can look at your own state of mind in this way and examine the happiness or suffering that follows a particular expression; and you can also look at how people respond to you. You've experienced a natural and spontaneous feeling of goodwill when other people are generous, kind, and loving. When you behave in these ways, you'll notice this same goodwill coming from those around you.

Try looking, too, at your state of mind when you undertake some task. How does it feel to be goal-driven? How does it feel to be present with the part of the task that's right in front of you? Are you approaching it with effort, energy, discernment, and wisdom — or with panic, impatience, resentment, and inattention? How do these feelings impact on the quality of your experience and the success of the task?

This is another aspect of present karma.

THE EXPERIENCE OF KARMA

The mind retains impressions of all our actions, and these impressions reappear, sometimes for many years afterward. We experience such memories as sources of great joy or great regret. Past wholesome actions arise in the mind coupled with delight, whereas memories of unwholesome actions can trigger painful remorse.

Remorse, as Sharon noted in Lesson Four, can be a purifying process. Bringing attentive awareness to an unresolved situation helps undo old knots and contractions. Significant karmic unburdening occurs when we allow these impressions, memories, feelings, and sensations to come up; bring compassionate, nonjudging mindfulness to them; and let them go.

I had a very painful, but ultimately liberating, experience of karmic unburdening in my own practice. After leaving college, I went to Hawaii to train for the Peace Corps. For some reason, the training included a lesson on how to kill chickens. I was going to Asia to teach English; but somehow the trainers felt I needed this particular skill.

I had not yet established a meditation practice at this stage of my life, so my mind was heavily influenced by delusion. I felt a sort of macho response, an impulse to rise to the challenge. I thought, "I ought to be able to do this." A friend who was training with me held the chicken, and I took a big knife and chopped its head off. It didn't feel good in the moment, but somehow it seemed like an important thing to do. I can see myself afterwards with a big grin on my face, holding up this scrawny, headless bird, as if to say, "Look what I accomplished!"

Years later, while I was meditating intensively in India, the memory of this incident started coming up in my mind. It was one of the most painful times in my practice. Reliving the experience with awareness and compassion, I realized that I had actually murdered this helpless being. The intensity of my remorse was immense. At the time I killed the chicken, I thought, "Well, I did it, and now it's over and done with." I didn't realize, then, that the mind retains impressions of all our actions.

It was very emotionally painful to see so clearly what I had done; but by just sitting through it again and again over a period of days, I experienced a softening of the difficult feelings. The intensity of the impression began to unwind, to loosen, to unburden. This was a very direct experience of how meditation practice allows these old karmic knots to come up, be seen, and begin to be released.

Karmic impressions can also come up as physical sensations. Once, when I was doing walking meditation, I suddenly felt an appalling pain in my shinbone. It was so intense that it seemed the bone must be protruding from the skin. I actually stopped to feel my leg, to make sure that wasn't the case. Just then, a memory leapt into my mind. I saw myself as a child, flying a kite out on a big field. I was running across the field to get the kite up in the air, not looking where I was going, and I ran straight into a cement bench. The bench connected with me right on the shinbone – the same place where I felt this intense pain so many years later.

It's interesting to note that this particular memory didn't reflect any unwholesome motivation, as the chicken incident had. The mere lack of attention that led to my running into that bench was enough to require resolution at a later, more aware period of my life.

As we practice meditation, many such impressions begin to emerge from their hiding places in the mind and body. If we can bring awareness, mindfulness, and bare attention to them, they can become agents of transformation. They can help us purify the karma of which they are manifestations. One Buddhist monk described this purifying process as a "general housekeeping of the mind."

How Karma Shapes Us

Our personalities are very accurate reflections of our individual karma. Every time we act in a certain way – say, cruelly or generously – we're practicing and strengthening that quality. Over time, the quality becomes ingrained in the mind, in the form of habits and patterns. This is how people become fearful or loving, greedy or generous, truthful or dishonest.

The English biologist Rupert Sheldrake developed a theory he called "morphic resonance." What this means is that after something in nature happens for the first time, it becomes easier for that same phenomenon to occur again. This theory resonates very much with my understanding of the law of karma. Every time we perform an action, it becomes easier to do it again. Gradually, inevitably, these actions establish themselves as character traits. This is why it's important not to underestimate the power of small actions. We need to pay as careful attention to these as to the larger, more evident or dramatic deeds we do.

According to Buddhist cosmology, our actions don't only develop personality traits; they catapult us into specific realms of existence. The Buddha taught that there are six such realms: the lower realms of suffering, the human realm, and higher realms of great happiness and bliss. We take rebirth in these realms depending on our karma – the skillful or unskillful, wholesome or unwholesome actions that we've cultivated.

To recognize the validity of the six realms, it isn't necessary to believe in reincarnation. It's said that each of us is reborn in a different realm every moment. A flash of strong ill will can take us to the hell realm — a claustrophobic world of hatred and frustration. In the next moment, a glimpse of spaciousness can lift us into the human realm, where we see clearly the extremes of joy and suffering, and our own capacity for cultivating each.

Somebody once asked the Buddha, "Why are there so many differences among people? Some are wealthy and some are poor; some are beautiful, others ugly; some are healthy and some are ill. What accounts for these differences?" The Buddha's reply was very clear: the differences between us, he said, reflect the working out of the law of karma. When we practice generosity, the karmic fruit is great abundance. The fruit of stinginess is lack of abundance. If we use gentle, loving speech, the result is beauty. The habit of angry speech produces lack of beauty. Nonharming leads to good health; harming leads to poor health. The practice of investigation bears the karmic fruit of wisdom; lack of inquiry leads to dullness of mind.

It's important, at this point, not to misinterpret the law of karma by confusing it with the attitude of blame: blaming either oneself or the victim of a painful situation. Whatever the causes and conditions behind present suffering, the appropriate response is always lovingkindness and compassion. A Mexican proverb says, "There is no excuse for not loving." The attitude of blame closes us off to the feeling of love.

THE BRAHMA-VIHARAS

All situations, as we've discussed, arise out of combinations of causes and conditions. Seldom is there a single, clear-cut reason for someone's painful or pleasant experiences — therefore, it makes no sense to react with judgment or envy. In determining how to respond to the fruits of karma in ourselves and others, the Buddha provided an invaluable guide called the *brahma-viharas.*

Brahma-vihara is a Pali term meaning "heavenly abode" or "best home." The Buddha taught that practicing these four qualities leads to "the liberation of the heart which is love." The brahma-viharas are:

- lovingkindness
- compassion
- sympathetic joy
- equanimity

LOVINGKINDNESS

The Pali word for lovingkindness is *metta*. More closely translated, *metta* means both "gentle" – as in a gentle rain that falls indiscriminately upon everything – and "friendship." Thus, metta refers to a steady, unconditional sense of connection that touches all beings without exception, including ourselves.

To understand this connection better, it helps to see karma as working over many lifetimes. It cannot be fully understood within the context of a single life. The clearest evidence for this is the suffering of infants and children. Often, people are born into situations of great deprivation, before they've had a chance to cultivate unskillful or unwholesome actions. The karma ripening now can only have its roots in previous lifetimes.

When you adopt a vaster vision – one that recognizes the many lifetimes each of us has known – you realize that we've all done everything. On our very long journeys, we've all acted out of ignorance, causing harm to ourselves and others.

Whether or not we accept that we've had previous lifetimes, we see this principle at work in this very existence. All of us have, at some time, had hateful, cruel, or greedy thoughts – and those of us who have acted on those impulses have had to deal with inevitable consequences. We all experience the fruit of unwholesome actions as suffering.

If you knew, as I do, the power of giving, you would not let a single meal pass without sharing some of it.

— THE BUDDHA

When we reflect on this, there's no blame or exclusion. Lovingkindness for both ourselves and others arises spontaneously, because we recognize that we're all capable of sowing unwholesome seeds, and we're all subject to the painful consequences that follow.

COMPASSION

Compassion is our caring human response to suffering. The compassionate heart is nonjudgmental. It recognizes that all suffering – our own and others' – is deserving of tenderness.

After his enlightenment, the Buddha is said to have decided not to teach his new understanding, because he was afraid no one would understand its profundity. Then he surveyed the world with his eye of wisdom. He saw beings everywhere seeking happiness and yet, out of ignorance of the true cause of happiness, doing the very things that cause suffering. It's said that this was what aroused the Buddha's heart of compassion and persuaded him to begin teaching.

We learn from this example that the skillful response to unwholesome actions and the ignorance that gives birth to them is compassion. If you see someone walking into a fire, your natural response is to try to awaken the person from the ignorance of that action. This is what the Buddha set out to do when he gave his teachings to the world.

SYMPATHETIC JOY

The third brahma-vihara refers to the realization that others' happiness is inseparable from our own. The practitioner rejoices in the joy of others, and is not threatened by another's success. Sympathetic joy is said to be the most difficult of the brahma-viharas to practice consistently.

Reflecting on karma is one way to arouse this quality of mind. When we see people enjoying good health, prosperity, beauty, and success — quite independent of their present actions — we recognize their good fortune as karmic fruit. This point of view can undercut our tendency to compare others' circumstances with our own, as well as the envy or judgment that typically accompany such comparisons. We can delight in others' well-being, knowing it to be evidence of past wholesome actions that have benefited us all.

EQUANIMITY

Equanimity is the spacious stillness of mind that provides the ground for the boundless nature of the other three brahma-viharas. This quality of radiant calm enables us to ride the waves of our experience without getting lost in our reactions. Sharon will explore this topic in depth in Lesson Eight; but for the purposes of this discussion, I want to touch on the intimate relationship between equanimity and wisdom.

Equanimity comes from seeing clearly that a complex interplay of causes and conditions has brought us to this moment, and will take us to the next. When we come upon difficult life passages, equanimity helps us navigate them without resentment. In the same way, we rejoice in good fortune without pride, because we understand that karma is playing itself out.

Wherever we go, our karma will present us with numerous opportunities to become wiser, happier, and more loving. What matters is not what seeds we sowed in the past. What matters is the seeds we plant now, and how we work with the ripening of those we've already planted. This understanding is the gift of equanimity.

Equanimity is inseparable from healthy compassion. Once we begin to open our hearts, the depth and range of the world's suffering comes home to us as never before. We realize that even with the greatest compassion in the world, we won't be able to alleviate all the suffering we see. Equanimity is the invaluable mind state that allows us to keep our hearts open, even in the face of tremendous anguish and ignorance that are beyond our ability to change.

The practice of equanimity is beautifully expressed in what the Zuni elders call "the fourfold path to enlightenment." This teaching says, "Show up, pay attention, tell the truth, stay open to outcome." That's a wonderful guideline for maintaining one's equanimity in everyday situations.

Personal Karma

Through understanding and reflecting on the law of karma, we start taking more responsibility for our actions. Our view of things expands. We can see the long-range effects of our actions in many arenas. We see that what we do in the present has far-reaching environmental and social consequences. Unless we take care with our present actions, we could end up with some very undesirable results.

The real challenge is to see how the law of cause and effect is at work within ourselves. Reflecting in this way leads to a strong and compelling interest in our own actions and choices. This requires great awareness and presence of mind – but the alternative is to live out our conditioned habitual tendencies, sowing seeds of karma and suffering everywhere we go.

All Buddhist traditions place tremendous importance on understanding the law of karma. Padmasambhava, the great Indian saint credited with establishing Buddhism in Tibet, said, "Though your vision or your understanding is as vast as the sky, your attention to the law of karma should be as fine as a grain of barley flour." So even when we understand the dharma and the emptiness of self very deeply, just living in that wisdom isn't enough. We need to pay keen attention to our smallest actions and their consequences.

Recognizing the importance of karma is another example of a quality the Buddha called "clear comprehension." Clear comprehension considers before acting whether the action is beneficial or unbeneficial to oneself and others. It examines the qualities that we develop with every act. Are they the ones we want strengthened?

Our actions, including the actions of mind – our thoughts and emotional patterns – are like drops of water falling into a bucket. We may not think that any one drop is particularly significant, but over time, drop by drop, the bucket fills up. In just the same way, drop by drop, the mind gets filled.

Very little in our culture or education recognizes this cumulative force. The blurb for a paperback novel I once saw proclaimed, "A novel of lust, passion, and greed – has something for everyone, a real delight." With this kind of reinforcement all around us, it's even more crucial that we pay attention to how we're filling our minds.

PURIFYING OUR KARMA

Karma is not a mechanistic, closed system. Nothing is fixed, because our present actions continuously feed in to a stream of cause and effect, influencing both its direction and its power. The Buddha talked of "covering" or "surrounding" unskillful acts with skillful ones. The present purity of our actions, he said, attracts the results of past wholesome karma; and likewise, present unskillful actions create a field that attracts the results of past unwholesome karma. What we do in the present powerfully affects the unfolding of the karmic journey.

In the secular Shambhala teachings of Chögyam Trungpa, Rinpoche, wholesome karma is personified in the form of beneficial beings called *dralas*. Cleanliness, kindness, and dignity attract the dralas. Sloppiness and ego-driven behavior repel them, leaving us literally "out of luck."

The Buddha taught that certain wholesome acts generate more power than others. Generous deeds, for example, purify the giver, the gift, and the receiver. Offering something to the Buddha or another enlightened person is a particularly powerful karmic act. But there is something even more powerful than making an offering to the entire order of enlightened beings, and that is having the mind fully concentrated in the feeling of lovingkindness.

According to the Buddha, however, even greater than the mind filled with lovingkindness is seeing clearly the momentary arising and passing away of all conditioned things. Perceiving the impermanence of arising phenomena holds the potential for freedom. And so we return to our practice of mindfulness meditation with a renewed appreciation of its importance, recognizing that developing bare attention is the only way we can truly experience the natural law of impermanence as a living truth.

Practicing meditation helps purify karma, but contemplating karma is also a strong motivation for practice. An understanding of karma awakens a natural affinity for the brahma-viharas, and a determination to accomplish them through our practice. Seeing that we are the heirs of our own actions also inspires us to pay closer attention to the seeds we plant in our minds. This is why karma is among the four reminders Tibetan Buddhists contemplate before every practice session.

The life of the great Tibetan saint Milarepa illustrates how understanding the law of karma can bring about tremendous spiritual ardency. Milarepa's father died when he was still quite young, and an unscrupulous uncle took over guardianship of his family. This uncle and his wife mistreated the family and cheated them out of their inheritance. When Milarepa grew up, he went off to the mountains to study black magic, with the intention of avenging his family. He became an accomplished magician, and subsequently used his arts to make a building collapse on his uncle and aunt. They and many others died.

Soon after, Milarepa discovered the law of karma. The tremendous remorse he felt for his actions drove him to the spiritual path. He met his teacher, Marpa, who put him through a series of tribulations designed to help him cleanse his evil karma. Later, Milarepa spent many years practicing in mountain caves, purifying his mind. He ultimately came to a place of great enlightenment, and his teachings were gathered in a collection of ecstatic songs in praise of the dharma called *The Hundred Thousand Songs of Milarepa*.

At the end of his life, Milarepa led his chief disciple, Gampopa, deep into the mountains of Tibet. It was here that he planned to transmit the ultimate secret teachings. Gampopa was filled with wonder and excitement at the prospect of receiving this precious transmission. Finally they came to the spot Milarepa had in mind, where they made the proper ritualistic preparations for the auspicious event. It's said that at last, when everything was ready, Milarepa bent over and showed Gampopa the calluses on his backside from all his years of sitting. That was his final transmission.

Sometimes, practitioners get sidetracked in search of exotic teachings, transmissions, and instructions. In the end, however, the single most powerful act we can perform in the service of spiritual awakening is simply to sit. Reflecting on the teachings and on the enlightened ones who truly understood them, we come to realize that awakening is not something "out there" that graces only a select group. Through the regular practice of meditation, we gradually attain the same levels of clarity, compassion, and equanimity that the enlightened ones have modeled for us over the millennia.

It's very rare, in the course of human history, that conditions come together to create the necessary environment for liberation. Authentic teachings have to be available; we must have the interest to pursue them; and we need the inspiration to practice. These conditions come about as the karmic fruit of our past skillful actions. To squander these precious advantages is to risk being reborn – either psychologically or literally – in a realm where they are no longer available to us. This is why

Padmasambhava's teaching is so relevant to our lives: though our vision may be as vast as the sky, our attention to the law of cause and effect should be as fine as a grain of barley flour.

KARMA: QUESTION AND ANSWER SESSION

Q: I don't believe in reincarnation, so it's hard for me to buy the view that I'm reaping the karma of actions I performed in a previous life. It's even harder for me to believe that innocent children are suffering because of something they did before they were born.

A: You don't have to believe in reincarnation to experience the effects of your actions. When you extend generosity and lovingkindness toward others, it comes back to you. When you approach the world with aggression or grasping, if you're aware, you feel the effects. The important point here is not where your present suffering came from so much as where you're going to take it from here. From this point of view, whether or not children suffer karma from previous incarnations is also a somewhat academic question. What counts is how you approach the situation right now. The appropriate response to suffering, whatever the cause, is compassion.

Q: If, as you've said, there's no continuous, solid self, then what is the vehicle for karma? Who is it who experiences the consequences of previous actions?

A: What we call "self" is actually a process made up of many elements, all of them in continual flux. The Buddha referred to it as "actions without an actor, doings without a doer." Within this nonpersonal process, our actions are like seeds that are planted and transformed by the shifting patterns of our lives. Some seeds are cultivated and nourished; some lie dormant for lifetimes, until the exact combination of conditions arises to germinate them. In every case, the fruit will bear a direct relationship to the seed. Just as an apple seed eventually brings apples into the world, and not mangoes, a loving act ends up bearing loving fruit — and hateful acts produce hateful fruit.

There is nowhere in the world — not in the sky, nor in the sea, nor in the depths of the earth — where one can escape unwholesome deeds.

— THE DHAMMAPADA

Some people take this understanding — that there is actually no self behind our actions — to discount our responsibility for the things we do. But karma is a powerful force that inevitably makes itself felt. We need to couple our understanding of selflessness with very mindful and respectful attention to our actions and their karmic fruit.

Q: Do animals have karma?

A: Yes. Most animals don't recognize and work with their karmic situations. This is why the Buddhist teachings regard human birth as very precious. We have the ability to discriminate between skillful and unskillful, wholesome and unwholesome acts. The force of karma operates wherever there is consciousness and intention. But only when mindfulness is present do the choices necessary for liberation from suffering come into play.

Guided Meditation: Intentions

Record or voice the following meditation and use it in your practice for the next week, and whenever you feel it could be helpful thereafter.

One of the ways in which we can make our attention to the law of karma as fine as a grain of barley flour, as Padmasambhava suggested, is to look at the factor of intention as it arises in our sitting and walking practice.

Intention is a very subtle object. It's that moment just preceding an action, in which we know that the action is about to happen. We could call it the "about to" moment. In that moment there is volition, or a willing aspect in the mind: a gathering of the energy that initiates the act.

Sometimes intention might be seen as a particular thought in the mind – a thought to do something, and then the doing of it. But often, it's not a thought. Often, it's simply an unarticulated impulse that leads to the action being carried out. Awareness of intention is crucially important in our practice because, as the Buddha taught, this factor of mind is the karmic seed. It's the intention arising in the mind before various activities, and through the activities themselves, that brings about different karmic results.

For this reason, it's very helpful to become aware of the intentions as they arise. Then we can make choices: "This is skillful, this is unskillful; this leads to happiness, this leads to suffering."

Notice, for example, how often you find your hand inside the refrigerator before you know how it got there. There might be an unnoticed impulse in the mind, an unnoticed desire, an unnoticed intention … and then the hand is in the door, reaching for food. When we are aware, or mindful, of intentions, we notice the intention as the desire arises. Only then do we have the information we need to make a wise choice: "Is this something that's helpful to do, or not helpful to do?"

So awareness of the intention begins to open up a wonderful space of freedom in our lives. No longer blindly driven by impulses or desires, we have the ability to see clearly and to assess with wise discernment.

Sit comfortably, in meditation posture. Notice the intention to adjust the hands into a comfortable position. Before the hand and arm move, there's an intention or a volition in the mind for that to happen.

It's as if there's a momentary pause before the action begins, in which you know that the movement is about to happen. Notice that "about to" moment.

You could make the soft mental note of "intending to move," or "about to move," or simply "intending." Notice the intention, and then notice how the movement follows from it.

The moment before your eyes close, you can notice the intention to close them. You might make a note of "about to close," and then notice the movement of the closing.

During this sitting period, notice the intention that arises before any shift of position. Perhaps you become aware of some discomfort or pain. Notice the discomfort. Notice the pain. If, at a certain point, there's a decision to move – to shift position even slightly – notice that the movement does not happen by itself. It happens as the result of an intention arising in the mind. Note "intending to move," and then note the moving.

Sometimes, you'll be aware of a very tangible feeling of impulse or volition. Sometimes, you may simply notice the space, the pause before the activity, the moment in which you know that you're about to do it.

Note the arising of intention in whatever way you experience it.

Begin to see the cause-and-effect relationship between intention in the mind and movement in the body.

Awareness of intention opens up a space of freedom for us. When we're aware of intention, we have the choice about whether to do the action or not.

When we're unaware of intentions in the mind, we're simply acting out our habitual patterns of conditioning.

When you notice the intention to move during a sitting, you can choose whether to carry out that movement or to simply be with the awareness of "intending, intending." You may choose to let that intention arise and pass away, continuing to maintain your posture. Or you might be aware of the intention to move, act on it, and be mindful of the movement that follows.

As our awareness becomes more subtly tuned to the arising of intentions in sitting, walking, and throughout the day, we can begin to investigate the motivations associated with those intentions.

Is the intention associated with greed? With generosity? With anger? With love? With ignorance? We can begin to see more clearly these qualities of motivation and make wise choices.

In walking meditation, you can be aware of the intention before each step – "intending to step" – and then the stepping.

As the mind becomes quieter, you can note the intention before each part of the step, at least for short periods of time: "intending to lift" and then the lifting...

... "intending to move," and then the moving ...

... "intending to place," and then the placing.

What's important here is to see the interrelationship of mind and body. Because of intention in the mind, the body moves.

At the end of the sitting, note the intention before opening the eyes – "intending to open" – and then the opening. Note the intention before moving your arms or legs – "intending to move" – and then the moving.

See if you can stay with this experience of cause and effect between mind and body as you go from sitting to standing and begin to engage in other activities.

EXERCISES FOR WORKING WITH INTENTIONS

Use the guided meditation with this lesson in your practice throughout this week. Then respond to at least five of the exercises below.

Exercise 1

Intentions may be experienced as words in the mind, an impulse or urge arising in the heart center, the coming together of energy before an action, or in several other subtle ways. When you pause before a major movement, like lifting your arm, do you notice an intention? What form does it take?

_____

_____

_____

Exercise 2

Intention is a key to seeing the interrelationship between body and mind. For example, you may have an unpleasant physical sensation. Based on that sensation, an intention arises to shift posture. The intention gives rise to the act of shifting the body, whereupon new sensations arise. Trace an experience of cause and effect in your own practice, noting the role of intention.

_____

_____

_____

_____

Exercise 3

Rather than acting automatically, resolve not to change your meditation posture or to get up from sitting until the intention to do so has arisen twice. For example, refrain from scratching an itch until you've first gently noted the intention to do so. Allow the intention to arise and pass away, pay attention to the breath or body, and watch the intention arise again. Describe your experience.

_____

_____

_____

_____

Exercise 4

Describe what happens during sitting meditation when, before opening your eyes, you note the intention to do so.

_____

_____

_____

_____

Exercise 5

During walking meditation, begin bringing in an awareness of intention every time you turn around. Before turning, pause for a moment and note the intention to turn. Then note the turning itself. Describe your experience.

_____

_____

_____

Exercise 6

Choose a brief, routine activity you perform several times each day — like opening a door, brushing your teeth, or making tea. Resolve to do that activity mindfully for a week, noting the intention before each component of the action (e.g. intending to reach for the door handle, reaching; intending to turn the handle, turning; intending to pull the door, pulling; and so on). At the end of the week, describe your experience.

_____

_____

_____

_____

Exercise 7

Select a period of time in your day (perhaps the hour after getting up from meditation practice) and resolve to become aware during that time of your intentions to speak. Direct your attention to the state of mind that directly precedes talking. Are you motivated by a need to defend yourself? By boredom or anxiety? Kindness or fear? Avoid judging or creating an image of yourself. Simply note whatever it is. Experience the feeling tone — the contracted or expansive nature of these different motivations. Describe your experience.

_____

_____

_____

_____

_____

GETTING THE MOST FROM YOUR MEDITATION

As we've learned in this lesson, karma is subtle and profound. It is not a system of reward and punishment. The karma we generate is born of our volitional actions. The guided meditation on intentions will help you identify and work with the seeds of karma during your formal sitting practice. The suggestions that follow are designed to broaden your awareness of cause and effect throughout the rest of your experience.

- Slow down. When we review those actions that have caused us remorse, we often find that they were undertaken in haste. Take the time to examine your motivations, and to bring mindfulness to the feelings associated with the act you're about to perform. This moment of meditation will make it possible for you to recognize a range of options of which you may not otherwise be aware.

- Practice noticing the immediate karma of your choices. An example with which many of us are familiar arises when we eat something we enjoy, but that we know doesn't agree with us. Notice any tendency to deny feelings of discomfort following an unwise snack or drink. Try to stay present with whatever experiences do unfold. Sometimes, this simple practice of awareness can play an important part in undoing a painful addiction.

- Review Lesson Three and contemplate the relationship between your impulses to grasp or push away and their consequences.

- Resolve to broaden your awareness of intentionality. See exercise 6 above, and experiment with it further. What happens when you stop momentarily to notice your intention every time you make a telephone call? Find other routine activities and regularly watch your intentions before performing these, too.

LESSON SEVEN GLOSSARY

"about to" moment: the moment before we act, in which we recognize the intention to act

brahma: "best" [Sanskrit, Pali]; highest

brahma-viharas: "best abode" [Sanskrit, Pali]; the four mind states said to create an ideal quality of experience

clear comprehension: The quality of mind that perceives the potential consequences of action before the act is performed

equanimity: the ability to maintain a spacious impartiality of mind in the midst of life's changing conditions

karma: "action, deed" [Sanskrit]; the law of cause and effect

realms of existence: the six states of existence the Buddha used to describe the different levels of human experience

right understanding: a view of reality that is unclouded by attachment to concepts, particularly the concept of self; an understanding of the law of karma; an aspect of the Noble Eightfold Path

LESSON EIGHT

EQUANIMITY

In the previous lesson, Joseph spoke about the role of equanimity in karma. But what exactly is "equanimity"?

Equanimity is considered a state of balance or poise. Sometimes it's called a "radiant calm of mind" or "spacious stillness of heart." The concept of equanimity is often confused with withdrawal, indifference, or hesitation, but this is a misunderstanding. Such states of disconnection are actually very subtle forms of aversion or hostility toward our experience. By contrast, equanimity is a state of complete openness. We're fully connected to what's going on, yet free of the exhausting, ceaseless grasping on to pleasure and pushing away of pain.

LIVING THE EXTREMES

Once, on our way to Australia, Joseph and I went to India. Our teacher Dipa Ma was getting rather old, so we took the opportunity to stop over and visit her. We arrived in Calcutta in the middle of the monsoon season. We went immediately to Dipa Ma's home, where we stayed all that day. Outside it was raining torrentially — sheets of rain were driving down. We were so happy to be with Dipa Ma that we didn't pay any attention to what was going on outside her little room.

When we left her at dusk and went down to the street, we discovered what happens in Calcutta after a monsoon. The sewers had flooded, and a river of sewage-strewn rainwater, maybe three feet deep, was churning past the front of the house. Of course, no cars could navigate the flood, so we would have to walk back to our hotel. As we stood on the curb, contemplating this extraordinary and unpleasant sight, Joseph remarked, "Well, this should be interesting." Now, Joseph, at six foot three, is quite a bit taller than I am. I thought, "Yeah, maybe if you're six foot three this is going to be interesting, but I don't think I'm going to find it quite so interesting!"

We stepped into the flood, and it was absolutely horrible. Rats floated by as we waded through the sewage. Every one of our senses was assaulted in the most vile unimaginable way. It smelled horrible, it felt horrible, and it was frightening.

Four or five days later, we arrived in Australia. A friend had bought us tickets to a symphony at the famous Sydney Opera House, an architectural marvel built right on the ocean harbor. We sat listening to the beautiful strains of Dvorak and Brahms, surrounded by beautifully dressed people who all smelled wonderful. Every sense was soothed and delighted. I thought, "What happened to Calcutta?"

Before the concert, our friend took us out to dinner. We went to the top of a very tall building, where a restaurant circled slowly to reveal a panoramic view of the city. Sydney is very beautiful, so the lovely vistas that swept by as we were eating were truly stunning. The food itself was delicious – wonderfully prepared and presented. We enjoyed ourselves immensely.

The next time this particular friend and I shared a meal was about six months later, at a retreat center in Burma. You don't have to pay to practice at retreat centers in Burma, because the lay people living nearby provide for you. They're so respectful and devoted to the practice of meditation that they're honored to be able to feed you while you're practicing. Every meal is an offering.

The Burmese people were very generous, but many of them were also very, very poor. Sometimes the food they would offer, although it was clearly the best they could provide, was of quite poor quality.

One day during our retreat, my friend and I found ourselves sitting at the same table. The main course was a very bitter vegetable floating in four or five inches of oil. As you chewed it, it turned into a ball of wooden pulp in your mouth. This meal, served at ten in the morning, was our main sustenance for the day.

My friend offered me the serving dish to see if I wanted seconds. At that moment, I remembered the last meal she and I had shared, in that lovely revolving restaurant in Sydney. I remembered the elegant service, exquisite food, and the panorama of that beautiful city sweeping by. Where was that reality in the next moment? Within six months – sometimes even within a single day or hour – we can experience polar extremes of pleasure and pain.

THE EIGHT VICISSITUDES

The Buddha taught that there are eight vicissitudes of life, which occur in four pairs of opposites: pleasure and pain, gain and loss, praise and blame, and fame and disrepute. These eight changing conditions constitute the very fabric of life. They rise and pass away as conditions warrant, completely beyond the reach of our whim or will or wish. Nobody can stop that flow. No matter how fervently we might want it to be otherwise, no one experiences only pleasure and no pain. No one experiences only praise and no blame. This is the very nature of the world: it continually manifests these changing circumstances.

It's said that a man once visited the Buddha's monastery to ask questions about his teachings. The first person he saw was a monk sitting in meditation. This monk had taken a temporary vow of silence, so when the visitor questioned him, he didn't respond at all. The man stomped away, furious.

He returned the next day and encountered a monk who, as well as being highly realized, was particularly erudite and scholarly. In response to his question, this monk launched into a very elaborate theoretical discourse about the Buddha's teaching. Again, the man became furious and left.

On his third visit, the man came upon another senior disciple of the Buddha named Ananda. Ananda had heard what had happened on the man's previous visits, so he was careful to respond, but not to say too much. The man again flew into a rage. "How dare you teach such profound and weighty matters so sketchily?" he demanded, and strode off angrily.

The monks went to the Buddha and asked him to cast some light on what had happened. The Buddha said, "If you say nothing, some people will blame you; if you say a lot, some people will blame you; if you say just a little, some people will blame you. There's always blame in this world." That's the nature of our lives. You can probably remember, at some point in your life, having received both strong praise and strong blame for the identical action. It's inevitable.

> As a solid boulder does not shake in the wind, the wise are not moved by censure or praise.
>
> — THE DHAMMAPADA

Of course, we prefer praise to blame. It's not a question of trying to pretend otherwise, or of entering some kind of gray, amorphous realm where we don't feel anything. The point is how attached we get to praise, and how resistant and fearful we get when blamed. By trying to hold on to all the praise and pleasure, we get lost in patterns of grasping and addiction. If we try to hold off, control, or deny the painful experiences of life, we're continually frustrated. We're shattered when things take their natural course. The heart/mind becomes brittle and rigid. The Buddha said that our hearts can wilt, just as a flower does when it's been out in the sun too long. For many of us, this is a familiar feeling.

Some years ago, I was interviewed by a Buddhist journal called *The Inquiring Mind*. I was in Australia when the interview came out, but when I returned, somebody mentioned it to me right away. He thought it was terrific. He went on and on about how it was one of the best things he had ever read. Of course, I liked that. I thought it was just wonderful.

The very next day, an old friend mentioned that a mutual acquaintance had seen the interview in *The Inquiring Mind* and had found it horrifying. I was stricken. I thought, "Horrifying! She didn't have to say it was horrifying!" She could have said she didn't like it, but – "horrifying"?

These two people were referring to exactly the same interview, which I had done with as much clarity and goodness of motivation as I could find in that moment. Somebody liked it; somebody didn't like it. So I needed to let go. It's not that I didn't care; I wasn't indifferent or cold. Rather, I had to recognize the vastness and complexity of the combined conditions that lead to someone having a reaction of any kind. How could I hope to control all of that? Maybe the person who didn't like what I said had been up all night in some stressful situation, or had just received bad news. Maybe the person who liked it was in love. So many things come together in any person's mind, in any person's life, in any given moment. Why must I feel responsible for all of that?

May you live all the days of your life.

— JONATHAN SWIFT

The practical implications of the eight vicissitudes came home to me quite forcefully when some friends and I were hiking in northern California. We had planned to hike in for three days and then turn around and come back out along the same trail. On the third day, we hiked steadily downhill for many hours. Suddenly, the friend walking beside me and I were struck by a simultaneous realization. He turned to me and said, "In a dualistic universe, downhill can mean only one thing." Sure enough, when we turned back the next day, we spent many hours hiking relentlessly uphill.

We live in a dualistic universe, as my friend so astutely noted. There will be downhill and uphill, pleasure and pain. There will be gain, loss, praise, blame, fame, and disrepute. How can a human heart – yours or mine, for instance – absorb all these continual contrasts without feeling shattered? How can we bear these unremitting transitions?

Our only sane option is to find a way to hold the changes with a sense of coherence, harmony, and wholeness. As it turns out, it is possible to survive going from Calcutta to Sydney to Burma — and more than that, to actually experience freedom in the midst of the most immense changes that keep rolling through our lives. We can even be happy with all of the continual arising and passing away. This happiness comes from the incredible spaciousness, sufficiency, and power of equanimity.

WISE ATTENTION

The basis for equanimity is called "wise attention": namely, recognizing the power of our own awareness and the crucial importance of how we relate to events. Wise attention is the antidote to the delusional thinking that replaces our direct experience with projections and interpretations. Equanimity is central to this state of nondelusion, because it doesn't resist the truth of how things are. It's spacious enough to see happiness as happiness and suffering as suffering, without judgments or attempts to control them.

The poet Ralph Waldo Emerson said, "What is life but the angle of vision? A person is measured by the angle at which he looks at objects." In other words, we can choose not to give in to anxiety, defeatism, or depression in the face of difficult challenges. We don't have to descend into apathy or hopelessness.

Recent psychological studies have examined how people explain their successes and failures to themselves as measures of their optimism or pessimism. It seems that optimists see failure as due to something that can be changed. They recognize that they might succeed the next time around. Pessimists, by contrast, take the blame for failure, ascribing it to some permanent character flaw.

An optimist, for example, won't assume that he was turned down for a job because of some lasting deficit of character. Where the pessimist says, "I'm a total failure and I always will be," the optimist will say — to use the language of Buddhist psychology — "A combination of conditions has come together to make this happen. These conditions are impermanent, and if I change some things, the result can be different." The difference between these two "angles of vision" is the spaciousness, openness, calm, and radiance that are present in the optimist's perspective and absent in the pessimist's.

Equanimity born of wise attention dawns when we recognize the naturalness of change. We recognize that there will inevitably be pleasure and pain, gain and loss, praise and blame, fame and disrepute. If we resist this fact of life or take it personally, we react in the same old ways — with grasping, hatred, fear, and delusion. When we understand that the vicissitudes of existence are natural, simply the way things are, we can open the mind, relax, and be balanced.

MOTIVATION AND SKILLFUL MEANS

In the constantly changing climate of praise and blame, our refuge lies in an understanding of our own motivation. According to the Buddha's teaching, the single most important factor in assessing any action is the intention that gives birth to it. A second factor, also as important, is what is called "skillful means." For example, you might be motivated by genuine compassion to tell someone something disagreeable to her, but it would probably not be all that skillful to shout it out across a crowded room. It would be more appropriate to take the person aside and tell her as gently as you can. This is what is meant by skillful means.

If you can feel good about both your motivation and your skillful execution, whether you receive praise or blame is completely out of your hands. You have to find a way to be at peace with your own integrity, knowing that the power of intention is the most important factor in everything you do. That's the "angle of vision" that will give you the most peace.

Again, this doesn't mean that what we do doesn't matter. It means that we must be incredibly honest and sensitive to our own motivation and to the level of skill with which we act — because that, more than anything, will reveal to us the nature of the action. What other people say may hurt or please us, but it's not an accurate reflection of our integrity.

Without wise attention, without equanimity, we lose perspective. Our minds tend to fixate on what is hurtful, and we forget that it's all arising and passing away. Equanimity is big — it's vast, it's open. In equanimity, the mind doesn't fixate on words like "terrific" or "horrifying." Instead, it lets go into a boundless field of possibilities. Then we can see praise and blame, fame and disrepute, as the ephemeral and conditional mind states they are.

PERSPECTIVE

Many years ago, Joseph and I were teaching a retreat on the big island of Hawaii. I was leading a sitting in the meditation hall, just after lunch. In the office below me, I could hear the phone ringing and ringing and ringing. It would stop and then immediately begin ringing again. I thought, "Something's really wrong." I ended the sitting and went downstairs to the office. Sure enough, the phone began ringing again. It was the civil defense department, calling to tell us that the largest tidal wave in history was coming our way and we had to evacuate immediately.

Now, this facility was right near the beach. I said to the caller, "There are seventy people here; we have two vehicles; any road we take will go right along the coast. I don't think we're going to be able to evacuate." The official said, "We'll call you back."

I went over to the building where Joseph was leading a group interview and waited in the back of the room. In the most doleful, embittered, distressed tone of voice, a participant was telling Joseph about his knee pain. I thought, "Boy, you think you have problems now; wait till you hear what I have to say!" It was a funny moment for me, listening to this person so consumed with self-pity and anguish. His experience was genuinely painful for him, no doubt – but the perspective I had in that moment cast his suffering in a very different light.

In the end, we all went up to the highest floor in the tallest building around. Nothing happened. No tidal wave came at all.

Equanimity, in this case, didn't mean ignoring the civil defense warning or shrugging off what seemed like the very real possibility of a terrible disaster. It meant stepping back from the personal implications of the situation and finding the safest option available to us – wise attention – and then implementing that option as calmly and efficiently as possible – skillful means.

I saw a striking metaphor for equanimity when I attended my first opera. The beautiful Santa Fe Opera House is an outdoor facility, wide open to the boundless New Mexico sky. From my seat I could see the stage, and behind it the sky, vast and endless. The people on the stage were behaving (one might say) operatically, dramatically; while behind them an immensity of spaciousness extended in every direction. I thought, "This is equanimity." Life goes on happening, with whatever degree of intensity, and we're not cut off from it – but it's held in the perspective of unconditional openness.

The Thai teacher Ajahn Chah said, "As you meditate, the mind will become quiet like a still forest pool. All of the wonderful and rare animals will come to drink at the pool, but you will be still. This is the happiness of the Buddha." We can apply this understanding of equanimity to all of life, not just to meditation practice itself. We try to pay attention to all our changing experiences, simply being aware of what's presenting itself in the moment; remaining unperturbed as the rare and wonderful animals come to drink at the pool of the mind.

To conceive the spirit of enlightenment, you first must develop equanimity toward all beings.

— ASANGA

EQUANIMITY IN RELATIONSHIPS

In the texts, equanimity is often likened to the appropriate relationship of a parent to an adult child. When the child is young, she needs nurturing and protection. After she grows up, her parents don't look at her and say, "Well, it's been fun, but it's all over between us now. I don't care about you any more." The parent has to accept that however much he loves and cares about this child, he also has to accept that this person is now making her own decisions and choices, and will suffer the consequences of her actions. We cannot control our children. We love them and we let go of them. That's the force of equanimity. And of course, it applies throughout the range of human relationships, not only in the context of parent and child.

Sometimes, we slip into a sense of owning people and trying to manage them. You might be in a helping relationship with somebody, trying to support her healing. It's easy, in this situation, to feel impatient: "Why aren't you better yet? Why aren't you moving along in line with my vision of what your happiness should look like?" When this happens, it takes balance, wisdom, and understanding to regain your equanimity. As much as you love someone and try to help her, as much compassion as you might have for her, things are the way that they are. Ultimately, you cannot control someone else's life. You can't control her choices, and by extension, you can't control her happiness or unhappiness.

Again, it's important to stress the difference between this approach and just not caring. We do care and we should care. We should always open our hearts and offer as much love and compassion as possible. But we can and must do that while also letting go of attachment to the results.

An example with which many of us can identify is that of a self-destructive friend. Perhaps this person is isolating himself, or drinking too much, or practicing unsafe sex. From the viewpoint of lovingkindness and compassion, you wish wholeheartedly and intensely that your friend be free of suffering. In the end, though, you have to recognize where the boundaries are. You have to clarify the limits of your own responsibility and understand where the source of his ultimate happiness really lies. If he doesn't change his behavior, your friend is going to suffer, no matter how ardently you wish it to be otherwise. Still, you continue to offer him lovingkindness and compassion. You try to help — but with the wisdom and acceptance to recognize that he's ultimately responsible for his own actions.

Rather than diminishing the force of love and compassion, acting from a ground of equanimity in this way actually strengthens it. To apply equanimity is to remove all conditions, so that your love and care remain consistent whether the outcome is to your liking or not. Equanimity adds a boundless dimension to love and compassion, because they're no longer just directed toward those people who behave according to your preferences. You can extend your heartfelt caring even to those people who aren't nice to you, or those whom disappoint you.

Equanimity endows lovingkindness with patience. It gives you the capacity to be present continually, even if your love and compassion are not returned — as is often the case in the ups and downs of human relationships. Equanimity is the antidote to burnout, because you're no longer wasting energy on trying to direct events that are beyond your control.

It's also said that equanimity endows compassion with courage. It's the key to being able to look at suffering directly, without needing to deny or avoid it. Genuine compassion depends on our ability to witness pain repeatedly without being overcome by sorrow, self-pity, or bitterness. So in order to be truly compassionate, we must first develop equanimity. This — gazing unflinchingly into the face of suffering, no matter how intense or relentless — is the act of courage that allows us to deepen and expand our compassion. From this perspective, accepting things as they are is not a sign of weakness or cowardice. It's the foundation of our greatest strength.

Not Standing Apart

As Joseph pointed out in Lesson Seven, classical Buddhist cosmology holds that we have all been born and died many, many times. In the course of all these previous lifetimes, according to this teaching, we have all been everything to one another — each other's mothers and fathers and saviors and murderers. We've stolen from each other and taken care of each other and betrayed and comforted each other. The Buddha said, "There's no place on this earth where we have not cried or been born or died." We've all done everything.

From this perspective, we can look at someone else's wrongful action and recognize its wrongfulness, but without a sense of self-righteousness. Since we, ourselves, have done everything in the entire repertoire of actions, we can hardly say, "I myself would never, ever, engage in such an activity." It's just not so. We've all done everything.

Whether or not you believe in this particular cosmology, you can reach the same conclusion through the practice of introspection. In a process like meditation, you see the tremendous array of motivations and impulses and thoughts and feelings that come and go in your own mind. What would happen if you followed every

THE SIX SENSE DOORS

According to classical Buddhist teachings, we experience the world through six "sense doors," or perceptual gateways. They are:

- seeing
- hearing
- smelling
- tasting
- touching
- mind

The door of mind refers to our thoughts, emotions, and mental images.

The Buddha taught that these six modes of perception define the totality of our experience — in other words, every moment of our lives involves experiences that are known by way of one of these sense doors. Further, the Buddha said that each experience received in this way is colored by a feeling tone, which is either pleasant, unpleasant, or neutral.

Understanding our experience in these terms reveals the importance of bringing mindfulness to every moment of our existence. Without it, we become mere creatures of mental conditioning, constantly trying to manipulate our experience so as to increase our pleasure and minimize our pain.

impulse that arises during a single hour of sitting meditation? You'd get up, you'd run out of the room, you'd buy a new car, you'd kill your enemy, you'd call all your friends and tell them you were running for president.

Behaving in that way would be insane. Yet — as Joseph pointed out in an earlier lesson — all of the insanity, greed, cruelty, violence, and oppression in this world begin with the very same kinds of thoughts that pass through our own minds. Thanks to our training in awareness, we may not act out all our rage and fear and anxiety, but that doesn't mean the impulses don't arise. So we have, in fact, experienced the precipitating cause, the essential nature, of everything that every other living being has ever done.

If we can accept that and have some compassion for ourselves, we can also have compassion for others. Once we witness the extremes of our own mind states, we no longer feel so separate, so immaculate, so above it all. We understand that in some way, we're all in this together. This realization is also a function of equanimity, and one of the ways it strengthens us.

Equanimity is the natural fruit of mindfulness. We're mindful of the changing sensations, thoughts and images, emotional states, and hindrances – pleasant, unpleasant, and indifferent. In meditation, particularly, we watch these experiences come and go, and we see that they're impermanent. So we hold them in a spacious, relaxed context, with a spacious, relaxed mind and heart. We acknowledge their existence, and at the same time we recognize them as passing flickers in an ocean of infinite space. In this way, every single moment of mindfulness becomes another step toward true equanimity.

EQUANIMITY: QUESTION AND ANSWER SESSION

Q: I have passions for many things: gardening and writing, to name just a few. Without these passions, my life would feel pretty meaningless. Does the cultivation of equanimity mean flattening out the intensity of my feelings about the things I care about?

A: Equanimity doesn't mean not caring. When we open our hearts, we can connect to all things, and that's as it should be. The point of equanimity is not to lose one's heartfelt connection with the things going on around us. Rather, it means balancing that connection with a clear recognition of the way things are. So, for example, we see what we genuinely cannot control, no matter how obsessed we might become with trying to. We see how much things are constantly changing. Even in the midst of intense, devoted activity, we can be served by seeing such truths clearly and remaining balanced.

Q: I have a friend who smokes three packs of cigarettes a day. She suffers from a chronic disease, which makes this addiction even more dangerous to her health. It's hard for me to keep my cool when I see her suffering so much, and then lighting up another cigarette on top of it. I mean, if someone won't wake up to something that's killing them, isn't it appropriate to yell?

A: We all wish ardently for the well-being of those we love. In the next lesson, we'll learn a specific meditation practice for putting those wishes into action. The gift of equanimity is to be able to recognize where our boundaries are and what our responsibility really is. The source of your friend's suffering is beyond your control. Your job, in this case, is to continue to offer her compassion and to support her health in whatever ways you can, but to maintain the perspective of wisdom. The fact is that she is ultimately responsible for her behavior. Psychologists would say that this understanding releases us from codependency. That release actually helps our lovingkindness endure, regardless of outcome.

Q: I often find myself identifying with my emotions, believing that they define my experience. Then I feel trapped and hopeless. How can I work with these feelings?

A: Tibetan Buddhists use an analogy I've found helpful. They liken the mind to a vast, clear sky. All our sensations, thoughts, and emotions are like weather that passes through without affecting the nature of the sky itself. The clouds, the winds, the snow and rainbows come and go, but beyond it all the sky remains clear and unperturbed. Let your mind be that sky, and let all these mental and physical phenomena arise and vanish like the changing weather. In this way, your mind can remain balanced and relaxed, without getting swept away in the drama of every passing storm.

GUIDED MEDITATION: PLEASANT AND UNPLEASANT FEELINGS

Use the following meditation to explore the feeling tone of your experience. Equanimity is brought to life and practiced through becoming aware of what Buddhist psychology calls "feeling." "Feeling" doesn't refer only to emotion, as we in the West tend to think of it. Rather, it refers specifically to the quality of pleasantness, unpleasantness, or neutrality that is a part of every single moment's experience.

The Buddha said that we experience the universe in six ways: through seeing, hearing, tasting, touching, smelling, and through the mind — that is, thoughts, emotions, images, and so on. Every single moment we're alive, we are experiencing the world in one of these six ways. Every moment of seeing or hearing or tasting or sensing through the body — touch sensation — or having an experience through the mind in thought or imagery or so on — every single one of these moments is known to us as either pleasant, unpleasant, or neutral.

Partly as a result of how we're perceiving it, partly as a result of interpretation, partly as a result of karmic consequences (according to the classical teachings) we feel a sensation in the body as pleasant, unpleasant or neutral. The same is true for sights, sounds, and so on. It's not that as the meditation evolves, all of this flattens out into nothingness. We still experience; we're still sensitive to pleasure, to pain; we're fully awake; we're alive. We experience all things in their own nature: "It's pleasant; it's unpleasant; it's neutral."

We are conditioned, when the feeling tone of something is pleasant, to cling, to grasp, to try to keep it, to hold on. We are conditioned, when the feeling tone of something is unpleasant, to condemn it, to have aversion toward it, to try to push it away or strike out against it. And we are conditioned, when the feeling tone of something is simply neutral, to space out, to lose touch with it, to disconnect.

We learn through mindfulness to open completely to the pleasant responses without clinging; to open completely to the unpleasant experiences without aversion; and to open completely to the neutral experiences without losing touch with them, without delusion.

A very famous teaching of the Buddha's is called "the wheel of dependent origination," in which he pointed to the possibility of our bondage or freedom in a single moment of hearing a sound, or feeling a sensation in the body – this very moment. The pleasant, unpleasant, or neutral qualities he taught are very wrapped up in the experience itself. They arise with the actual moment of contact, of seeing or hearing.

The Buddha said that if we can feel the pleasantness without clinging, if we can feel the unpleasantness without condemning, if we can feel the neutrality of this very moment's experience without delusion, then we are free.

In a moment of seeing, a moment of hearing, a moment of tasting, whatever – we're free right then because we are not driven by our old reactions to the feeling tone of the experience. If we are driven by these old reactions, then we're bound, we're trapped, we're limited right then, in that moment.

Right here in this moment, we can open up. We can experience a liberation of our being, feeling the pleasure, feeling the pain, feeling the neutrality.

As you sit in an easy relaxed way, with the breath, with sounds, sensations in the body, emotions, thoughts, all the different things that come and go, pay attention to the quality of pleasantness, unpleasantness, or neutrality. Don't struggle with it. If you can do it in an easy way, that's fine. If not, allow your attention to rest on the object itself.

See if you can label the particular nature of the feeling as pleasant, unpleasant, or neutral.

It's because of the feeling tone of each experience that we cling, or we condemn, or we space out, or we get lost. It's therefore quite important to become sensitive to the feeling associated with our different changing experiences – sights and sounds and thoughts, images, sensations in the body – whatever they might be.

It's because we want to prolong a certain feeling that we cling. It's because we want to push away another feeling that we condemn. It's because we're not awake for a neutral feeling that we get lost.

It's especially important not to struggle to try to discern what is a neutral experience. Sometimes it's difficult to distinguish between subtle pleasure or subtle pain and neutrality. Let the mind be at ease in this exercise.

If you notice the pleasantness, unpleasantness, or neutrality, make a mental note of it.

Often when we find the mind clinging, we're not actually clinging to a particular object; we're clinging to the feeling of pleasure the object gives us. If you notice clinging in the mind, look for the feeling, the quality of pleasure, rather than getting lost in or fixated on the object. This is very freeing.

If you find anger or condemnation coming up in the mind, it's because of a certain feeling that an object is giving us. Pay attention to the feeling, not just the object.

You may find that the mind is lost in fantasy. The reason that we get lost in the fantasy is because a particular thought gives us a feeling of pleasure. Rather than focusing exclusively on the content of the thought, notice the feeling of pleasure that it's giving you. Pay attention to that, note it. This is the hook for our attachment – it's this feeling.

Perhaps you're finding yourself lost in vengeful, angry fantasy.

It is not the thought itself that we get lost in; it's because of the feeling that it gives us. If you pay careful attention to anger, you will notice it's not actually a very pleasant feeling.

Sensations in the body are a very good avenue for developing sensitivity to feeling. You might have blissful, light, tingling feelings. We find them very pleasant. Can you enjoy them fully without clinging?

You might have painful, tense, itching, heavy sensations in the body; they might be quite unpleasant. Can you open to them fully without condemning?

The rising and falling of the abdomen or the sensation of the in and out breath might tend to be neutral. Can you open to it fully?

"Those who are mindful or heedful are on the path to the deathless; those who are mindless or heedless are as if dead already." If we don't open up to neutral experience, which makes up so much of our ordinary day, we are as if dead already. If we don't open to painful experiences, we are as if dead already, because we're trying to shut down, to close off, to push away an inevitable part of our experience. And in fact, if we try to cling to pleasant experience, we are as if dead already, because we cannot successfully hold on. We become fearful, we become agitated, we become defensive.

Try to experience the pleasant feeling completely, without the clinging; the unpleasant experience completely, without the aversion; the neutral experience completely, without the delusion, the spacing out, the losing touch. This is done through relaxing. Just relax. There's nothing you have to do about any of it: make it stay, make it go away, or replace it with something more exciting. Simply be with it, be sensitive, be aware of the component of feeling.

All the experiences will still come and go; there's nothing to impede, nothing to control. Equanimity is a great open spaciousness of mind and heart that feels fully what is happening. We're fully connected to all the joys and all of the sorrows, the good feelings and the difficult feelings and the ordinary feelings. We let them come, we let them go.

Your attention is like the earth – it's stable. It's not ruined or destroyed as different things come and go. You sit like a mountain where the wind may come and go. It's not because you're repressing anything or pushing anything away, but because you can accept it, you can see it for what it is. You can let it go.

Before you open your eyes, see if you can note the intention to open them. Before you make any movement, try to note the intention and then the movement, the sensations of the movement. Pay attention as best you can throughout the day to all of the changing feelings that come and go. See if you can be aware of them without being driven by old reactions. Stay aware of them within the spaciousness of great equanimity.

EXERCISES FOR WORKING WITH PLEASANT AND UNPLEASANT FEELINGS

Use this guided meditation for the next week, as you explore the role of feelings in your experience. Because feelings are so pervasive and distracting in our lives, you may find it particularly helpful to return to this meditation from time to time.

Exercise 1

Choose a visual experience and note the quality of pleasant or unpleasant feeling that accompanies the seeing. Write down what you notice.

_____

_____

Exercise 2

Now do the same thing with an experience of hearing.

_____

_____

Exercise 3

Repeat the exercise with an experience of smelling.

_____

Exercise 4

Repeat the exercise with an experience of tasting.

_____

_____

Exercise 5

Now describe the feeling tone associated with an experience of touching or bodily sensation.

_____

_____

Exercise 6

Finally, repeat the exercise with an experience of an emotion.

_____

_____

Exercise 7

It can be liberating to understand that we're often in a cycle of reaction to the feeling tone associated with objects of consciousness. When you find yourself caught in a state of attachment, look back at your experience and notice the quality of pleasant feeling that led to the reaction. Describe your experience.

_____

_____

Exercise 8

When you find yourself caught in aversion (anger or fear), look back at your experience and notice the quality of unpleasant feeling that led to the reaction. Make a note of your experience.

_____

_____

GETTING THE MOST FROM YOUR MEDITATION

In Lesson Two, Joseph challenged us to see ourselves as the one sane person who maintains calm on a sinking ship, thereby saving the lives of all on board. To manifest that kind of wisdom and clarity, we must develop the quality of equanimity – not just on the meditation cushion, but especially in those areas of our lives most likely to trigger strong responses. The suggestions that follow will help you to bring the power of equanimity to those parts of your experience where it can be of benefit to yourself and others.

- Practice recognizing the eight vicissitudes. When someone pays you a gratifying compliment, or you're blamed for something, remember that conditions always change. This places the experience in a larger perspective that defuses tendencies to grasp, reject, or space out. (It doesn't, however, mean that you should avoid responding graciously to a kind remark.)

- Practice identifying the sense doors and feeling tones. When you feel something strongly, notice through which perceptual gateway it arrives. Notice whether the feeling tone is pleasant, unpleasant, or neutral. Then watch what happens to the experience. Does your new awareness change the feeling tone? Does it change the level of intensity? Does it help you to chart a steadier course through the ups and downs of your daily experience?

- Contemplate the truth of change. When we examine our experience with curiosity and honesty, we see that every part of it is constantly changing. The tide comes in, but recedes the moment it's full. The new moon gives way to the crescent. Inside ourselves, too, are waves of hunger, joy, sleepiness, fear, and kindness in endless motion. The more we perceive the reality of these ebbing and flowing cycles, the less likely we are to lose our balance.

LESSON EIGHT GLOSSARY

feeling tone: the pleasant, unpleasant, or neutral tone that colors every experience

sense doors: the six perceptual gates through which we experience the world

skillful means: action based on kindness, respect, truthfulness, and timeliness

vicissitudes: changing conditions

wise attention: a way of seeing that relies on awareness; the opposite of delusion

LESSON NINE
LOVINGKINDNESS

Throughout this course, we've been exploring the possibilities of a mind free of the forces of craving, aggression, and delusion. One of the great fruits of such a mind is the power of unobstructed, unconditional lovingkindness.

The Pali word for lovingkindness is *metta*. Sometimes, *metta* is translated simply as "love." We often speak of love, but "lovingkindness" is a less familiar term to most of us. In our culture, the notion of love has assumed a complexity that obscures its true nature. Typically, the word *love* conjures up thoughts of passion or sentimentality. Metta is neither of these, and this distinction is crucial.

Passion is associated with attachment, wanting, owning, and possessing. When we "love" in this way, we expect things to proceed as we think they should. The voice of attachment says, "I'll love you as long as you love me in return," or "as long as you meet these ten behavioral requirements," or "as long as you never change." This is actually a state of great fear and anxiety, because, as we've seen, we can't control the nature of change. This kind of "love" is a conditional offering, much like a business transaction.

In contrast, the spirit of metta is like a freely offered gift. Like water pouring from one vessel to another, it flows freely, taking the shape of each situation without changing its essence. If somebody disappoints you or fails to meet your expectations, your feeling of lovingkindness for him can still remain. By the same token, your lovingkindness toward yourself need not be destroyed when you feel, as we all do sometimes, that you've let yourself down.

Sentimentality masquerading as love is an ally of delusion. It smears a little petroleum jelly on the lens through which you look at the world, creating an effect photographers call "soft focus." Sentimentality blots out life's rough edges, trouble spots, and defects. It's a state of denial. Painful experience is considered unbearable, so sentimentality rejects it. Through the lens of this kind of "love," everything looks perfect.

I once read an interview with the former Miss Kentucky. Thirty or forty years after her reign, this one-time beauty queen was asked what she thought about life. "I'm so tired," she said. "I'm so tired of smiling." She had spent decades composing her face into a fatuous, camera-perfect smile that had no meaning whatsoever.

A truly loving person doesn't dissemble in this way. Metta has nothing to do with sweetly accepting abuse while repressing feelings of rage or pain. Having a loving heart is not the same as masking your experience with a veneer of Miss Kentuckyism. That isn't lovingkindness. Rather, it's a splitting off from life's realities, provoked and sustained by fear of pain.

It's said that the Buddha first taught metta meditation as an antidote to fear. According to legend, he sent a group of monks off to meditate in a forest that was inhabited by tree spirits. The tree spirits resented the monks' presence, so they decided to scare them away. They transformed themselves into ghoulish visions, made terrible shrieking sounds, and created awful smells. The monks, appropriately terrified, fled the forest. "Please, Lord Buddha," they begged, "send us to meditate in some other forest."

The Buddha said, "I'm going to send you back to the very same forest — but this time, I'll give you the only protection you need." And so the Buddha gave the first-ever teaching of metta meditation. He encouraged the monks to recite the phrases we'll learn later in this lesson — but more importantly, to actually do the heartfelt practice of lovingkindness.

> *Our practice is not simply following the heart, but training the heart.*
>
> — ACHAAN SUMEDO

Like many such stories, this one has a happy ending. It's said that the monks returned to the forest and practiced metta. The tree spirits were so moved by the energy of lovingkindness they generated that they decided they quite liked the monks being there, after all. They decided to serve and protect them.

Whether or not this parable is literally true, its inner meaning endures: a mind filled with fear can be penetrated by the quality of lovingkindness. Moreover, a mind filled with lovingkindness cannot be overcome by fear. Even if fear should arise, it can't overpower such a mind.

The practice of lovingkindness is, at a certain level, the fruition of everything we've discussed so far. It relies on our ability to open continuously to the truth of our actual experience, not cutting off the painful parts, and not trying to pretend things are other than they are. Just as spiritual growth grinds to a halt when we indulge our tendency to grasp and cling, metta can't thrive in an environment that is bound to desire or to getting our expectations met.

In lovingkindness, our minds are open and expansive — spacious enough to contain all the pleasures and pains of a life fully lived. Pain, in this context, doesn't feel like a betrayal or an overwhelming force. It is part of the reality of human experience, and an opportunity for us to practice maintaining our authentic presence.

THE SEARCH FOR HAPPINESS

All human beings are united by an urge for happiness. We want an experience that takes us beyond our small, separate sense of self; a feeling of being at home with ourselves and one another. At the root of even the most terrible addiction or violence lies this urge to be happy. It may be twisted and distorted by ignorance of where happiness is actually to be found — yet still, that fundamental longing for genuine happiness is there.

The ultimate lesson all of us have to learn is unconditional love, which includes not only others but ourselves as well.

— ELISABETH KÜBLER-ROSS

The fact that every one of us wants to be happy is one of our most beautiful attributes. It's not something we need be afraid or ashamed of, or that we should feel tentative about. We deserve to be happy, so this urge is actually appropriate. All beings deserve to be happy. When we can combine the yearning for happiness with wisdom, it becomes a homing instinct for freedom. Then we can be inspired to overcome any obstacle.

The practice of metta helps us to honor the urge toward happiness in both ourselves and others. We develop the ability to embrace all parts of ourselves: the difficult aspects as well as the noble. As we continue practicing from that base of inner generosity, metta gives us the ability to embrace all parts of the world.

Ultimately, metta overcomes the illusion of separateness. The unconditional experience of lovingkindness is a radical sense of nonseparation. Thus, the nature of metta is to dissolve all the states associated with the fundamental error of separateness: fear, alienation, loneliness, despair, and feelings of fragmentation.

Overcoming Inner Torment

The Buddha said, "The mind is naturally radiant and pure; it is because of visiting forces known as defilements that we suffer." In Pali, the word "defilement" is *klesha* – which, more literally translated, means "torment of the mind." It's unfortunate that kilesa came to be understood as "defilement" – a word redolent of prudish and judgmental connotations. "Torment of the mind," on the other hand, is an experience we all recognize. When certain mind states arise strongly, they do have a tormenting quality. States like the five hindrances – grasping, aversion, sleepiness, restlessness, and doubt – can make us feel this way. So can guilt, fear, and jealousy.

Yet all of these so-called "defilements" are only temporary visitors. I sometimes use a particular image to help me remember that. In this fantasy, I'm just sitting happily at home, minding my own business. Suddenly, there's a knock at the door. I open it, and standing right there on my doorstep is grasping or greed or hatred or jealousy – one of the defilements. Almost reflexively, I fling the door open wide. "Come right in," I tell the defilement. "Just take over the house. It's all yours." I forget who actually lives here.

It's because of our mistaken relationship to these unwholesome qualities that we invite them to take over. In an instant, we lose touch with the fundamentally pure nature of our own minds – and then we suffer. But, as Joseph explained in a previous lesson, we can learn not to identify with the torments that come knocking. Through the practice of mindfulness, we realize that they're only visiting. They're adventitious; they're not inherent to our being. They don't reflect who we really are.

The defilements are manifestations of our conditioning, so there's no reason to dislike ourselves for experiencing them. Our challenge is to see them for what they are, as changing and conditioned, and to remember our own true nature. We come back to that natural radiance and purity of our minds by experiencing metta.

The Buddha taught that the mental forces that bring suffering can temporarily obstruct positive forces like love or wisdom, but they can never destroy them. Although the positive forces can't be destroyed by the negative, positive forces can actually uproot the negative. Love is a greater power than fear or anger or guilt, so it has the capacity to undo painful mind states.

The sense of metta can extend anywhere, any time. The late Indian teacher Nisargadatta Maharaj once had an exchange with a man who complained a great deal about his mother.

"She was neither a good person nor a good mother," the man grumbled.

"Did you love your mother?" Nisargadatta asked.

"She wouldn't let me."

"Well," Nisargadatta replied, "she couldn't stop you."

With that simple remark, this great teacher drove home the reality that no external condition can prevent love. No one and nothing can stop it. The awakening of metta is not contingent upon things or people being a certain way. By perceiving this boundless quality of mind through meditation practice, we contact the essence of metta.

BEING A GOOD FRIEND

The Pali word *metta* has two root meanings. One is "gentle"; so metta is likened to a gentle rain that falls impartially upon the entire earth, neither selecting nor excluding where it will land. But the principal root meaning of *metta* is "friend." To understand the power of metta is to understand the power of friendship.

Consider the qualities that make a good friend. She's constant; there for you in both happiness and adversity. She doesn't forsake you when you're in trouble or down on your luck. A friend helps you, and protects you when you're unable to take care of yourself. He's a refuge when you're afraid; he won't talk about you behind your back. The foundation of metta practice is knowing how to be this kind of friend.

My friend and colleague Sylvia Boorstein was once on a plane from Chicago to San Francisco. About forty-five minutes into the flight, the pilot announced that there was a problem with the plane's hydraulic system. "There's nothing to worry about," he said, "but rather than fly over the Rockies with faulty hydraulics, we're going to turn back. The flight attendants will instruct you in the proper position to take in the event of an emergency landing. They will also come around to collect your shoes, eyeglasses, and pens."

Sylvia was stricken. Sitting there without her shoes, she began to do lovingkindness meditation. She did it in the same way she normally did every day, enveloping the dozen or so people in her immediate family with aspirations for their happiness, peace, and well-being. "May Collin be happy, may Nathan be happy, may Grace be happy." When Sylvia reached the end of her list of beloved family members, she went back to the beginning and did it again.

For some reason, the pilot felt the need to update his passengers at five-minute intervals. His voice would come over the PA system: "We're going to be landing in thirty-five minutes." "We're going to be landing in thirty minutes." "We're going to be landing in twenty-five minutes." Sylvia just kept doing her metta meditation: "May Seymour be happy, may Nathan be happy, may Collin be happy..." and back around again.

Finally, the pilot announced that the plane would be landing in five minutes. Sylvia thought, "Well, in five minutes, either I'll be dead or I'll still be alive." But when she returned to her metta practice, she found she couldn't restrict herself to her list of special beings. The only logical way she could send metta was to all beings everywhere. With perhaps only five minutes left to live, it made no sense to isolate or exclude. (As it turned out, the plane came down safely. Sylvia said the landing was like any other.)

Like Sylvia, when we open to the immediacy of our experience, we find a genuine sense of friendship arising for all beings everywhere. This feeling isn't the same as approving indiscriminately of others' actions; nor does it mean that we suddenly become passive or complacent. What it does mean is that we don't have to feel separate. We can become friends of everything that lives.

The Taoist sage Chuang-tzu said,

> There was a man so displeased by the sight of his own shadow and so displeased with his own footsteps that he determined to get rid of both. The method he hit upon was to run away from them. So he got up and ran. But every time he put his foot down, there was another step, while his shadow kept up with him without the slightest difficulty. He attributed his failure to the fact that he was not running fast enough, so he ran faster and faster without stopping until he finally dropped dead. He failed to realize that if he merely stepped into the shade, his shadow would vanish, and if he sat down and stayed still, there would be no more footsteps.

When we make the courageous choice to be still rather than run away, we have a chance to establish a relationship with what is – which gives rise to lovingkindness.

FRIENDLINESS TO YOURSELF

The beginning of metta practice is learning how to be your own friend. As the Buddha said, "You can search the entire universe for someone more deserving of your love and affection than you are yourself, but that person is not to be found anywhere. You, yourself, more than anybody in the universe, deserve your own love and affection."

This is not an attitude that has taken root in Western culture. Very few of us embrace ourselves in the way the Buddha suggested. Metta practice is the key to this treasure: the possibility of truly respecting, honoring, and supporting ourselves. It brings us to the realization so eloquently described by the poet Walt Whitman: "I am larger and better than I thought; I did not think I held so much goodness."

Certain Indian philosophical systems during the time of the Buddha taught that, in order for the spirit to soar free, the body must be tortured, mortified, and abused. Although most of us would agree that this is hardly the way to liberation, we seem to have our own variation on the theme. Self-judgment is so prevalent in our society that it's attained the status of a virtue. Contemporary Western students often fall into the trap of embracing self-condemnation as a path to awakening. "If I continually malign myself," they reason, "I'll vanquish this troublesome ego and become spiritually pure." If that were the case, of course, we would all have been free a long time ago.

A spirituality based on self-hatred will never sustain itself over the long haul. Generosity, for example, is intrinsic to the path of liberation. Yet if our motivation for practicing generosity is self-judgment, it ceases to be true generosity and becomes a kind of martyrdom. The same is true of morality, another essential component of spiritual transformation. When rooted in self-hatred, morality turns into rigidity and repression.

Loving others without any love for ourselves tramples on healthy boundaries, leading to what we've learned to call "codependency." Instead of resting in loving-kindness, we spend our lives searching painfully and fruitlessly for intimacy. Yet we have only to contact our own true nature in order to experience the natural radiance and purity of our minds. That's the beginning of being able to extend lovingkindness toward all beings everywhere. It's also an essential requirement for experiencing the quality of love we all so deeply want to give and receive.

In Buddhist psychology, metta is identified as the cohesive factor in consciousness. In other words, metta brings all beings together. When someone experiences anger, for example, the heart is very dry. We know that dry substances — say, two pieces of paper — don't naturally cohere. Add a little wetness, and the paper bonds easily. Love moistens the heart, so that it can join with others in an authentic expression of connectedness.

The beauty of this realization moved the Buddha to say that sustaining a loving heart, even for the duration of a finger snap, makes one a truly spiritual being.

THE PRACTICE OF METTA

To begin learning how to do metta, use the guided meditation on CD 2, track 3. The following description is a visual aid to support your ongoing practice.

Begin by sending metta to yourself. The traditional practice uses a series of phrases. These are:

> May I be free from danger.
> May I be happy.
> May I be healthy.
> May I live with ease.

If these phrases don't touch your heart, come up with your own. The important thing is not to recite the "correct" lines, but to use words that are meaningful to you. You could say, "May I be free of confusion," or "May I find relief from suffering." Experiment until you find the phrases that seem right.

From here, the practice proceeds in a very structured and specific way. After directing metta to yourself, you move on to someone you find inspiring, or to whom you feel grateful. Traditionally, this person is called "the benefactor." Bring this person's presence into your mind and direct the metta phrases toward him or her:

> May you be free from danger.
> May you be happy.
> May you be healthy.
> May you live with ease.

Next, move on to a beloved friend, sending unconditional lovingkindness to that person in the same way: "May you be free from danger," and so on. At this point, begin extending metta still further, toward those who don't typically arouse feelings of love. Going beyond the safe, familiar circle of loved ones strengthens and increases your capacity for benevolence. This is a powerful practice for challenging your sense of limitation.

The next person you go to is traditionally called "neutral." This is somebody you neither like nor dislike. Some of us find it difficult to bring to mind anyone whom we haven't already deemed likable or unlikable. In that case, there may seem to be hardly any neutral people in your life. Others of us feel our world is filled with too many neutral people. If this is your experience, you may see most people as roughly equivalent to pieces of furniture.

If you have trouble coming up with a suitable neutral person, try thinking of a clerk you've seen at the supermarket, or perhaps someone who walks his dog past your house. You can usually find people who have passed through your life casually enough to have aroused neither your attachment nor your aversion. Again, use the same phrases you've used before, but this time, direct them to the neutral person: "May you be free from danger," and so on.

Now you're ready to send lovingkindness to someone with whom you've had difficulty or conflict. To send lovingkindness to difficult or threatening people is not to forget about your own needs. It doesn't require denial of your own pain, anger, or fear. Nor does doing this practice mean you're excusing abuse or cruelty. Rather, you're engaging in the marvelous process of discovering and cultivating your inherent capacity for unconditional love. It doesn't have to do with being passive or complacent in terms of the other person; it has to do with your own spiritual expansion. This adversary stands at the turning point between a finite and an infinite sense of lovingkindness. Directing metta toward a difficult person leads to the discovery of your own capacity for lovingkindness that's born of freedom.

In the final phase of the practice, we move on to offer metta to all beings everywhere, without distinction or exception.

THE FRUITS OF METTA

There was a time when I was practicing metta intensively in Burma. It took me about six weeks of concentrated practice to go through the five categories: myself, my benefactor, my friend, the neutral person, and the difficult person. After those first weeks, my teacher Sayadaw U Pandita called me into his room for an interview. He asked me, "Suppose you're walking in the forest with your benefactor, your friend, your neutral person, and your difficult person. You run into a group of bandits, who tell you that someone in your group must be sacrificed. You have to decide who that will be. Which one do you choose?"

The question shocked me. I looked deep into my heart, trying to find a basis on which to make that terrible choice. I realized that I didn't perceive any distinction between these people, including myself. I told U Pandita, "I can't make that choice. Everyone seems the same. They all seem equal to me."

"You wouldn't choose your difficult person?" he asked.

"No," I replied. "I wouldn't choose her." After all those weeks of genuinely feeling into this person's pain and wish to be happy, I truly didn't want her to suffer harm.

"Wouldn't you choose yourself?" U Pandita persisted.

"Uh-oh," I thought. My conditioning welled up, generating a great urge to please him by giving what I thought was the right answer. But there was no way I could honestly say I would choose myself, because I didn't feel that I deserved to live any less than anyone else in the group. So I said, "No, I don't see any difference between myself and any of the others." U Pandita simply nodded, and I left.

Later that day, I was reading the *Visuddhimagga,* a classic Buddhist commentary known in English as *The Path of Purification.* I was surprised to come across the very same question about the bandits. There it was: metta practitioners have been presented with this riddle for more than two thousand years. It turned out that my answer — that I couldn't choose to sacrifice anyone, including myself — is considered the correct one.

Of course, different life situations require different courses of action. An answer that's appropriate in one circumstance may be entirely inappropriate in another. The point of this story, however, is that lovingkindness doesn't require us to denigrate ourselves in the interests of other people's happiness. Metta implies equality, oneness, wholeness. Authentic intimacy doesn't arise from martyr-like deference to others any more than from narcissistic deference to ourselves.

Ultimately, the practice of metta is not about contriving any kind of feelings. The waves of feeling that come and go are less relevant to the cultivation of metta than is harnessing the considerable power of intention in the mind. This is why we repeat the metta phrases. Each time we say them, we plant a seed of intention. Those seeds bear fruit in their own time, in their own way.

Some seeds come to fruition quickly, yielding the satisfying experience of instant gratification. Others take much longer to bear fruit. That process is beyond our control; our work is simply to plant the seeds. Every time we form the intention to further our own happiness or that of others, we're doing exactly what we need to do. Beyond that, we learn to simply trust in the laws of nature to cultivate our seeds appropriately.

In 1976, some of us who had been involved in founding the Insight Meditation Society decided we would inaugurate the center with a month-long, self-guided retreat. We had no teacher to supervise our practice — just what we had learned about meditation so far. This was before my intensive metta retreat in Burma, but I had already done a little metta. I knew the basic instructions and the structure I've described in this lesson. I decided to take this opportunity to do intensive and systematic metta meditation.

I spent the first week of the retreat directing lovingkindness toward myself. All day long, sitting, walking, standing, and lying down, I would direct the metta phrases toward myself: "May I be happy, may I be peaceful," and so on. But I felt absolutely nothing. It was a dreary, boring week, not what I had expected at all.

Then, as it happened, a few of us suddenly had to leave the retreat. Now I felt really miserable. Not only had I spent the week in fruitless practice, I'd never even gotten beyond directing metta to myself. I was inadequate, and on top of that, I was selfish, too!

While hurrying to pack, I dropped a jar of something on the bathroom floor. It shattered into pieces. The first thought that came into my mind was, "You are really a klutz, but I love you." The second thought was, "Look at that! Something actually did happen in this week of practice." I would have sworn that absolutely nothing was happening all through that week – but it seems that something transforming had been, on a level I couldn't discern.

This is a very different experience from struggling to fabricate a particular feeling. Love can't be magically created through force of will. Instead, we just settle back and plant the seeds without worrying about the result. This is our work.

METTA AND THE BRAHMA-VIHARAS

As we learned in Lesson Seven, lovingkindness is the first of the brahma-viharas, or "best homes." Each brahma-vihara enriches, supports, and sustains the others. The second of them is compassion, which is defined as the quivering or trembling of the heart in response to suffering. Rather than seeking to reject pain or deny its presence, compassion faces it with an open heart. This is contrasted with responding to pain with bitterness, anger, or fear.

Let those love now who
never loved before;
Let those who always loved,
now love the more.

— THOMAS PARNELL

The third brahma-vihara is sympathetic joy: the cultivation of happiness when seeing someone else's good fortune or happy circumstance. It keeps us from being threatened by another's good fortune. It keeps us from contrasting ourselves with that person and feeling poverty-stricken in comparison. Sympathetic joy recognizes that someone else's happiness doesn't have to take away from our happiness, but can actually enhance our own joy.

Equanimity, the fourth brahma-vihara, supports the other three. Equanimity, as we've seen, is not indifference, but balance of mind. It protects us from plunging into despair or becoming complacent. Equanimity provides the spaciousness in which lovingkindness, compassion, and sympathetic joy can arise, grow, and expand outward to all living things.

The manifestation of these brahma-viharas in our lives is quite unfeigned. It's a natural expression of the heart. This is very different from a self-conscious construction of ourselves as peaceful, loving, happy people.

We might find the brahma-viharas manifesting as generosity, rooted in a sense of inner abundance. Having enough for ourselves, we're willing to share, let go, and offer to others with uncontrived graciousness and joy. A loving heart can also express itself through morality. This goes back to the Buddha's teaching that if you truly loved yourself, you would never harm another. The natural expression of a loving heart is a sense of oneness, so harming another is like harming yourself.

CHANGING THE WORLD WITH LOVINGKINDNESS

Ashoka was an emperor who lived in northern India about two hundred and fifty years after the time of the Buddha. When he first ascended to the throne, Ashoka was greedy to expand his territory at any cost. Not surprisingly, it's also said that he was a very unhappy man. One day he sent his army out to fight for some territory. After the terrible, brutal battle was over, Ashoka walked out onto the battlefield, aghast at the bloodshed he had caused.

Just then, a Buddhist monk walked by. He didn't say a word, but his entire being radiated serenity. Ashoka thought, "Why is it that I, who have everything a human being could want, feel so miserable? Yet this monk, who has nothing but his robes and begging bowl, seems deeply happy and at peace."

Ashoka followed the monk off the battlefield. "Are you happy?" he asked him; "And if so, how did you come to be so happy?" The monk who had nothing responded by introducing the Buddha's teaching to the emperor who had everything. After that, Ashoka devoted himself to the practice and study of Buddhism. The nature of his reign changed completely. He stopped waging wars; he made sure his people were fed; he planted trees and built hospitals. Ashoka transformed himself from a tyrant into one of history's most revered and beloved rulers.

Ashoka's son and daughter carried Buddhism from India to Sri Lanka. From there, it spread to Burma, Thailand, and eventually the whole world. We have access to these teachings today, so many centuries and cultural transitions later, as a result of Ashoka's transformation. The radiance of that single monk changed the course of history.

Every one of us can be that monk. Every single one of us can cultivate lovingkindness and wisdom, so that happiness becomes our powerful and natural expression of being.

SIX CATEGORIES, FOUR PHRASES

Traditional metta practice is a carefully structured path to a fully opened heart. The practice comprises six graduated categories that gently expand our lovingkindness from ourselves to all beings everywhere. With each category, we use four phrases that express lovingkindness through the focus of our attention. These phrases can be used just as they appear here, or may be adjusted to conform more closely to your own experience of lovingkindness.

Six Categories

In the six categories of classical metta practice, we extend lovingkindness to beings in this order:

- ourselves
- a benefactor, or person who has benefited us
- a good friend
- a neutral person, about whom we have no strong feelings
- a person we find difficult, or with whom we're in conflict
- all beings without exception

There is a further step, which can help us take "all beings" out of the conceptual arena and into our hearts. We do this by sending metta to pairs of opposites, or complementary sets of beings. Examples are men and women; those who suffer and those who are happy; humans and animals; and so forth. This step can often reveal to us the more subtle levels of judgment that separate us from others.

Four Phrases

The four phrases with which we begin our practice are:

May I be free from danger.
May I be happy.
May I be healthy.
May I live with ease.

In the first stages of metta meditation, we use these phrases to extend lovingkindness to ourselves. They reflect our wish to experience safety, health, and freedom from struggle. As we unfold into the further phases of the practice, we change the pronoun: "May *you* be free from danger."

It's not uncommon to encounter resistance when trying to extend lovingkindness to someone we find difficult. When this happens, it can be helpful to include yourself along with the difficult person: "May *we* be free from danger," and so on.

METTA: QUESTION AND ANSWER SESSION

Q: My boss is extremely rude and arrogant. He seems to respect me only when I behave in the same way. I think if I treated him with the kind of gentleness you describe, he'd take it as a sign of weakness.

A: To be able to have metta is, in fact, our greatest strength. Practicing metta doesn't mean letting people walk all over us. Responding to rudeness from a motivation of lovingkindness is not the same as letting rudeness rule the interaction. It does mean that we aren't caught in a downward spiral of resentment and revenge. We discover that, in fact, we can be very strong without the angry reaction.

Q: I want to feel lovingkindness toward others, but most of the time I really don't. So many people do so much harm through their ignorance and selfishness. How can I cultivate real metta toward these people?

A: It helps to bring your attention to people's good qualities. That doesn't mean ignoring their hurtful actions, but recognizing that each of us is a mixed bag of wholesome and unwholesome impulses. If you can't think of anything good about someone, reflect on the fact that he, like you, wants to be happy, and that he creates suffering out of ignorance. A certain feeling of connection naturally arises through contemplating that fact.

Actually, a wonderful and pragmatic way to cultivate lovingkindness is through the formal practice presented in this lesson. Even though it may feel artificial at first, the feeling of metta grows stronger the more we practice. Be patient with yourself. It takes time to retrain our hearts.

Q: Is anyone beyond the power of lovingkindness? What about psychopaths who are incapable of feeling empathy for their victims? What about rabid dogs? Can it help such beings at all to extend lovingkindness to them? Can it reduce the amount of harm they do?

A: Whether or not it's helpful to them, it is helpful to us. Metta is taught as the antidote to fear. That doesn't mean that we behave foolishly in the face of danger, but that we remember we are ultimately not separate from one another. The beings you describe are in tremendous pain, which drives their destructive actions. We practice metta for them in recognition of that suffering, and to express the deep truth of our nonseparation. My personal belief is that this expression is helpful to all, even though we can't control someone else's behavior (hence the need for great equanimity, as well!).

THE BENEFITS OF LOVINGKINDNESS

Most of us appreciate intuitively that the more we open our hearts to all beings, the happier our lives will be. However, the Buddha didn't stop at that general recognition. He taught that those who practice metta experience eleven particular benefits:

1. You sleep well.
2. You awaken easily.
3. You enjoy pleasant dreams.
4. People love you.
5. Celestial beings *(devas)* love you.
6. The devas protect you.
7. You're safe from external dangers.
8. Your face is radiant.
9. Your mind is serene.
10. You will be unconfused at the moment of death.
11. You'll take rebirth in the higher, happier realms.

GUIDED MEDITATION: METTA

You will find a recorded version of this guided meditation on CD 2, track 3. Use either that one or the one that follows (or both) to become familiar with the structure of metta practice. This is a meditation you can return to again and again, particularly in times of difficulty.

The first instruction the Buddha gave for doing metta meditation is to sit comfortably. That means literally — that is physically. Sit comfortably, relax, be at ease in your body. It also means to be at ease in your mind, symbolically or psychologically. Relax. Don't try to force anything or make anything special happen. Don't try to contrive extraordinary loving feelings. Just relax, be at ease, sit comfortably. Imagine that you are out in a big, wide-open field, just planting seeds, seeds of intention.

Begin metta meditation by opening to, directing the sense of loving care, of friendship, of kindness, of connection, to yourself.

See if you can think of one thing you like about yourself, even just a small thing. It might be a particular quality or attribute, some part of yourself that you respect. Or it might be something good that you've done; a time when you've been generous, when you've been careful, you've been honorable. Maybe it's a time when it would have been easy to tell a lie but you chose to speak the truth.

If you can't find one good thing that you've done or one thing you like about yourself, then simply rest your mind in the awareness of your wish to be happy. This wish is rightful, appropriate, and beautiful. Like all beings everywhere, you simply want to be happy.

Spend a few moments either contemplating the good within you or the rightfulness of this wish to be happy.

See if you can find three or four phrases that express what you wish most deeply for yourself – not just for today or the short term, but in a deep and enduring way. What would you wish most for yourself?

The traditional phrases are four in number. The first is, "May I be free from danger" or "May I live in safety." "Danger," here, refers to both inner and outer danger – inner danger from being completely lost in tormenting mind states, and outer danger in the obvious sense. "May I be free from danger" or "May I live in safety." And then the other three phrases are, "May I be happy," "May I be healthy," and "May I live with ease."

The last phrase refers to the experiences of day-to-day life, like family and livelihood – "May it go easily, may it not be a struggle. May I live with ease." "May I be free from danger; may I be happy; may I be healthy; may I live with ease." You can use these phrases or whatever phrases you choose. The ones that are most meaningful to you are the best. See if you can have these phrases emerge from your heart rather than from a pounding insistence in your head. Cherish each phrase; connect to it.

It's as though you're holding something very precious and fragile in your hand, like an object made of glass. If you clutch it too tightly, it will shatter and break, and if you become negligent, if you just let your hand fall open, it will drop and break. You hold it, cherish it, stay connected to it … not too tightly, not too loosely.

Let each phrase emerge from your heart. Connect to it, simply connect to it. Without trying to force any special feeling or to make anything happen, allow it to come up. Be with it. This is the power of intention in the mind. Let it work.

"May I be free from danger. May I be happy. May I be healthy. May I live with ease." You can develop a rhythm that's pleasing to you. You don't have to hurry. There can be space; there can be silence. Once again, have the phrases emerge.

If you find your attention wandering, you don't need to judge that. You don't need to try to figure out how your mind made those connections, how you ended up thinking about what you've been thinking about. You don't have to analyze. You don't have to elaborate on the thought. If anything arises in your field of awareness other than these phrases and the feelings that may come with the phrases, see if you can simply let go gently. Bring your attention back to the phrases.

The next expansion of the field of metta is toward someone traditionally called "the benefactor" – that is, somebody who has been good to you, taken care of you, been generous toward you, helped you. Or it could be somebody who inspires you: someone who reminds you of your own full capacity as a human being to be loving, compassionate, and aware. If somebody comes to mind, you can either bring forth an image or visualization of that person, or maybe say her name quietly to yourself. Get a feeling for her as though she were here in front of you.

Remember the good that this person has done for you or her good qualities, and begin offering her lovingkindness through the phrases, through the intentions.

"May you be free from danger. May you be happy. May you be healthy. May you live with ease."

If no one comes to mind that serves as a benefactor, you can simply continue directing the feeling of lovingkindness toward yourself.

Now open your heart further to include a really good friend. Remember, metta itself means "friendship." If you think of a friend, once again you can visualize him or say his name. Bring him here and include him in this power of intention, of friendship, of lovingkindness.

See if you can wish for this person just what it is you've wished for yourself.

Remember that this person also just wants to be happy.

The next person that you choose is known as the "neutral person" — someone for whom you don't have strong liking or a strong disliking. If you can think of such a person, once again contemplate the fact that all beings everywhere want to be happy. With this person as well, though perhaps you don't know her very well and don't understand her particular conditioning, you do know this: all beings everywhere want to be happy. And so you wish for this person the happiness, the freedom, the love, the joy that you would wish for yourself.

Again, if you can't find a neutral person, you can continue with yourself or with a friend.

Now we move on to a difficult person. It's best not to begin right away with the most difficult person in your life, the one who has hurt you the most grievously. Don't start where there's the most anger or fear or conflict, but rather with somebody who is mildly difficult, someone who's irritating or annoying to you.

Only very slowly and gradually do we work to incorporate the more and more difficult people. Remember that when we offer friendship or lovingkindness, it is not at all in a sense of condoning everyone's actions or saying, "It didn't matter how much I got hurt, really." It's not about pretending or feeling something other than what we're actually feeling.

It is about recognizing and understanding our oneness, or nonseparateness.

To offer this difficult person lovingkindness, loving care, does not diminish you in any way, but rather brings you back in touch with your deepest and most perfect capacity to love, which is an enormous strength. The capacity to love is not a weakness.

If you find it hard to work with the difficult person, as it often is, try visualizing yourself along with that person. Rather than running into the feeling that you're abandoning your own needs and you're not going to take care of yourself and you'll just be hurt again, you are in effect saying, "May we be happy, may we be peaceful, may we be free from danger." You're putting yourself in there on an equal footing with this person.

If you find painful feelings like anger and grief coming up, don't try to force your way through them. It might be time to feel the pain of those states and direct some lovingkindness toward yourself. Then go back once again, to see if you can include this person in your field of loving care.

If the painful emotions that come up are very intense, just drop the phrases for a little while and open to the feeling itself. Be aware of it. Use all the tools of mindfulness to create space around it. A little bit later you can move on, back to sending metta.

We move from sending metta to the difficult person to sending metta to all beings everywhere, without distinction, without exclusion. We open to a sense of the boundlessness of life. The traditional categories we pass through on our way to total inclusion are deliberately many in number, because they progressively open us to a sense of the boundlessness and magnitude of life. So we say, "May all beings be free from danger. May they – or may we – be happy … be healthy … live with ease. May all living beings, all creatures, all individuals, all those in existence be free from danger … be happy … be healthy … live with ease." We open and open, recognizing our inevitable connection to all beings everywhere, so that there's no limit.

From here, go on to send metta to pairs of opposites. You may, for example, send metta to all females and then to all males; to all enlightened beings, those who are free, those who are good-hearted, and then all unenlightened beings. You can tell from that particular example that the two halves don't actually have to be equal parts of a whole. The benefit of sending metta in this way, using either opposites or many parts of a whole, is that we see for ourselves where our resistance may be. We see where we withhold, where our challenges are. And, again, we don't do this in order to judge ourselves about what we discover, but to gently offer ourselves loving care.

We begin to see how many of these limitations are actual and how many of them are simply constructed. We see where we can gently open through.

All females ... all males ... all enlightened ones ... all unenlightened ones ... those beings who are happy ... those who are really suffering ... those who are causing suffering.

Beings being born ... those dying. Whatever comes to your mind.

All parts, when taken together, make up the whole.

Finish by directing the force of lovingkindness, of friendship, of loving care, to all beings everywhere without distinction, without exclusion, and without separation.

You can gently open your eyes ... feel the various sensations in your body, your heart space ... and see if, as you get up and begin other activities, you can have the mind rest in these phrases. Continue to extend, to offer, to open to the power of lovingkindness throughout the day.

METTA EXERCISES

Work with at least five of these exercises after you've had an opportunity to practice metta consistently for a week.

Exercise 1

What arose in your mind as you sent metta to yourself? Describe any images or feelings that arose during this phase of the meditation.

_____

_____

_____

Exercise 2

Imagine yourself sitting in the center of a circle, surrounded by the most loving people you know or have heard of. All of them are sending metta to you. What is your experience of this visualization?

_____

_____

_____

Exercise 3

Describe the process you underwent in finding a benefactor to whom to send metta.

_____

_____

_____

Exercise 4

Describe how you went about finding a neutral person to use in your metta practice.

_____

_____

_____

Exercise 5

Describe the easiest and most difficult parts of this practice.

_____

_____

_____

Exercise 6

What was your experience of working with a difficult person? Did you include yourself with that person when sending metta?

_____

_____

_____

Exercise 7

Describe your experience of moving from the finite (yourself, the benefactor, and so on) to the infinite (all beings everywhere).

_____

_____

_____

Exercise 8

Describe your experience in working with pairs of opposites or complementary sets (men/women, rich/poor, and so on). Did you encounter resistance? Fear? Curiosity?

_____

_____

_____

GETTING THE MOST FROM YOUR MEDITATION

- Review the section on the brahma-viharas in Lesson Seven (page 145).

- Follow the five precepts. Our moral conduct reflects the true extent of our love, concern, and care for ourselves and others. Review Lesson One and display the card listing the five precepts where you can see it every day. Resolve to work with the precepts in every area of your life.

- Contemplate the meaning and effects of karma. When we comprehend the full impact of our actions, we see how lovingkindness tangibly affects our own experience and that of all those with whom we come into contact. We begin to feel the immediate and long-term effects of opening our hearts to all beings. Review Lesson Seven to refresh yourself on the role of karma in our lives.

- Reflect on the truth of our nonseparation. Recognize that the potential for every kind of act exists in you. When you encounter unfairness, deviousness, and other violations, remember that you also carry the potential for such acts. You may have the strength or the awareness not to act on them, but the people who don't have that advantage are also trying to be happy. The suffering they create arises out of ignorance. Try to extend the power of lovingkindness.

- During the course of your day, try using the metta phrases to send loving-kindness to strangers and associates. Notice the difference between feeling isolated in your own world and feeling connected by means of your practice.

LESSON NINE GLOSSARY

benefactor: someone who has treated you with kindness and generosity; a person who has enriched your life or inspired you

deva: "shining one" [Sanskrit, Pali]; a celestial being who dwells in a pleasant realm of existence

kilesa: "trouble, defilement" [Pali]; a factor of mind that obscures clear seeing; a hindrance to meditation

neutral person: in the context of metta practice, someone for whom you feel no particular liking or disliking

LAST WORDS

Athletes know that the benefits of physical exercise can't be stored, but they can be built upon. The same is true of spiritual wisdom. The Buddha made this crystal clear: when we practice, he said, wisdom grows, and when we don't practice, it wanes.

There is no substitute for deepening the mindfulness habit through daily meditation. But formal practice is only one part of the equation. For wisdom to flourish, we must bring this same effort and focus to every aspect of our lives. The process of awakening can be furthered with every single thought, word, and action – not just by what happens on the meditation cushion. Wisdom increases when practice permeates all of life.

Your own experience is a constant, reliable source of further teachings. Continue to bring your clear, unjudging attention to everything you do, sense, and say. You'll find that this practice will enrich your daily meditation sessions – and conversely, that your formal practice will open the way for new outlooks and choices in your work, home, and social life.

If you should drift away from your meditation practice for a while, don't become discouraged. Remember that the essence of meditation is to start over, again and again. When you notice the absence of mindfulness in your life, simply return to your meditation cushion and renew your practice.

MEDITATION IN ACTION

One of the Tibetan *lojong,* or mind training, slogans says, "Whatever you suddenly meet should be joined with meditation." In other words, the meditative process – quieting the mind, bringing awareness to all experience, recognizing the impermanence of thoughts and impulses – this way of living can be applied to everything, even the unexpected. The more formal sitting you do, the more you'll become habituated to shining the light of mindful attention on all the situations and circumstances of your life. You will no longer be "caught unaware."

As you proceed from this point on the path of awakening, take with you these words of encouragement from Zen teacher Charlotte Joko Beck:

> To continue practice through severe difficulties we must have patience, persistence, and courage. Why? Because our usual mode of living – one of seeking happiness, battling to fulfill desires, struggling to avoid mental and physical pain – is always undermined by determined practice. We learn in our guts, not just in our brain, that a life of joy is not in seeking happiness, but in experiencing and simply being the circumstances of our life as they are; not in fulfilling personal wants, but in fulfilling the needs of life; not in avoiding pain, but in being pain when it is necessary to do so. Too large an order? Too hard? On the contrary, it is the easy way.

EXERCISES FOR TAKING YOUR PRACTICE INTO THE WORLD

Use these exercises for a few days each month to help you maintain clarity, compassion, and mindfulness throughout the full range of your experience.

Exercise 1

Practice acting on the thoughts of generosity that arise in the mind.

Exercise 2

Determine not to gossip or speak about any third party who isn't with you at the time.

Exercise 3

Pick a person in your life that you usually ignore or feel indifferent to. Consciously pay attention to them and make them an object of your metta.

Exercise 4

Observe whatever desire arises strongly in your mind. Note whatever emotions you find associated with it (such as loneliness, fear, longing, boredom, and so on).

Exercise 5

Use times of suffering or unhappiness as opportunities to pay particular attention. What are the sources of the discomfort? Is an expectation not being met, or a desire going unfulfilled? Do you find, at the heart of the suffering, a sense of being out of control?

Exercise 6

Choose a simple activity and be as mindful of it as you can. Note the intention preceding each component of the activity. Note the experience of following through on these intentions. (See the exercises in Lesson Seven to refresh yourself on this technique.)

Exercise 7

When you find yourself waiting in line, stuck in traffic, sitting in a meeting, or otherwise "between worlds," practice awareness of the breath or of sounds, sights, and so on (see Lessons One and Two for reminders of basic awareness techniques).

GETTING THE MOST FROM YOUR MEDITATION

All of the instructions and suggestions in *Insight Meditation* come down to the cultivation of mindfulness. Here are some powerful exercises that can help you strengthen mindfulness in every area of your life.

- Keep a daily sitting log. Each day, record in a small notebook how long you practiced and the quality of your meditative experience, such as "sleepy," "mind full of planning," or "calm and spacious." Then use another sentence or two to describe the general quality of your day: "overwhelmed"; "frustrated"; "happy." After a month or two, review your log and see whether you can identify any trends or relationships between your sitting practice and your daily life. Pay special attention to any areas in need of particular mindfulness and support.

- Use everyday activities as reminders to be mindful. Choose some daily activity that you do routinely, without thinking. Shaving, brushing your teeth, or opening your car door are possible candidates. Resolve, every day for a week, to pause for a few seconds just as you're about to begin the chosen activity. Then do it with the full attention you would bring to a breath or step during meditation. At the end of the week, add another activity. Do this every week for four weeks, so that by the end of a month you're bringing mindfulness to four everyday activities. (You can, of course, continue adding activities week after week for as many months as you like.)

- Simplify your life. Remove yourself from the bustle of daily activity for a full day. Then sit quietly and reflect on your life — your home, schedule, job, finances, relationships, recreational activities, possessions, goals, spirituality. In each area, ask yourself what you might do to simplify that part of your experience. Continue to sit quietly, letting any answers arise. Use these answers to contemplate a gentle, mindful process of change.

- Go back over this course whenever you feel the need to be refreshed and inspired in your practice. You can replay certain guided meditations at any time they seem helpful. It's important to remember that you have this resource available to you.

- Use the list of recommended books and tapes in this workbook. So many teachers have written and spoken about meditation and the path of clear seeing. You can draw on their wisdom daily, or whenever you feel the need. There are also some suggestions in this workbook for ways to find meditation groups. Many meditators find it especially helpful to sit regularly with others who are also committed to the practice.

- Going on a retreat led by a teacher is another good opportunity to go more deeply into the practice in an intensive, supportive structure. And finally, the more you keep up a daily practice, the more you will gain confidence in the dharma itself. It will guide you.

APPENDIX A

MEDITATION SUPPLIES

The three most common types of meditation support are:

- *Zafus (zah-foos):* The most traditional and widespread of the meditation cushions, the zafu is a flattened, round cotton case filled with kapok or buckwheat. It is generally about fourteen inches in diameter and ten inches in height. The crescent zafu is an innovation designed to provide extra hip support. Inflatable zafus are also available for traveling meditators.

- *Gomdens:* These firm, rectangular cushions were designed for Western practitioners by a Tibetan meditation teacher. Although only six inches thick, their firm foam interior creates a higher perch than the softer zafu.

- *Meditation benches:* These simple wooden benches provide an angled sitting surface – sometimes padded – with room underneath for legs. The meditator sits in a supported kneeling position, rather than cross-legged.

See the next page for photos of these items.

Other supports might also be helpful:

- A *zabuton:* (zah-boo-ton), or thick mat you can place under your cushion or bench. Zabutons soften the impact of hard floor surfaces on your legs and ankles.

- A *support cushion:* Made in sizes that fit zafus, gomdens, and benches, these small, flat cushions are placed under or on top of the meditation support to provide a little more height (or, in the case of benches, to cushion the seat). Some practitioners also use them to tuck under a knee.

- A *gomden raiser:* These wooden platforms are made specifically for gomdens, raising them a couple of inches off the floor or zabuton. Tall meditators who use gomdens sometimes find them useful.

The zafu is the most commonly used meditation cushion among Western practitioners.

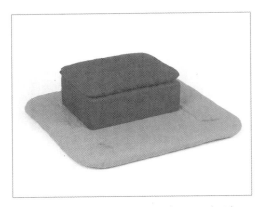

The rectangular gomden (shown here on a zabuton and with a support cushion) is firmer and higher than the zafu.

Meditation benches offer an alternative to the more traditional cross-legged posture.

RESOURCE LIST

The following is a partial list of sources. Although no single outlet carries all the items listed above, you'll be able to find the item of your choice from one of these merchants.

Carolina Morning Designs
PO Box 509, Micaville, NC 28723
(888)267-5366 / http://www.zafu.net
Cushions and benches.
(Website has a helpful article on selecting your mode of support.)

Peter Catizone
PO Box 380495, Cambridge, MA 02238
(617)548-4444 / http://www.catizone.com
Specialized meditation benches.

DharmaCrafts, Inc.
405 Waltham Street, Ste. 234, Lexington, MA 02421
(800)794-9862 / http://www.dharmacrafts.com
Cushions and benches.

Samadhi Cushions
Box INT
30 Church Street
Barnet, VT 05821
(800)331-7751 / http://www.samadhicushions.com
The only source for gomdens.

Zen Home Stitchery
120 East 18th Street
Costa Mesa, CA 92627
(949)631-5389
Cushions, including a unique "wedge" support.

Ananda Woodworking
14618 Tyler Foote Road
Nevada City, CA 95959
(800)515-3294 / http://www.meditationbench.com
A variety of meditation benches.

APPENDIX B

THE FIVE HINDRANCES

Classical Buddhism teaches that five mental hindrances are chiefly responsible for distracting our minds from awareness of the present moment. These five hindrances are:

- desire
- aversion
- sleepiness
- restlessness
- doubt

Desire (attachment, clinging, craving)

In the context of meditation, "desire" refers to the futile attempt to hang on to pleasant experiences by trying to stop the natural flow of changing conditions. This tendency can manifest in something as innocuous as a fleeting yearning for something we see in a shop window, and in states as extreme as addiction.

The illusion of desire is that we can find satisfaction by acquiring the thing or person or experience we crave. The irony of desire is that it can never fulfill its promise. Desire only creates more desire. This is because lasting satisfaction can't be attained through external objects and experiences, so the pursuit of desire is bound to end in disappointment. In the process, we also lose our peace of mind to the continual quest for the unattainable. Instead of living in the immediacy of the present moment, our minds are constantly darting ahead to a moment of fulfillment that never comes.

Aversion (anger, hatred, depression)

Aversion tends to manifest in two primary forms: the outward channel of anger, and the introverted channels of fear, depression, and guilt. The outward channel of anger may be perceived as empowering, but it is actually limiting, painful, and debilitating. We become beguiled by the energy of anger, and may not see or know how to handle its destructive force. Some contemporary psychologists recommend "getting your anger out" by screaming, beating on pillows, and so on. Others point out that the more we express our anger, the more anger we seem to generate.

In meditation, we work with anger by entering the inner experience mindfully, without acting it out. This practice lets us examine all the components that make up this particular feeling – and, ultimately, allows us to recognize that both the experience of anger and the self experiencing it are constantly changing shape. None of it is as solid as it appears.

Sleepiness (sloth, sluggishness)

Sleepiness during meditation may be caused by many things, including:

- energy imbalance
- resistance to painful experience
- physical exhaustion

In meditation, we try to find the middle way between relaxation and alertness. An energy imbalance arises when we lean too far in one direction or the other. When relaxation overtakes alertness, the result is often sleepiness. We tend to feel murky, disconnected, "spaced out."

Another frequent cause of sleepiness is resistance to painful feelings. Sometimes this is an expression of the mind/body's wisdom. When suffering becomes too great, the cloudiness of mind that accompanies sleepiness helps us to step back a little from our pain. At other times, sleepiness can be a habit-driven attempt to avoid difficult emotions or sensations.

Physical exhaustion is another cause of sleepiness. It is suggested that you explore the other two possibilities thoroughly before concluding that you need to sleep. Excessive relaxation and resistance often masquerade as tiredness.

Restlessness

Restlessness is the other side of the energy imbalance: an overemphasis on alertness, at the expense of relaxation. Common manifestations of restlessness are:

- physical agitation
- obsessive planning
- guilt

Sometimes, it can feel extremely difficult to keep still for the duration of your meditation session. Your limbs yearn to stretch; your neck itches; you want to look around the room. Although it may feel entirely physical, this kind of agitation is a manifestation of the mental hindrance of restlessness.

Restlessness can arise as a tendency to plan your life, your vacation, even your dinner. The obsessive nature of this pastime becomes clear in the way it develops, becoming more and more elaborate and speedy. Obsessive planning takes you into an imagined world of mental events, removing you from the immediacy of your present experience.

Restlessness expressed as guilt arises out of the experience, familiar to many meditators, of using our time on the cushion to take a moral inventory. This can lead to remorse — considered a wholesome attitude in Buddhist psychology — or guilt, which is characterized as destructive. Remorse is a healthy recognition of wrongdoing, a form of awareness that opens the possibility of making amends. Guilt, on the other hand, is a form of self-flagellation that tends to escalate rather than help you resolve your feelings. Like any other obsessive mental activity, guilt obscures your experience of the moment you're in.

Doubt (indecision, skepticism)

The Buddha encouraged his students to question everything, including his own teachings. In this sense, doubt is a healthy response to new information. It prompts us to ask the questions that help us find our own way on the spiritual path.

Doubt becomes a hindrance when it manifests as chronic indecision. When faced with a choice, we have to commit to one course or another. Sometimes, indulging in doubt is a way of avoiding that commitment and the risk that goes along with it.

Another way of avoiding commitment is to analyze it into the ground. This type of skeptical doubt functions to distance us from the vulnerability of our experience. We remain standing at the crossroads, avoiding the potential of having made the "wrong" choice. Skeptical doubt makes it difficult to enter anything wholeheartedly, including the practice of meditation. It abandons us to our mental fabrications, robbing us of in-depth experience.

APPENDIX C

THE THREE GREAT MYTHS

Concepts become obstacles to clear seeing when we identify with them as solid, unchanging realities. Many concepts are deeply ingrained in our minds, creating a world of perception that has little to do with our actual experience. Three of the most pervasive and limiting concepts are the notions of time, place, and self.

Time

Although we know that "time" is an artificial construct, most of us take this concept very seriously. We label our experience of memories and reflections "past," and behave as though these thoughts actually represent something solid that exists continuously behind us. Similarly, we plan and imagine a "future," on which we project all manner of expectations, hopes, and fears. In fact, the thoughts of both "past" and "future" are happening right now. When we take them for reality, we get stuck in past traumas and triumphs, burdened with anticipated problems, and misled by projected outcomes.

Place

The idea of place is another example of a concept we seldom question. A young Greek woman tells a story about traveling to India. One day, she came across a desert border crossing: a dry riverbed, spanned by a large iron bridge. Half of the bridge was painted red, the other half green. In the middle of the bridge was a great iron gate. There was nothing else out there but this huge red and green bridge with its locked gate. To allow the traveler to cross from one "country" to the other, the guards on one side of the bridge called to those on the other side and both walked up to the gate. Then, at the same moment, they turned their keys in the lock. The gate opened, and the young woman crossed the border.

Many of the tensions and hostilities in our world today are founded on the notion that such borders exist, separating "my country" from "your country." In fact, the planet doesn't naturally recognize such divisions. They exist only as concepts, on which we build great, elaborate structures. When we get too attached to these structures, they often become the cause of great conflict and suffering.

Self

Our deepest and most persistent concept is the notion of self: the idea that a permanent entity exists as the essence of our being. As we meditate, we discover that "self," "I," and "mine" are mistaken ideas arising from our identification with different aspects of the mind/body process. Many of the world's problems are born from our attempts to justify and defend this imaginary, separate self. This misunderstanding, which we call "ego," can also be seen as the source of our individual suffering.

It's important to remember that these concepts, as well as many others, serve useful functions in our lives. If we remember, though, that they are constructs of our minds, then we can use them when appropriate, and avoid being imprisoned by them.

APPENDIX D

THE THREE KINDS OF SUFFERING

Classical Buddhist texts identify three categories of human suffering:

- the suffering of painful experiences
- the suffering of change
- the suffering of conditionality

The Suffering of Painful Experiences

This is the kind of suffering most of us think of when we contemplate the pain of existence. It includes all kinds of physical, mental, and emotional discomforts, like sickness, rage, addiction, and so forth. This category of suffering is the inescapable consequence of having a physical body and a human mind.

The Suffering of Change

Ordinarily, we spend much of our lives trying to create an unchanging, permanent pleasure state. Our culture supports this pursuit, most notably through advertising that promises an end to pain through material consumption. Yet the truth of existence is that all things and experiences are transitory. We create suffering for ourselves whenever we try to avoid the inherent uncertainty of our lives.

The Suffering of Conditionality

Everything in this world comes into being through a combination of conditions. In order to take care of ourselves in this life, we need to make continuous effort to sustain those conditions. Without this application of energy, things fall apart. This is known as the suffering of conditionality.

APPENDIX E

THE FOUR BRAHMA-VIHARAS

"Brahma-vihara" is a Pali term meaning "heavenly abode" or "best home." The Buddha taught that practicing these four qualities leads to "the liberation of the heart which is love." The brahma-viharas are:

- lovingkindness
- compassion
- sympathetic joy
- equanimity

Lovingkindness

The Pali word for lovingkindness is *metta*. More closely translated, metta means both "gentle" – as in a gentle rain that falls indiscriminately upon everything – and "friendship." Thus, *metta* refers to a steady, unconditional sense of connection that touches all beings without exception, including ourselves.

Compassion

Compassion is our caring, human response to suffering. The compassionate heart is nonjudgmental. It recognizes all suffering – our own and others' – as deserving of tenderness.

Sympathetic Joy

The third brahma-vihara refers to the realization that others' happiness is inseparable from our own. The practitioner rejoices in the joy of others, and is not threatened by another's success. Sympathetic joy is said to be the most difficult of the brahma-viharas to practice consistently.

Equanimity

Equanimity is the spacious stillness of mind that provides the ground for the boundless nature of the other three brahma-viharas. This quality of radiant calm enables us to ride the waves of our experience without getting lost in our reactions. (See Lesson Eight for an in-depth discussion of equanimity.)

APPENDIX F

THE SIX REALMS OF EXISTENCE

The Buddha taught that there are six realms of existence. These can be understood both as realms of future existence and also as mind states we're reborn into from one second to the next. Which one we find ourselves in is a function of our karma. Nobody but ourselves determines what our state of mind will be in any given moment. Our experience is conditioned by our own volitional actions.

The Three Lower Realms

These three realms of suffering are conditioned by aversion, desire, and delusion, respectively. The *hell realm* is a claustrophobic torment of frustration and rage. The *realm of the hungry ghosts* is peopled by beings with huge stomachs and pinhole mouths, whose persistent craving can never be satisfied. In the *animal realm,* we dully repeat thoughtless routines without awareness.

The Human Realm

The human realm represents a bridge between the suffering of the lower realms and the experience of freedom, because here we are able to cultivate more wholesome states of mind and create a path to liberation from suffering. It's said that the combination of pain and pleasure we experience in the human realm provides the ideal conditions for true realization.

The Deva Realm

When we use our opportunity in the human realm to practice generosity and nonharming, we lay the foundations for rebirth in the higher, more pleasurable realms. These realms are characterized by an exquisitely refined existence.

The Brahma Realms

The experience of the brahma realms is one of happiness that arises not from conventional pleasure, but from deep concentration or meditative absorption. These are realms of profound calm, great rapture, and boundless consciousness.

APPENDIX G

THE EIGHT VICISSITUDES

Ancient Taoists referred to "the ten thousand joys and the ten thousand sorrows" of existence. The Buddha was more specific. He defined four particular joys and their respective opposites as conditions that we should expect to encounter again and again throughout our lives — not because we're being rewarded or punished, but simply because these conditions reflect the fullness of our experience.

The "eight vicissitudes" the Buddha taught are:

- pleasure and pain
- gain and loss
- praise and blame
- fame and disrepute

In our culture, we're routinely encouraged to aspire to lives of unchanging pleasure, gain, praise, and fame. One consequence of this expectation is that we come to believe we're necessarily at fault when we experience pain, loss, blame, and disrepute. The power of the Buddha's teaching on this subject is that it releases us from unrealistic expectations about what our lives should be, and reminds us that painful and unpleasant experiences are also natural in life.

GLOSSARY

"about to" moment: the moment before we act, in which we recognize the intention to act

Abhidhamma: "special doctrine" [Pali]; the body of Buddhist teachings devoted to human psychology

anatta: "selflessness" [Pali]; insubstantiality

asuras: "demons" [Sanskrit]; the jealous gods who dwell in a realm characterized by envy and conflict

aversion: hatred; anger; the tendency to push away unpleasant experiences

beginner's mind: a mind that is open to the experience of the moment, free of conceptual overlays (coined by Suzuki Roshi – see resource list, page 226)

benefactor: someone who has treated you with kindness and generosity; a person who has enriched your life or inspired you

bodhi: "awake" [Pali, Sanskrit]

bodhisattva: "enlightenment being" [Sanskrit]; a Buddhist saint; the Buddha's title before he became enlightened

brahma: "best" [Sanskrit, Pali]; highest

brahma-viharas: "best abode" [Sanskrit, Pali]; the four mind states said to create an ideal quality of experience

buddha: "awakened one" [Sanskrit]; specifically, Sakyamuni Buddha

clear comprehension: the quality of mind that perceives the potential consequences of action before the act is performed

desire: greed; addiction; the tendency to grasp at and try to prolong pleasurable experiences

deva: "shining one" [Sanskrit, Pali]; a celestial being who dwells in a pleasant realm of existence

dharma: "carrying, holding"; "that which supports" [Sanskrit]; the teachings of Sakyamuni Buddha

discriminating wisdom: the capacity to distinguish between direct and conceptual experience; sometimes used to distinguish wholesome or beneficial thoughts and actions from unwholesome or harmful ones

dukkha: "suffering" [Pali]; the pain that arises out of the ungovernable nature of events

ego: the pattern of conditioned habits that we mistake for a solid self

enlightenment: a state of clear understanding about the nature of reality; a state of mind that is free of greed, hatred, and ignorance

equanimity: the ability to maintain a spacious impartiality of mind in the midst of life's changing conditions

feeling tone: the pleasant, unpleasant, or neutral tone that colors every experience

gomden: "meditation place" [Tibetan]; a firm, rectangular meditation support

"in order to" mind: a goal-oriented motivation; a mind filled with expectation

kalyana mitta: "spiritual friend" [Pali]

karma: "action, deed" [Sanskrit]; the law of cause and effect

kilesa: "trouble, defilement" [Pali]; a factor of mind that obscures clear seeing; a hindrance to meditation

mental noting: a technique used in meditation to help direct the mind to the object of meditation

merit: the spiritual benefits we derive from practicing generosity, ethical conduct, and meditation

metta: "kindness, gentle friendship" [Pali]; unlimited friendliness; lovingkindness

Middle Way: a spiritual path that avoids extremes of self-mortification and self-indulgence, as taught by the Buddha

mindfulness: the state of being fully present, without habitual reactions

mudra: "gesture" [Sanskrit]; usually refers to particular hand positions used in meditation practices

neutral person: in the context of metta practice, someone for whom you feel no particular liking or disliking

nirvana: "extinction of suffering" [Sanskrit]; a state of freedom that is attained through fully apprehending the nature of reality

non-doing: meditation; the practice of refraining from reacting to internal and external events and situations

object of meditation: the activity (like the breath) or event (like sound) to which one directs attention during meditation

"plop" mind: immediate awareness, like the sudden sound of a frog plopping into a pond

precept: a principle that defines a certain standard of conduct

realms of existence: six states of existence the Buddha used to describe the different realms of human existence

retreat: an extended period of meditation

right aim: mindful modulation of concentration, so that meditation is neither rigid nor sloppy; an aspect of the Noble Eightfold Path

right effort: the energy to undertake the spiritual journey; an aspect of the Noble Eightfold Path

right understanding: a view of reality that is unclouded by attachment to concepts, particularly the concept of self; an understanding of the law of karma; an aspect of the Noble Eightfold Path

samsara: "journeying" [Sanskrit]; the ocean of worldly suffering; the state of being governed by the five hindrances

sense doors: the six perceptual gates through which we experience the world

síla: "precepts" [Pali]; moral conduct

sinking mind: a dreamlike state in which mindfulness is not in balance with concentration

sit: to sit in formal meditation

skeptical doubt: doubt whose function is to undermine faith

skillful means: action based on kindness, respect, truthfulness, and timeliness

Theravada: "path of the elders" [Pali]; the form of Buddhism found through most of Southeast Asia (vipassana meditation is a central part of this tradition)

sustaining attention: a gentle concentration of the mind on a single, present object; antidote to the hindrance of doubt

vicissitudes: changing conditions

vipassana: "to see clearly" [Pali]; insight; the style of meditation taught in this course

viriya: "exertion" [Pali]; the strong, courageous heart of energy

walk: to practice formal walking meditation

wise attention: a way of seeing that relies on awareness; the opposite of delusion

wrong view: the tendency of the mind to cling to concepts at the expense of reality; taking what is impermanent to be permanent, what is dissatisfying to be satisfying, what is selfless to be self

zabuton: "sitting mat" [Japanese]

zafu: "sitting cushion" [Japanese]

RESOURCE LIST

Explore the following list of books and other publications for more comprehensive coverage of the topics introduced in *Insight Meditation.*

Works by Joseph Goldstein:

The Experience of Insight: A Simple and Direct Guide to Buddhist Meditation. Boston: Shambhala Publications, 1987.

(with Sharon Salzberg; audio) *Insight Meditation: An In-Depth Correspondence Course.* Boulder, CO: Sounds True, 1996.

Insight Meditation: The Practice of Freedom. Boston: Shambhala Publications, 1994.

One Dharma. San Francisco: HarperSanFrancisco, 2002.

(with Jack Kornfield) *The Path of Insight Meditation.* Boston: Shambhala Publications Pocket Edition, 1995.

(with Jack Kornfield) *Seeking the Heart of Wisdom: The Path of Insight Meditation.* Boston: Shambhala Publications, 2001.

Transforming the Mind, Healing the World. Minneapolis: Paulist Press, 1994.

(contributor) *Voices of Insight.* Boston: Shambhala Publications, 1999.

Works by Sharon Salzberg:

Beginner's Mind (with Jack Kornfield and Shinzen Young; audio) Boulder, CO: Sounds True, 1999.

A Heart As Wide As the World: Stories on the Path of Lovingkindness. New York: Random House, 1999.

Faith. New York: Riverhead Books, 2002

(audio) *A Heart As Wide As the World.* Boston: Shambhala Publications, 1999.

(with Joseph Goldstein; audio) *Insight Meditation: An In-Depth Correspondence Course.* Boulder, CO: Sounds True, 1996.

Lovingkindness: The Revolutionary Art of Happiness. Boston: Shambhala Publications, 1997.

(audio) *Lovingkindness Meditation.* Boulder, CO: Sounds True, 1996.

(editor) *Voices of Insight.* Boston: Shambhala Publications, 1999.

Other Books and Tapes

Batchelor, Stephen. *Buddhism without Beliefs: A Contemporary Guide to Awakening.* New York: Riverhead Books, 1998.

Beck, Charlotte Joko. *Everyday Zen: Love and Work.* San Francisco: HarperCollins, 1989.

Boorstein, Sylvia. *It's Easier Than You Think: The Buddhist Way to Happiness.* San Francisco: HarperSanFrancisco, 1995.

—. *Don't Just Do Something, Sit There: A Mindfulness Retreat with Sylvia Boorstein.* San Francisco: HarperSanFrancisco, 1996.

—. *The Courage to Be Happy.* Boulder, CO: Sounds True, 2000.

Chödrön, Pema. *When Things Fall Apart: Heart Advice for Difficult Times.* Boston: Shambhala Publications, 1997.

—. *Start Where You Are: A Guide to Compassionate Living.* Boston: Shambhala Publications, 1994.

—. *The Wisdom of No Escape and the Path of Loving-Kindness.* Boston: Shambhala Publications, 1991.

—. *Noble Heart.* Boulder, CO: Sounds True, 1998.

—. *Pure Meditation.* Boulder, CO: Sounds True, 2000.

Cleary, Thomas, trans. *Dhammapada: The Sayings of the Buddha.* New York: Bantam Books, 1995.

Epstein, Mark. *Going to Pieces without Falling Apart.* New York: Broadway Books, 1998.

—. *Going on Being.* New York: Broadway Books, 2001

Friedman, Lenore. *Meetings with Remarkable Women: Buddhist Teachers in America.* Boston: Shambhala Publications, 1987.

Friedman, Lenore. *Meetings with Remarkable Women: Buddhist Teachers in America.* Boston: Shambhala Publications, 1987.

Gunaratana, Henepola, Ven. *Mindfulness in Plain English.* Somerville, MA: Wisdom Publications, 1993.

Hope, Jane, and Borin Van Loon. *Introducing Buddha.* New York: Totem Books, 1995.

Kabat-Zinn, Jon. *Full Catastrophe Living: Using the Wisdom of Your Body and Mind to Face Stress, Pain, and Illness.* New York: Dell, 1990.

Kornfield, Jack. *The Inner Art of Meditation.* Boulder, CO: Sounds True, 1993.

—. *A Path with Heart.* New York: Bantam, 1993.

—. *Living Dharma: Teachings of Twelve Buddhist Masters.* Boston: Shambhala Publications, 1977.

—. *The Roots of Buddhist Psychology.* Boulder, CO: Sounds True, 1995.

—. *Your Buddha Nature.* Boulder, CO: Sounds True, 1997.

Kornfield, Jack, and Christina Feldman. *Stories of the Spirit, Stories of the Heart.* New York: HarperCollins, 1991.

Kornfield, Jack and Paul Breiter. *A Still Forest Pool: The Insight Meditation of Achaan Chah.* Wheaton, Illinois: Theosophical Publishing House, 1985.

Levine, Stephen. *Healing into Life and Death.* New York: Bantam, 1989.

—. *Exploring Sacred Emptiness.* Boulder, CO: Sounds True, 1989.

Mahasi Sayadaw. *The Progress of Insight: A Treatise on Satipatthana Meditation.* Igatpuri, India: *Vipassana Research Publications,* 1994.

Morreale, Don. *The Complete Guide to Buddhist America*. Boston: Shambhala Publications, 1998.

Muller, Wayne. *Legacy of the Heart: The Spiritual Advantages of a Painful Childhood*. New York: Simon & Schuster, 1993.

—. *Touching the Divine*. Boulder, CO: Sounds True, 1994.

Nhat Hanh, Thich. *Peace Is Every Step: The Path of Mindfulness in Everyday Life*. New York: Bantam, 1991.

—. *Transformation and Healing: The Sutra on the Four Establishments of Mindfulness*. Berkeley: Parallax Press, 1990.

—. *The Miracle of Mindfulness: An Introduction to the Practice of Meditation*. Boston: Beacon Books, 1975.

—. *Teachings on Love*. Boulder, CO: Sounds True, 1996.

—. *The Art of Mindful Living*. Boulder, CO: Sounds True, 1991.

—. *The Present Moment*. Boulder, CO: Sounds True, 1999.

Nisker, Wes. *Buddha's Nature: Evolution As a Practical Guide to Enlightenment*. New York: Bantam Books, 2000.

O'Hara, Nancy. *Find a Quiet Corner: A Simple Guide to Self-Peace*. New York: Warner Books, 1995.

Pandita, U Sayadaw. *In This Very Life: The Liberation Teachings of the Buddha*. Somerville, MA: Wisdom Publications, 1993.

Ram Dass. *Journey of Awakening: A Meditator's Guidebook*. New York: Bantam, 1990.

—. *Spiritual Practices and Perspectives for Daily Life*. Boulder, CO: Sounds True, 1992.

Ram Das and Paul Gorman. *How Can I Help? Stories and Reflections on Service*. New York: Alfred A. Knopf, 1985.

Rosenberg, Larry. *Breath by Breath: The Liberating Practice of Insight Meditation*. Boston: Shambhala Publications, 1998.

Smith, Rodney. *Lessons from the Dying*. Somerville, MA: Wisdom Publications, 1998.

Sogyal Rinpoche. *The Tibetan Book of Living and Dying*. New York: HarperCollins, 1994.

Steindl-Rast, Br. David. *Gratefulness, the Heart of Prayer: An Approach to Life in Fullness*. Minneapolis: Paulist Press, 1984.

Surya Das, Lama. *Awakening the Buddha Within: Tibetan Wisdom for the Western World*. New York: Broadway Books, 1997.

Suzuki, Shunryu. *Zen Mind, Beginner's Mind*. New York: Weatherhill, 1970.

Chang, Garma C.C., trans. *The Hundred Thousand Songs of Milarepa*. Boston: Shambhala Publications, 1999.

Thera, Nyanaponika. *The Vision of Dhamma: Buddhist Writings of Nyanoponika Thera*. Igatpuri, India: Vipassana Research Publications of America, 2000.

Trungpa, Chögyam. *Meditation in Action*. Boston: Shambhala Publications, 1991.

—. *Glimpses of Abhidharma: From a Seminar on Buddhist Psychology*. Halifax, NS: Vajradhatu Publications, 1986.

—. *Cutting through Spiritual Materialism*. Boston: Shambhala Publications, 1973.

Meditation Groups and Centers

It is highly recommended that you join other meditators to practice together on a regular basis. Another excellent way to support your practice is to attend extended meditation retreats whenever possible. The following list will help you find meditation groups, retreat centers, and qualified meditation instructors in your area.

Insight Meditation Society
1230 Pleasant Street – Barre, MA 01005
Phone 978-355-4378 / FAX 978-355-6398 / www.dharma.org
(Sharon Salzberg and Joseph Goldstein are resident guiding teachers)

Barre Center for Buddhist Studies
149 Lockwood Road – Barre, MA 01005
Phone 978-355-2347 / FAX 978-355-2798 / www.dharma.org

Cambridge Insight Meditation Center
331 Broadway – Cambridge, MA 02139
Phone 617-441-9038 / www.@world.std.com

New York Insight
PO Box 1790 Murray Hill Station – New York, NY 10156
Phone 917-441-0915 / FAX 212-979-2943 / www.nyimc.org

Insight Meditation Community of Washington
c/o Dori Langevin – 1206 Dale Drive – Silver Spring, MD 20910
Phone 301-562-7000 / www.erols.com/imcw

Spirit Rock Meditation Center
PO Box 169 – Woodacre, CA 94973
Phone 415-488-0164 / FAX 415-488-0170 / www.spiritrock.org

Seattle Insight Meditation Society
PO Box 95817 – Seattle, WA 98145-2817
Phone 206-366-2111 / www.seattleinsight.org

Vipassana Hawaii
PO Box 240547 – Honolulu, HI 96824
Phone 808-396-5888 / www.vipassanahawaii.org

Vipassana Metta
PO Box 1188 – Kula, HI 96790-1188
Phone 808-573-3450 / www.maui.net/~metta

Gaia House
West Ogwell, Newton Abbot – Devon TQ12 6EN – UK
Phone ++44 (0)1626-333613 / www.gn.apc.org/gaiahouse

Meditationszentrum Beatenberg
Waldegg, 3803 Beatenberg – Switzerland
Phone ++41 (0) 33 841 2131 / FAX ++44 (0) 33 841 2132 / www.karuna.ch

Online Resources

The following is a list of websites with links to meditation centers throughout North America and around the world.

http://www.buddhanet.net
http://www.tricycle.com/dharmacenters
http://www.dharmanet.org
http://www.accesstoinsight.org
http://www.dharma.org

Other Resources

The Inquiring Mind is a semiannual newspaper for the North American and European mindfulness community. In addition to articles dealing with all aspects of practice, this publication lists meditation groups and retreats by region.
Contact: The Inquiring Mind / PO Box 9999, North Berkeley Station, Berkeley, CA 94709

For information about Insight Meditation audio and video cassette recordings featuring Sharon Salzberg, Joseph Goldstein, and other meditation teachers, write: Dharma Seed Tape Library, Box 66, Wendell Depot, MA 01380

ABOUT THE AUTHORS

Sharon Salzberg has been a student of Buddhism since 1970, and has been leading meditation retreats worldwide since 1974. She teaches both intensive awareness practice (vipassana or insight meditation) and the profound cultivation of lovingkindness and compassion (the Brahma-viharas). She is a cofounder of the Insight Meditation Society in Barre, Massachusetts, The Barre Center for Buddhist Studies, and The Forest Refuge, a new project for long term meditation practice.

Sharon is the author of *Lovingkindness: The Revolutionary Art of Happiness* and *A Heart As Wide As the World,* by Shambhala Publications; *Lovingkindness Meditation* (audio) by Sounds True; and coauthor with Joseph Goldstein of *Insight Meditation, an In-Depth Correspondence Course,* also from Sounds True. She recently edited *Voices of Insight,* an anthology of writings by vipassana teachers in the West, published by Shambhala. Sharon is currently writing a book about the spiritual quality of Faith.

Joseph Goldstein is a senior teacher of Insight (Vipassana) and Lovingkindness (Metta) Meditation. He studied with many leading Buddhist teachers in India, Burma, and Nepal and has led retreats worldwide since 1974. He is a cofounder and guiding teacher of the Insight Meditation Society in Barre, Massachusetts, The Barre Center for Buddhist Studies, and The Forest Refuge, a new project for long term meditation practice.

Joseph's books include *The Experience of Insight; Insight Meditation: The Practice of Freedom;* and *Seeking the Heart of Wisdom* (with Jack Kornfield), published by Shambhala Publications. He is also coauthor with Sharon Salzberg of *Insight Meditation, an In-Depth Correspondence Course* (audio), published by Sounds True. Joseph is currently writing a new book, *One Dharma,* on the integration of different Buddhist teachings and traditions.

The Spiritual University You Have Been Listening For.